Events

International Library of Philosophy

Editor: Ted Honderich
Professor of Philosophy, University College London

A catalogue of books already published in the
International Library of Philosophy
will be found at the the end of this volume

Events

A metaphysical study

Lawrence Brian Lombard

Associate Professor of Philosophy
Wayne State University, Detroit

ROUTLEDGE & KEGAN PAUL

London, Boston and Henley

First published in 1986
by Routledge & Kegan Paul plc
14 Leicester Square, London WC2H 7PH, England
9 Park Street, Boston, Mass. 02108, USA and
Broadway House, Newtown Road,
Henley on Thames, Oxon RG9 1EN, England
Set in Times
by Columns of Reading
and printed in Great Britain
by T J Press (Padstow) Ltd
Padstow, Cornwall

Library of Congress Cataloging in Publication Data
Lombard, Lawrence Brian, 1944-

Events a metaphysical study.

(International library of philosophy)
Bibliography: p.
Includes index.
1. Events (Philosophy) I. Title. II. Series.
B105.E7L65   1986   110   85-10710
British Library CIP data also available

ISBN 0-7102-0354-3

CONTENTS

Contents

PREFACE
AND
ACKNOWLEDGEMENTS

This book is about events. The theory of events I offer in it tries to take seriously the idea that events are changes in objects. The concept of change figured centrally among the philosophical concerns of the ancient Greeks. I think the reason for this was the threat that change appeared to pose for the principle of non-contradiction: change seems to involve an object's becoming what it is not. Aristotle appears to have satisfied philosophers that the principle of non-contradiction was not in any danger of being refuted by an admission that things change (or *vice versa*); and as a result, the concept of change ceased for a long time to be a central topic of philosophical concern. It became a vital issue again in the nineteenth century, when the principle of non-contradiction again came under scrutiny. In more recent times, the concept of an event and that of change have captured the attention of philosophers, due this time to a re-awakening of interest in metaphysical issues generally, and to the idea that these concepts must play an important role in any serious discussions of the theory of action, the mind-body problem, the concept of causation, and moral philosophy. In this book, however, I shall neither try to trace the history of the discussion of the concept of an event, nor try to discuss the connections between events and change and these other philosophical issues; I've had difficulties enough just trying to think about events.

The theory I shall propose is a theory about events construed as concrete particulars; it is about what it is to be an event, about what events are like, about when events are identical, about what properties they have essentially and about what relations events bear to objects of other kinds. The theory embodies an attempt to construe events as the changes that objects undergo when they change. I should like to believe that no view about events could be correct unless it begins with the idea that the concept of an event must be explicated, somehow, in terms of the concept of change. I shall not argue for that belief, however; the success, or lack thereof, of my theory will serve as partial evidence for the truth or falsity of that belief.

In the course of my thinking about events, I have been drawn to and forced to think about some methodological and meta-philosophical issues. These issues chiefly revolve around the issue of how philosophical arguments concerning what there is ought to be construed and what the role of criteria of identity (e.g., distinct physical objects cannot occupy the same place simultaneously) is in such arguments and in theories about what there is. Since my views on these subjects have not merely served as part of the background against which I have been thinking about events, but also have influenced the form and content of my views on events, it seemed important that my views on these topics be included in this work on events.

Chapter I offers a reconstruction of arguments whose conclusions are that entities belonging to some metaphysically significant kind exist; the suggestion is that such arguments are deductive arguments whose premises are claims of common sense and whose validity is supported by inductive considerations. A proposal is made concerning the determination of which kinds of entity are metaphysically significant. The proposal makes use of the idea of a criterion of identity, a principle specifying conditions necessary and sufficient for the numerical identity of entities belonging to a given kind. Chapter II is concerned with the specification of the conditions that would have to be met by claims purporting to be criteria of identity in order for them to serve the metaphysical functions assigned to such principles in Chapter I. I then argue that if a criterion of identity meeting these conditions can be given for the entities belonging to a given kind, one can formulate a principle giving conditions necessary and sufficient for belonging to that kind. Since criteria of identity help in saying not only what the ultimate kinds are but also what it is to belong to such a kind, a criterion of identity must play an important role in any theory about the nature of the entities that there are. Chapter III consists of a brief look at three recent proposals for a criterion of identity for events. My primary objective is to show how these proposals are in fact linked, in the way envisioned in Chapter II, with their defenders' views about what events are. My secondary objective is to explain why I find those proposals unsatisfactory.

Since my basic thesis is that events are changes in objects, Chapter IV is devoted to an incomplete examination of the concept of change; it takes the form of a discussion of the idea that an object changes if and only if it has a property at one time and lacks it at another. In Chapter V, the connection between the concept of change and that of an event is formally introduced. The notion of a 'respect' in which things change is explicated in terms of the notion of a 'quality space', a set of mutually exclusive properties such that, when an object changes by having and then lacking a property belonging to a given quality space, the object comes to have another property from that same space. The rest of the chapter is devoted to a discussion of some of the spatial and temporal features of events and to a discussion of the subjects of events.

I begin Chapter VI by employing the resources afforded by the notion of a quality space for the purpose of arguing against the view that events are identical just in case they have the same spatio-temporal features. This leads to a refining of the picture of the relation between events and quality spaces. I then draw a distinction between 'atomic' and 'non-atomic' events and suggest that certain descriptions of events can be said to be 'canonical'. This leads directly to my proposal for a criterion of identity for events.

Chapter VII is a discussion concerned with determining which properties of events are essential. I argue that events do not have their causes or effects essentially. I argue, however, that events are necessarily changes in the objects that are in fact their subjects and that events necessarily occur at the times at which they in fact occur. Chapter VIII is speculative; I explore the idea that events have individual essences and the idea that some entities can be said to be 'ontologically supervenient' on objects belonging to other kinds. Some lingering issues, not treated at all or at a sufficient length in the rest of the book, are mentioned in a short Appendix.

Preface and acknowledgements

There are many to whom I wish to express my gratitude and appreciation for their various contributions to me and my thinking, contributions without which I doubt that I would have written this book. Through his lectures and seminars at Stanford and his writings, Donald Davidson made me aware of the subject of events; and, though I do not know how much of what I say about events he would agree with, I have felt his influence at many points. Alexander Rosenberg was among the first who thought that I might have something interesting to say about events and that I should write a book on the subject. Though this is perhaps not the book he thought I should write, he has been, since 1976, a source of encouragement and good advice, as well as a good friend. Peter van Inwagen and Myles Brand have also, for a long time, been generous and helpful with their encouragement and good philosophical sense.

There has been a long tradition of cooperative philosophical interaction among the philosophers of Wayne State University, and I am happy to report that that tradition lives on. My colleagues have never failed to put their learning, their critical abilities, and their time at my disposal. I have long since stopped counting the hours that Michael McKinsey has spent discussing events with me and reading and commenting on drafts of this book and the preliminary studies thereof. I shudder to think of what this book would have been like (if, indeed, it would have been written at all) apart from my philosophical association with him; I am greatly in his debt. Larry Powers played a similar role; his trenchant criticisms have helped a great deal. In addition, what sensible ideas I have about metaphilosophy, I owe to his systematic and penetrating thinking on that subject and to his discussions with me of my metaphilosophical views. William Stine has given freely of his encouragement, good advice, and good humour. Thanks are also due to the members of my seminar on events, in the Autumn of 1981, for forcing me to present my views more clearly. In this connection, I must mention Patrick Francken, who is responsible for making me see that certain views of mine needed serious re-working, and Sherrill Hines, whose transcriptions of tapes, made during that seminar, were most helpful in organizing my thoughts. My correspondence over the past few years with Cynthia Macdonald, of the University of Manchester, gave me the opportunity to test certain ideas that have found their way into this book; I am grateful for her friendship and her services as sounding-board and critic. And I must thank Nancy Tokarz, Karen White and Sam Miller, for their parts in turning an illegibile manuscript into a typescript of an early draft, and Jeanette H. Piccirelli of Words/Numbers for the typing of the final draft.

Material that originally appeared in various talks and articles of mine has found its way into this book. In some cases, serious revision was called for; in others, outright rejection. I here express my thanks to the publishers of those articles for permitting me to make free use of the material I published in their journals. *Philosophical Studies*: 'Events, changes, and the non-extensionality of "Become" ', vol. 28 (1975), pp. 131-6; 'Relational change and relational changes', vol. 34 (1978), pp. 63-79. *Canadian Journal of Philosophy*: 'Events', vol. IX (1979), pp. 425-60; 'Events and the essentiality of time', vol. XII (1982), pp. 1-17. *Pacific Philosophical Quarterly*: 'Events and their subjects', vol. 62 (1981), pp. 138-47. *Philosophia*: 'Actions, results and the time of a killing', vol. 8 (1978), pp. 341-54.

Wayne State University is to be thanked for a Summer 1983 Research Grant; and my thanks go also to VT for giving me the strength to go on.

My greatest debt is owed to Marge, whose love, whose pleasure at even my small achievements, whose encouragement during disappointing times, and whose presence and willingness to put up with me give my work a non-philosophical purpose. This book is dedicated to her.

I
EXISTENTIAL PROOFS

1 INTRODUCTION

Metaphysical problems, like all philosophical problems, arise from a sense of puzzlement. What is puzzling is that the world should really be by and large the way we believe it to be. We sometimes discover that the ways we think the world to be appear to conflict. When what is called for in order to resolve such a conflict is, not a rejection of one or more of those apparently conflicting beliefs, but an explanation of how the appearance of conflict can be seen to be mere, we have an occasion for philosophy. Thus, a philosophical problem generally has the form: how is it possible for apparently conflicting beliefs to be, appearances to the contrary notwithstanding, true? A solution to such a problem calls, not for the discovery of a new fact, but for the discovery of a way to understand the facts and the beliefs we have about them, a way that shows how it is possible for those beliefs to be true.[1]

The idea of philosophy, in general, and of metaphysics, in particular, as explanatory in nature is not incompatible with the idea that philosophers should be interested in offering arguments and proofs in support of their views.[2] Indeed, I want now to discuss the structure of arguments that purport to prove the existence of entities belonging to metaphysically interesting kinds. In such arguments it can be seen how intimately connected are the projects of explaining how it is possible for our beliefs to be for the most part true and of proving that things belonging to certain kinds exist.

1

2 EXISTENTIAL PROOFS

Metaphysicians are often concerned with ontological issues. This concern is a proper one, for they are interested in giving accounts of how it is possible for our beliefs to be by and large true; and it seems clear that many of those beliefs are such that they would not be true unless certain objects exist. This concern with ontological issues often leads metaphysicians to offer arguments for the existence of entities that purportedly comprise certain metaphysically interesting sorts. I want, in this chapter, to say something about the structure of such arguments and to say something about what makes a sort of thing metaphysically interesting. I begin with a sketch of what I call 'existential proofs', arguments whose conclusions are existential claims concerning entities, φs, comprising metaphysically interesting sorts. I will fill in that sketch as the dialectic develops between those who advance them, the friends of φs, and those who resist them, the foes of φs.

In saying what an existential proof is, I do not suppose that I am giving an account of how metaphysicians have conceived of their endeavours to prove the existence of entities of this or that sort, though some no doubt have seen and some do see these endeavours more or less in the way I shall describe. I want rather to engage in some rational reconstruction; I am proposing that existential proofs are what in effect are offered and defended by the friends of φs when advancing their ontological views properly and appropriately. And it is such arguments that are resisted, when the view that there are φs is resisted properly and appropriately, by the foes of φs. Thus, in so far as a metaphysician presents arguments for the existence of φs that cannot be reconstructed as existential proofs, that metaphysician has not offered a relevant reason for thinking that there are φs and is no true friend of φs. And if a metaphysician's objections to φs cannot be reconstructed as a response to an existential proof, that metaphysician is no true foe of φs.

2.1 *The structure of an existential proof*

An existential proof for the existence of some entities, φs, that comprise a metaphysically interesting sort consists of a pair of arguments. The first member of the pair, the 'existence' argument, is a *deductive* argument whose premise is a perfectly ordinary, commonsensical and commonplace claim about the world, and whose conclusion is a claim asserting the existence of an entity (an F) allegedly belonging to a species of the metaphysically interesting sort in question (the φs). The second member of the pair, the 'significance' argument, has as its premise the conclusion of the existence argument, and its conclusion is a claim asserting the existence of entities belonging to the metaphysically interesting sort in question. The significance argument, too, is deductive, involving nothing more than an inference from species to genus. Thus, an existential proof has this form:

p
∴ There is at least one F

There is at least one F
All Fs are φs
∴ There is at least one φ.

The following are examples of existential proofs:

My car and your book have the same colour
∴ There is a colour (that my car and your book have)
All colours are properties
∴ There are properties;

Mt St Helens is erupting
∴ There is an eruption
All eruptions are events
∴ There are events.

In some cases, the existence and significance arguments get collapsed into one (sometimes with the universal generalisation suppressed), as in

Here is a hand
∴ There are physical objects.

In other cases, the significance argument may proceed from premise to conclusion through one or more intermediary stages involving larger and larger species, as in

> There is at least one colour
> Colours are properties
> Properties are universals
> ∴ There are universals.

I intend to think of the inference in significance arguments as obvious and trivial, as valid arguments whose first premise is established by the associated existence argument and whose second premise(s) (the universal generalisation(s)) as trivially true in at least one sense. And the questions which will arise concerning significance arguments will have to do with the 'significance' of their conclusions. There is, however, an alternative way of approaching significance arguments and the 'significance' issue they raise. In the way just mentioned, the significance argument is taken to be obviously valid and sound, and the significance issue concerns the 'meaning' of its conclusion. This assumes that we do not know what it is really to be a φ; telling that story, of what it is to be a φ, gives the 'meaning' of the conclusion. And it assumes that, despite that ignorance, we know that the Fs are φs. An alternate approach consists in supposing that we know a lot about what it is to be a φ, about what φs would be like if there were any. What would then be in question is whether the Fs, whose existence is established by the existence argument, are indeed φs. Here, the 'significance' issue would be raised, not by asking after the 'meaning' of the conclusion of the significance argument, but by questioning the truth of the claim that Fs are φs. Since what is required in order to settle this issue is a theory about what φs are, just as is required by the former approach, I believe that these two approaches force just the same issues out into the open. And I shall proceed by taking the significance issue to be raised by the former approach.

What can the foes of φs object to in the first stage of an existential proof (the existence argument)? Since the argument is *deductive*, anyone wishing to deny that its conclusion has been established must object either to the *truth* of the premise of the argument or to the *validity* of the inference (or both).

2.2 *Objecting to the premise*

The premise of an existence argument is a perfectly ordinary claim about the world: Mt St Helens erupted, my car and your book have the same colour. One might, of course, object to the particular claim appearing as premise; perhaps the friend of properties or the friend of events has got the facts wrong. But, this objection is surely uninteresting. The friend of events will grant that Mt St Helens might not have erupted, and the friend of properties will grant that my car and your book only seemed to have the same colour because of the lighting conditions. But having granted that, it will be insisted that even if Mt St Helens hadn't erupted, surely Vesuvius erupted, and if not Vesuvius, then some volcano somewhere, sometime erupted. And if it is not my car and your book that have the same colour, it is the first and third stripes on an American flag which do, and if not, then it is some other pair of objects somewhere, some time that have the same colour. The friends of events and properties are willing to replace their original premises with any other having to do with the fact that some entity erupted and the fact that some pair of objects have the same colour. So, if the foes of events wish to make a serious objection to the premise of an existence argument, they must claim that nothing ever erupts; and the foes of properties must claim that no pair of objects ever has the same colour. The foes of events cannot, if their objection here is serious, be persuaded even by being taken directly to the site of an erupting volcano; and the foes of properties cannot be persuaded by being shown two sheets of yellow paper. The dispute here cannot be taken to be merely a dispute over the facts; the foes of events and properties cannot be seen as interested in merely denying that there are events and properties, respectively, while allowing that there *could* have been events and properties. In the course of objecting to the premise, the view of the foes of events and properties must be that it is not possible that anything should ever erupt and that it is not possible that any pair of objects should have the same colour. Otherwise, the friends of events and properties can find suitable premises for arguments leading to the conclusion that there at least could be eruptions and colours. And surely that would be enough.

But clearly the net of the objection made by the foes of events and properties must be cast much wider than is indicated above. The friend of events is no more interested in eruptions than is the friend of physical objects in chairs. As will be discussed when the issue of what counts as a metaphysically interesting sort of entity is broached, a metaphysician is interested in eruptions and chairs only to the extent that they are species of broader genera; it is with those broader, more inclusive sorts that the metaphysician's concern lies. What motivates the friends of properties' idea that there are such things as properties is not the apparent fact that my car and your book have the same colour, but is rather the apparent general fact that some objects are *similar* to each other in some respect. What impresses the friends of events is not the particular fact that some volcano erupted or even the general fact that volcanoes erupt. What is impressive in such facts is that they indicate about some objects that they change. So, the friends of properties are willing to use as a premise in the first stage of their argument for the existence of properties *any* true claim asserting a similarity between any pair of objects. And the friends of events are willing to use as a premise in the first stage of their argument for the existence of events *any* true claim asserting of any object that it changes.[3]

Thus, the original attack on the truth of the particular premise used by the friends of φs is not really to the point. The scope of the attack must be broadened. The foes of properties must be asserting, as a matter of principle, that no objects are or could ever be similar; and the foes of events must be asserting, as a matter of principle, that no object does or could ever change. It seems then that a foe of φs (be the φs properties, events, numbers, etc.) who objects to the premise of the first stage of an existential proof is just a *sceptic*. The task of metaphysics, as I suggested above, is to explain how it is possible for most of our ordinary beliefs about the world to be true, to say what the world would have to be like if most of what we believe to be true is really true. But it is surely the case that ordinary claims about, for example, similarities between objects and changes in objects do express ordinary, commonsensical beliefs we have about the world, beliefs at least some of which must be counted as true if any of our beliefs are true. Those who attack the friends of φs' argument in this way, however, are just asserting that, appearances to the contrary notwithstanding, nothing ever changes, and nothing is ever similar to anything else. These foes of properties and events are not simply denying the starting point for the debate between themselves and the friends of properties and events; they are denying a pre-condition of the possibility of metaphysics itself. There is no debate possible, in my view, between this foe of φs and the friends of φs. For the former is no true foe of φs; he is a foe of metaphysics! I envision the debate about the existence of properties to be one pitting one metaphysician's views and arguments against those of another metaphysician. Thus, they must agree that most of what we commonly believe about the world is indeed true. Their disagreement is over what makes that possible. There must be, then, some version of an existence argument whose premise all the disputants can accept. So, both the true friend and the true foe of φs agree that the first stage, the existence argument, of an existential proof for the existence of φs is a deductive argument whose premise is either true or could be replaced by one that is true.

It may be the case that the objection to a premise is not after all a sceptical objection. The objection might be based instead on a certain construal of the premise, a construal according to which it entails a falsehood. I wish to make two remarks about this possibility. First, such an objection to the premise must be based on a fallacy of equivocation. For if the foe's construal shows the premise to have a false implication, and if I'm right in thinking that the premise is an obvious truth, then it must be the case that the foe is confusing the premise, which is true and hence cannot entail a falsehood, with a similar claim that does entail a falsehood. Such an objection is not sceptical, just confused. Second, the alleged false implication cannot be thought, at this stage of the debate between the friend and foe of φs, to be the conclusion of the existence argument; for if so, the objection begs the question at issue.

2.3 *Objecting to the validity of the existence argument*

An objection to the validity of the inference involved in the first stage of an existential proof is a *semantic* objection. What is at stake is the validity of a deductive argument. Such an argument is valid just in case its premises entail its conclusion; and entailment relations are relations that hold in virtue of meaning. So, the friends of φs are claiming that the meanings of certain commonsensical claims are such that those claims entail that objects belonging to a species of φ exist. And the foes of φs who attack the argument at this stage deny this.

This dispute between the friends and foes of φs is to be dealt with, of course, by an inquiry into meaning. We want to know how to understand certain commonsensical claims, at least to the extent of being able to say what entities they speak of. Because of the work of philosophers such as Russell, Quine, Davidson and others, we know that this is a matter of providing a semantic theory for such claims. The relevant data for such a theory consist in part of a catalogue of known relations such claims bear to others on the basis of their meaning. And the question around which the theory will turn is this: how is it possible for the claim in question (the premise of the existence argument) to stand in these logical, semantical and meaning relations? But, of course, there may be many ways of showing this, many semantic theories that account for the semantic relations our ordinary claim about the world bears to other claims. Thus, what is sought is the best of them, the semantic theory providing the best explanation of the facts due to meaning about the claim in question. Of course, this theory is not just about the claim in question; it must also be about the claims to which that claim is semantically related, and about the metatheory in which the semantic theory is to be embedded (e.g., Tarski-type, Montague-type, etc.). And the friends of φs will insist that this best semantic theory assigns to the premise of an existence argument a meaning such that it can be seen to follow that that premise has another implication – that there are entities belonging to a species of the φs. The foes of φs may attack this theory, this explanation of how it is possible for the premise in question to mean what it does, by arguing that it is inadequate to certain data, or that it is defective in some other respect, or that some alternative semantic theory is a better one.

The issue is to be decided by deciding whether it is the friends or the foes of φs who have the best explanation of the semantic facts. And it is clear that the argument that establishes that some semantic theory, T, is the best one to offer to account for the semantic facts is an *inductive* argument, an inference to the best explanation, for the truth of T. If T happens to be the semantic theory offered and defended by the friends of φs, then it will turn out that, though the existence of φs is established (pending the outcome of the rest of the friend of φs' argument) by a deductive inference from an ordinary, obvious claim about the world, the validity of that inference will be established by induction. That is, an inductive argument will establish (to whatever extent the conclusions of inductive arguments are 'established') that a certain theory about the meaning of the premise of an existence argument is true. That theory, however, shows that that premise entails the existence of φs. Thus, the validity of the deductive argument for the existence of φs is established by induction.

2.4 *An example*

A large portion of this book is aimed at giving a theory about events. Such a theory would have little point if there were no events. The little point it would have would be that such a theory would say what events would be like if there were any. But that little point would vanish if there could be no events. It would then seem incumbent upon me to argue that there indeed are, or at least could be, events. That apparent obligation notwithstanding, I do not intend to do that, but not because I think the existence of events is obvious and therefore in need of no proof. The existence of events may be obvious, but it is still in need of proof.[4] The existence of entities belonging to all the metaphysically interesting sorts (whichever they may be) stands in need of existential proof in my view. My reason is rather more mundane. There has been a wealth of discussion already in the recent philosophical literature on the semantics of claims reporting actions and change and on whether such claims imply that there are such things as actions and events.[5] And I have nothing of interest to add to the discussion of the validity of any argument that purports to be an existential proof of the existence of events. There is, however, a sense in which I believe I can add something to the discussion of whether or not there are events; as I shall argue later, the providing of a theory of events plays an important role in the settling of the question of the existence of events; and it is in the providing of such a theory that I am interested. What I do wish to do in this section is to show very briefly that some well-known arguments for the existence of events are existential proofs.

The arguments I have in mind are Davidson's. In 'The logical form of action sentences',[6] Davidson offers an argument for the existence of events. What is actually offered is an argument whose conclusion is that there are actions. But Davidson believes that actions are events, and I shall not concern myself with the truth of this belief, since it does not affect the point I shall be making. And in 'Causal relations',[7] Davidson offers another argument whose conclusion is that there are events.

In 'The logical form of action sentences', the sentence

(1) Jones buttered the toast in the bathroom with the knife at midnight

is offered up for semantic analysis. The principal considerations in terms of which to judge the success for any proposed analysis are that such a proposal should (a) explain the fact that (1) entails each of the following:

(2) Jones buttered the toast in the bathroom with the knife,
(3) Jones buttered the toast in the bathroom,
(4) Jones buttered the toast,

and (b) be embeddable in a Tarski-type metatheory. Various proposals are considered. One construes (1) as expressing a five-place relational claim relating Jones, the toast, the bathroom, the knife and midnight, and construes (2)-(4) as expressing, respectively, analogous four-, three-, and two-place relational claims. A second proposal interprets (1) as 'Jones brought it about that the toast was buttered in the bathroom with the knife at midnight'. A third takes (1) to be equivalent to 'Jones brought it about that a state where it is not the case that Jones has buttered the toast in the bathroom with the knife at midnight changes into a state where Jones has buttered . . .'. And a fourth construes (1) to have the structure of 'There is an x such that x consists in the fact that Jones buttered . . .'. Each of these proposals is rejected by Davidson, who then suggests that what we wish to have explained by a semantical account of (1) can be explained by supposing that (1)'s true semantic colours are that of

(5) There is something that was a buttering of the toast by Jones, and it was done in the bathroom, and it was done with the knife, and it was done at midnight.

And (5) fairly straightforwardly entails that there are butterings, which in turn entails that there are actions.[8]

It is obvious that we have here an existential proof of the existence of events. It is claimed that the inference from (1) to 'there is a buttering (of the toast by Jones)' is deductively valid, and that seeing the validity of the inference from the existence of a buttering to the existence of events is just a matter of seeing that butterings are actions and that actions are events. The validity of the existence argument for the existence of a buttering is established, for Davidson, by offering a semantical analysis of its premise, (1), and by comparing that analysis with others and finding it superior to them. And in doing that, inductive support is offered for the validity of Davidson's existence argument. The comments on Davidson's proposal from Chisholm, Clarke, Horgan *et al.*, all involve suggesting that the proposed semantic analysis fails to satisfy other requirements or that it is not as good an explanation of the semantic facts as some other and that some other explanation has the right to the title of best explanation.

The same dialectical pattern is seen in Davidson's 'Causal relations' and the responses to it; here, however, the common-sensical claims said to entail that there are events are singular causal statements such as

(6)   The short circuit caused the fire.

And Davidson argues that the semantic relations that (6) bears to other claims are best captured by a theory that interprets (6) as containing a two-place causal relational expression relating a short circuit and a fire; and short circuits and fires are events. Discussion of this proposal has sometimes concerned an alternative that treats the causal relation as one relating fact-like entities and takes that relation to be non-truth-functional though extensional.

It is not just in Davidson's arguments for events and actions that this pattern can be discerned. One can see an existential proof of the existence of the Forms in Plato's *Phaedo*, a proof motivated by the need for an explanation of how it is possible for obvious claims involving 'incomplete predication' (e.g., this thing is tall with respect to one thing but short with respect to another) to mean what they do; it is argued, I believe, that such claims always involve a comparison with a standard whose applicability is never 'incomplete' (tallness is never short with respect to any

11

thing). The proof in Wittgenstein's *Tractatus* for the existence of simples is an existential proof whose premise is any claim with a sense and is motivated by the idea that every claim has an analysis and by a theory about semantics according to which the analysis of any claim's meaning must 'picture' or replicate in some way the fact or facts that make that claim true or false. And there is a clear example of an existential proof and the appropriate discussion thereof in 'Holes', by David Lewis and Stephanie Lewis.[9] There, one argument under discussion has as its premise the claim 'there are remarkably many holes in this piece (of Gruyère)'; the conclusion, 'there are holes', is then used as a premise for a significance argument whose conclusion is that there are non-material entities.

Not all arguments with existential conclusions that one is likely to run across in philosophy appear to be existial proofs, however. For example, the pattern of existential proof seems not to be exhibited in Aquinas's Cosmological Proofs for the existence of God. The reason for this may be as follows. One difference between 'philosophical' arguments for the existence of entities of certain kinds (existential proofs, by my lights) and 'scientific' arguments whose conclusions are existence claims has to do with the generality of the kinds in questions; philosophers are not interested in the existence of entities belonging to the kind 'egg-laying mammal'. More importantly, the relevant difference is that, while both philosophical and scientific arguments for the existence of entities involve an inductive inference to the best explanation, the philosopher is seeking an explanation of certain *semantic* phenomena, while the scientist is not. The Cosmological Proofs are responses to a demand that, for example, the existence of motion and the existence of a world of contingent beings be explained. What are to be explained here do *not* seem to be semantic facts. Of course, to the extent that no firm distinction can be made out between facts about meaning and facts about phenomena, there can be no firm distinction between metaphysical and scientific arguments for the existence of things. Still, when an argument for the existence of things belonging to a certain kind is being taken as philosophical, it must be taken, I am suggesting, to have the structure of an existential proof, a deductive argument with commonsensical premise whose validity is defended inductively by providing support for a semantic theory.

2.5 *The significance issue*

Let us suppose that the foes of φs become convinced that the friends of φs' existence argument is sound. Then, supposing that no one has been hoodwinked, there are Fs. The friends of φs will then insist that the existence of φs is established, for they claim that if there are Fs then there must be φs, since the Fs are just a species of the φs. The friends of φs, that is, accept the significance argument. However, the battle between friend and foe of φs is not yet over. For the foes of φs can accept the inference to the existence of φs and yet not give up the fight. The issue, however, undergoes a shift. The issue no longer concerns whether or not there are Fs or φs; it concerns rather the 'significance' of the fact that there are φs. The significance issue arises once the significance argument is accepted; it is responsive to a concern with the 'meaning' of the conclusion that there are φs.

One becomes convinced that there are Fs and one sees that, whatever else the Fs are, they are φs. It is, after all, obvious that hands are physical objects, that colours are properties, that avalanches are events, and so on. This one can be said to know independently of knowing in any precise or detailed way what physical objects, properties, or events are. And that is the issue. In agreeing, by accepting an existential proof, that there are φs, one has *not* yet made any commitment with respect to the nature of those entities whose existence has just been admitted. The argument for the existence of φs does not involve a theory about what it is to be a φ (except that it requires that the Fs be a species of φ). And until a theory about the nature of the φs is given, it is not determined whether or not the friends of φs, in establishing the existence of φs by means of an existential proof, have established something of true metaphysical importance.

Suppose that a would-be foe of propositions becomes convinced of their existence by an existential proof; but further suppose that, when a theory specifying what propositions are is finally given, it turns out that propositions are really just sets. We can imagine the following response by the would-be foe of propositions. 'I thought that when the friends of propositions said they were going to prove that there are propositions, contrary to what I (formerly) believed, they were going to prove the existence of certain entities, entities whose existence I doubted and which allegedly comprised a sort I believed was (necessarily) empty. But I've always believed that there were sets; so if that's all the friends of propositions were trying to convince me of (that there are propositions, for there are sets), then they have been, in a sense, preaching to the converted and I apologize for raising such a fuss. I have been told of something that is new, something related to what might be called the "taxonomy" of the world's ontology; it is important to know which entities are species of what others. But the existential proof for propositions has established nothing of "ontological" significance, for two reasons. First, admitting its conclusion does not require belief that there are (previously unbeknownst to me) entities belonging to some wholly *new*, unrecognized kind (that's what happened when I became convinced that there are sets, for I had previously believed that *all* entities were physical objects); and second, these propositions are just a species of set, and metaphysical discussions of what there is should focus on the most *general* kinds of thing. My list of the basic, most fundamental kinds of entity has not been lengthened by the arguments of the friends of propositions; indeed, it may be that their list has been shortened, for they may have thought, prior to seeing that propositions are sets, that the propositions did comprise a basic kind of thing, distinct from the kind the sets comprise.'

I think that this response is perfectly appropriate. If the friends of φs' conclusion is to be metaphysically significant, what must be shown is not just that there are φs, but also that the φs comprise a 'new' kind of thing, a kind such that no other already admitted existent truly belongs to it. But we cannot determine whether the existence of φs is truly significant until we have a theory about what it is to be a φ. For such a theory will, in the course of saying what it is to be a φ, reveal how the φs stand in relation to objects of other kinds and whether or not the φs are among those objects of other kinds.

Some 'how is it possible'-questions concern how it is possible for certain commonsensical claims that we make to mean what they in fact mean. The answering of such a question calls for a semantic investigation. And since it may, on occasion, turn out that the answer shows a certain existential proof to be sound, it follows that in order for those commonsensical claims to mean what they mean certain entities must exist. So far, this only demonstrates what certain speakers of English are 'committed' to. But there is the presumption that by and large most of what we commonsensically say is, to the extent that we say what we believe, *true*. Thus, to say what entities there must be in order for the things we say to mean what they mean is to say, by and large, what entities there must be if what we say is true. The 'ontology' of English is an ontology of the world, on the assumption that English can be and is used to say true things about the world. Not all of that ontology, however, is of ontological interest to philosophers. To determine what interest there is or should be in some proof that there are φs, we must determine what the φs are, what it is to be a φ. And that calls for a metaphysical, not a semantic, theory.

3 METAPHYSICAL CATEGORIES

In many cases where we ask a question of the form, 'What is it to be a φ?', we are asking what might be called, in a broad sense, a scientific question. Though there is some overlapping of interests, philosophers (*qua* philosophers) are not interested in what it is to be a tiger or a prime number. We are, however, interested in the existence and nature of physical objects, sets, properties, events, etc. But this is *not* because we know *a priori* something special about the entities in the latter groups. We can and do change our minds about which entities ought to occupy our attention. Rather it is that we suspect something true of those latter groups: that they are, in some sense, among the basic, ultimate, or fundamental kinds of things. To the extent that we think that the numbers, for example, are just special kinds of sets, our interest in the existence of numbers would really be an interest in the existence of sets. For if numbers are sets, then if it were shown that there are no sets, then there would be no numbers either. If our conviction that there are numbers remained unshaken by the non-existence of sets, then that would show (apart from obtuseness) that we were wrong to think that numbers were sets. Philosophical interest in what there is centres around the basic, the overarching, the general. But we do not know in advance of giving a theory about the φs whether they are basic, general, or fundamental; and in the course of giving such a theory, we may change our minds. If it is the most basic and fundamental kinds of things whose existence is of central concern to philosophers interested in what there is, we ought to have a principle that gives conditions under which some group of things does indeed count as a basic kind of thing. Such a principle would also serve as an analysis of what it is to be a thing belonging to a metaphysically basic kind.

3.1 *Essences*

The bachelors do not form a kind of thing. This fact is connected with the idea that no bachelor is necessarily a bachelor; while it is necessary that anyone who is a bachelor is one who has certain bachelor-making properties (being unmarried, being male, etc.), it is not the case that anyone who is a bachelor is one who necessarily has those bachelor-making properties. But, if we wish to speak about kinds of entity, we want to speak of those groups that are such that any thing in such a group must be in it. In that way, when we say what kind a certain thing belongs to we are saying something important about that thing; we are saying what it has to be like, if it is to be at all. We are saying something about that thing's *essence*.

By and large, any property determines a sort of thing in so far as it determines a class whose members are just those objects that have that property. Such a property, ϕ, however, is an *essence* of the entities belonging to the class of things having ϕ if and only if

(i)   it is possible that there are entities that have ϕ, and
(ii) it is necessarily true that if some entity has ϕ, then it is necessary that if that entity exists it has ϕ.

Several comments on (i) and (ii) are in order here. (a) Impossible properties, those that no object can have, all determine the same class. And it would be pointless and bizarre to say that round squares, things that are red and blue all over, and furious green ideas all belong to the same kind. Thus, to rule such 'groups' out of consideration, (i) is imposed. Impossible properties are not essences.

(b)   Condition (ii) may be read either as

(ii') $\Box(x)(\phi x \supset \Box(x \text{ exists} \supset \phi x))$, or as
(ii'') $\Box(x)(\phi x \supset \Box(y)(y = x \supset \phi y))$.

16

I am indifferent with respect to these two renderings; for my purposes, it does not matter whether 'exists' stands for a property. It is, however, of concern to me to point out that both (ii′) and (ii″) are readings of (ii) that are to be preferred to

(ii‴) $\Box(x)(\phi x \supset \Box(\phi x))$.

The reason for this preference is that (ii‴) commits one either to the view that objects have their essences even in possible worlds in which they do not exist or to the view that each object exists in all possible worlds. Each of these views is stronger than any relevant view I need to maintain on possible worlds; so I will think of (ii) as either (ii′) or (ii″) and not take a position on those stronger views.[10]

(c)   Tautological properties, e.g., the property of being either green or not green, are properties of everything, and are essences of everything. If there is a property of existence, it too is a property of everything.

(d)   Some properties are such that some objects have them in every possible world in which they exist, while other objects have them in only some of the worlds in which they exist. For example, the property of being either prime or prim is had by the number five in every world in which it exists, but is had by some librarians in only some of the worlds in which they exist. The properties satisfying (i) and (ii), and hence qualifying as essences, however, are had by any objects having them at all in every possible world in which they exist. That is, essences are had essentially by any objects that have them at all.

I am interested in those properties that are essences, for I am interested in saying something about how objects divide into kinds (some of which are metaphysically important). And it is clear that properties that can be had essentially by some objects and accidentally by others are unsuitable for such a purpose. And if there is a sense in which the number five and Nancy the librarian belong to the same kind, it is surely not a metaphysically interesting sense, given that what we think we know about numbers and librarians is even roughly true. The properties, the sharing of which is relevant to inclusion in a kind, should be properties had essentially by every object that has them.

It is not, however, sufficient for the purposes at hand to insist that the properties that will figure in the attempt to say which

17

kinds of entities constitute metaphysically interesting kinds be properties had in every possible world by anything that in fact has them. For suppose that in fact there are no prim things; then the only things in fact prime or prim will be the prime numbers. And the prime numbers will have that property in every world in which they exist. Now, while it is certainly true that the prime numbers deserve grouping together, they do not deserve grouping together under the rubric 'things that are either prime or prim'. The things that are in fact prime or prim and that are so in every possible world in which they exist should not be said to form a kind just because of the accidental non-existence of prim things. It should not be the case that whether or not the φs form a kind should be determined by which φs in fact exist. Thus, we should insist that essences be properties that are had in every possible world by any objects that *could* have them, and not merely by those objects that do in fact have them. The appearance of outermost, *de dicto*, modal operator in (ii) (and in (ii′)) ensures this.

3.2 *Groups that are too large*

Some groups of things sharing an essence are 'too large' to be basic kinds of things. Now, in light of the fact that metaphysicians are interested in discovering which groups of things are the metaphysically most basic, the idea that certain groups whose members share an essence encompass too many entities ought initially to strike one as rather odd. Oughtn't we to be interested in the broadest categories? How, then, could a class be too wide for such a purpose?

I imagine that if asked to mention a class of entities which ought to count as an ultimate sort of thing from a metaphysical point of view, or whose non-emptiness clearly ought to be of concern to metaphysicians, one would mention the Abstract Entities, those entities sharing the essence of being abstract (however that property is to be analysed). Surely that group isn't too small; for while the abstract entities constitute a species, a species of existent thing, that latter group is clearly too large with respect to the dividing of things into metaphysically interesting sorts. I want to suggest, however, that the class of abstract entities is indeed too large, and that it would be a mistake for metaphysicians interested in what there is to focus their attention on the abstract entities as such.

Let us suppose that there are good reasons for thinking that there are abstract entities and that they come in the usual species: propositions, sets, properties, and perhaps some others. But suppose also that some reason emerges for thinking that there could be, after all, no propositions, for example. In such a case, it seems that that fact would *not* make us uneasy about the other species of abstract entity. If, on the other hand, we thought we had some good reason for thinking that there could be no rocks, that fact *would* make us uneasy about the rest of the species of physical object, for it is very difficult, if not impossible, to see what the reason could be like that could cast doubt on the possibility of the rocks but would not also infect the possibility of other physical objects. In the case of the abstract entities, however, we can imagine special problems attached to the propositions that would have nothing to do with the sets or the properties. The general idea here is that some species are, in some important sense, more closely tied to other species of their genera than other species are tied to other species of their genera. And it is in the latter cases, of loose ties between species, that I am inclined to say that those genera are too large. What are the ties that bind?

The abstract entities should not be taken to comprise a single, basic kind simply because that group would include such diverse sorts of things as sets, properties and propositions. Of course, if it were to turn out that of the abstract entities there could be, for example, *only* sets, or if, for another example, propositions and sets (and the other species of abstract entity) were all just properties, then there would be no objection to treating the property of being an abstract thing as an essence that determines a basic kind of thing. Of course, the different species (assuming them to be truly diverse) of abstract entity (when that genus includes the sets, properties and propositions) do all have something important in common which justifies their being subsumed under a common rubric 'abstract entity'. But, if what we are after are the basic kinds of thing, then that rubric, that essence that all abstract entities have in common, subsumes too much. No distinct, unique metaphysically interesting category of thing is such that its members have the property of being an abstract entity as its distinguishing essence. That class, when it includes those diverse species, is 'super-categorical'. And what irks about treating the abstract things (when that group contains properties, sets, propositions, etc.) as a single metaphysically interesting kind of entity is what irks about the existent things (in so far as there could be more than one kind of existent thing) and what would irk about the 'spatio-temporal' things (in so far as there could be more than one kind of spatio-temporal thing).

What condition, in addition to (i) and (ii), must be placed on properties, in order to ensure that a property meeting those conditions will determine a kind that is metaphysically interesting? Such kinds must not contain species that are too diverse and only loosely tied to other species. My conjecture is that the kinds that are too large, for their species are too diverse, are the groups of things for which there is no criterion of identity, and that the requisite groups can be got hold of by requiring that such groups be determined by properties satisfying not only (i) and (ii), but also

(iii)   There is a criterion of identity for the things having ϕ.

I state this third condition without discussion here. I shall, however, have a good deal to say about criteria of identity in Chapter II; and I hope to explain there why it is reasonable to suppose that the abstract entities, for example, should not be taken to have a criterion of identity.

Any property meeting conditions (i) and (ii) is an essence. But a property meeting conditions (i), (ii) and (iii) is an essence that determines a class of objects whose members, we might be inclined to say, form a 'kind'. What kind is formed will of course depend on what ϕ is. ϕ might be such that it includes only biological creatures of a certain sort; so, ϕ determines a 'biological' kind (e.g., tiger). ϕ might determine a 'numerical' kind (e.g., prime number), or a 'physical' kind (e.g., water), etc. On this conception, the kinds are just those groups of entities sharing an essence and for which there exists a criterion of identity.

The addition of (iii) is supposed to rule out certain properties, e.g., that of being an abstract entity, that of being an existent thing, and that of being either a number or a physical object, as properties determining metaphysically interesting kinds. It will do that because of certain conditions that will be placed (in Chapter

II) on what is to count as a criterion of identity, conditions that will make it clear that there can be no criterion of identity for, e.g., the abstract entities that meets them.

3.3 *Metaphysical categories*

There is, of course, interest, some of which is philosophical, in discovering which groups are such that their members form kinds. It is clear, however, that not all kinds are metaphysically interesting kinds. For some kinds are too small and are recognizable as mere species. The prime numbers are just numbers that are so-and-so, the numbers are (perhaps) just sets that are such-and-such, and the colours are just properties that are thus-and-so. We can rule out such kinds, however, and focus in on just those kinds whose members form the most basic kinds, from a metaphysical point of view, by insisting that the properties the possession of which determines membership in such a basic kind, a metaphysical category, meet not only conditions (i), (ii) and (iii), but also the following condition:

(iv) There is *no* essence ψ, which is such that
  (a) necessarily, anything having ϕ has ψ (but not *vice versa*), and
  (b) there is a criterion of identity for the things having ψ.

The metaphysical categories, that is, the basic kinds to which metaphysicians direct or ought to direct their attention when wondering about what there is, are just the broadest kinds whose members share an essence and a criterion of identity.

Certain commonsensical and true claims apparently entail that certain entities exist. The entailed existential claims in turn entail, in conjunction with obvious claims about which entities belong to which species and genera, claims about the non-emptiness of certain groups of things. And some of those groups arouse metaphysical interest. Among those groups are some that give rise to the suspicion that they are among the most fundamental, basic, or general kinds of things that there are or can be. Whether or not a group does qualify as such a kind, as a metaphysical category, is determined, I have suggested, by whether or not the members of that group share an essence and a criterion of identity, and belong to no larger group whose members share an essence and a criterion of identity. And such determinations can only be made in the course of giving a theory about the entities in question, a theory responsive to the premises of the existential proof establishing their existence.[11] Thus, we are lead from considerations about metaphysics, as a discipline involved, in part, in the explaining of how it is possible for most of our beliefs about the world to be true, to a concern with what the ultimate kinds of existent, the metaphysical categories, are.

II

CRITERIA OF IDENTITY AND THE NATURES OF OBJECTS

---

1 WHAT IS A CRITERION OF IDENTITY?

A fair amount of the weight of my characterization in Chapter I of kinds and metaphysical categories is borne by the idea of a criterion of identity. There are certain metaphysical tasks, centred principally on getting a grip on what it is for a group of entities to constitute a metaphysically significant one, to be performed by the discovery and articulation of criteria of identity. It has also been said that philosophers ought not to suppose there are entities belonging to a certain sort unless there is, or is reason to believe that there is, a criterion of identity for the entities belonging to that sort. Among the things I want to do in this chapter is to say what conditions would have to be met by a claim purporting to be a criterion of identity in order for it to be plausible to suppose that the metaphysical roles I and others say such principles can play can in fact be played by them. That is, I assume that criteria of identity can do much of the metaphysical work assigned to them; and I will try to say what such criteria would have to be like in order for that assumption to be justified.[1]

1.1 *Form*

When I speak of criteria of identity, I have in mind metaphysical principles such as these:

(1) Distinct physical objects cannot have the same spatio-temporal history,

(2)   Distinct sets cannot have exactly the same members.

The term 'criterion of identity' has been used to refer not only to such principles as (1) and (2), but also to principles that I should think would be more aptly termed 'criteria of persistence'.[2] That fact notwithstanding, I shall always have principles like (1) and (2) in mind when discussing criteria of identity.

Apparently, a criterion of identity is a principle having the following form:

(3) $(x)(y)(\phi x \wedge \phi y \supset (x = y \equiv R(x,y)))$,

though there will emerge a reason to amend this slightly. Such a principle gives a condition – $R(x,y)$ – the satisfaction of which by an entity, x, and an entity, y, is both necessary and sufficient for x and y to be one and the same entity, provided that x and y share a feature, ϕ. However, not every claim of the form (3) (or any revision thereof) can count as a criterion of identity, if a criterion of identity is to perform certain metaphysical functions. More will have to be said about what can take the places of 'ϕ' and '$R(x,y)$' and other conditions will have to be mentioned in order for it to be seen that a claim having the requisite form is a criterion of identity, that is, is a principle capable of performing certain tasks. A criterion of identity is a principle capable of performing certain tasks. A criterion of identity is a principle having a certain form and content, a form and content that permit it to serve certain functions. Before discussing these further constraints on criteria of identity, I want to make a brief comment on the concept of identity in order to forestall some potential misunderstandings.

A criterion of identity for the ϕs is *not* a definition of 'identity' as that notion is applied to ϕs.[3] I take it that 'x=y' always means the same thing no matter what replaces 'x' and 'y'. If identity can be defined at all, it can perhaps be defined as the only two-place relation that is reflexive, symmetric and transitive, and satisfies both the principles of the indiscernibility of identicals and (I shall presume throughout) the principle of the identity of indiscernibles. What a criterion of identity does is to specify a condition on ϕs such that ϕs satisfying it will be alike with respect to all properties, and hence, by the identity of indiscernibles, be numerically identical. And the fact that we get different criteria of identity for different choices of what is to replace 'φ' does not mean that '=' means something different when surrounded by, say, terms for or variables whose values are sets from what it means when surrounded by terms for or variables whose values are physical objects. Nor does it mean that 'x=y', when applied to φs, means 'is the same φ as', unless the latter just means 'x and y are φs and x=y' (which is how I take it). Identity, so far as I am concerned, is not relative.[4]

A criterion of identity is, in part, a vehicle for the articulation of a view concerning what it is for an entity to belong to the kind for which it is given; and it does this by specifying a condition on entities belonging to that kind, a condition the satisfaction of which is both necessary and sufficient for the numerical identity of those entities. The question of how it is possible for a criterion of identity to say something important about what it is to belong to a certain kind by specifying a condition on the identity of the kind's members is one of the issues I shall be addressing.

1.2   *The φs*

Philosophers who have been interested in giving criteria of identity have been concerned with what the identity criteria are for entities construed as physical objects, sets, propositions, properties, events and the like. This concern displays their interest in what are thought to be the broadest, most general sorts of things that there are, if indeed there are things of those sorts. But they have not been interested in the criteria of identity for the red things, the bachelors, or the beloved things. And the reason for this lack of interest is, I suspect, that those groups of things do not form kinds; moreover, if both sets and events were beloved, then a criterion of identity for the beloved things would specify a condition under which some set, x, and some event, y, were identical without mentioning the fact that that condition could not be satisfied by x and y in light of the fact that events and sets belong to different kinds.

In so far, then, as what replaces 'φ' in a criterion of identity expresses a property of the entities for which the criterion is being given, we should insist that the predicate replacing 'φ' express an essence (in the sense defined in Chapter I, section 3.1). By so insisting we help to ensure that the entities to which a

25

given criterion of identity applies will, in a natural way, all belong to a single kind. It should be pointed out, however, that this restriction, that in a criterion of identity what replaces 'φ' be a predicate expressing an essence, is not sufficient to this purpose; more will be said on this matter below.

1.3 *The condition of identity*

What replaces 'R(x,y)' is an open sentence whose only free variables are 'x' and 'y'; and it is satisfied when the values of those variables are alike with respect to the possession and non-possession of all of a certain class of properties, S. What replaces 'R(x,y)' in a criterion of identity will be called that criterion's 'condition of identity' (or 'identity condition'). So, a criterion of identity says of objects sharing an essence, φ, that they are one and the same object just in case they share certain properties in common.

Leibniz's Law, the conjunction of the principles of the indiscernibility of identicals and the identity of indiscernibles, is usually formulated in the following way:

(4) $(x)(x)(x=y \equiv (F)(Fx \equiv Fy))$.

But obviously it can be reformulated so as to have (3)'s form and meet the conditions already mentioned for being a criterion of identity, so long as we allow existence as a property and 'F' to range over all properties (except, of course, intensional ones):

(5) $(x)(y)(\text{Exists } x \wedge \text{Exists } y \supset (x=y \equiv (F)(Fx \equiv Fy)))$.

From a certain perspective, then, Leibniz's Law can be thought of as a criterion of identity for the existent things. But if so, it is a criterion of identity in a 'degenerate' sense, and I want to rule it out, not as false surely, but as a criterion of identity, for it is by employing the idea of a criterion of identity that I hope to get a grip on what it is that divides things into kinds and categories. And in so far as there is more than one kind of thing, it is clear that Leibniz's Law is not up to that task.

Thus, I shall insist that for a sentence of the form (3) to count as a criterion of identity, it must be *stronger* than Leibniz's Law. What I mean by 'stronger' is this. A criterion of identity for the φs states a condition, R(x,y), which φs meet if and only if they are identical. This condition specifies a set of properties, S, which identical φs must have in common. A criterion of identity for the φs is stronger than Leibniz's Law if and only if its condition of identity specifies a *proper* subset, S, of all the properties the objects sharing the essence φ can have.[5] So, a criterion of identity for the objects sharing an essence will spell out a condition the satisfaction of which by φs guarantees numerical identity; and the condition's being satisfied by φs x and y requires that x and y be alike with respect to certain properties constituting a proper subclass of all the properties φs can have. Thus, in (1), the identity of physical objects requires likeness with respect to spatio-temporal features; and in (2), the identity of sets is guaranteed by likeness of membership properties. Of course, Leibniz's Law cannot satisfy the requirement of being stronger than Leibniz's Law.

I know of no non-trivial identity condition that (a) could replace the usual one in Leibniz's Law and (b) would result in a criterion of identity for everything that is both true and stronger than Leibniz's Law. If I am right about this, then the entities to which a criterion of identity stronger than Leibniz's Law applies must be a proper subset of the existent things. Thus, a criterion of identity is given only for a group of things such that not every thing belongs to that group.

1.4   *A puzzle*

Leibniz's Law, which I presume to be true, together with some facts about some entities, which happen to be φs, will have consequences concerning whether or not those φs are identical. A criterion of identity for the φs, together with some facts about those same φs, will also have consequences concerning whether or not those φs are identical. The two sets of consequences cannot conflict. That is, if a and b are φs, then a=b according to the criterion of identity for the φs if and only if a=b according to Leibniz's Law. Were this not so, then either the criterion of identity in question is false or Leibniz's Law is false or contradictions are true. But I assume that we have a true criterion for the φs, that Leibniz's Law is true, and that contradictions aren't true. What this shows is that φs alike with respect to the properties specified in the φs' condition of identity

27

are also alike with respect to *all* properties, and hence, by the identity of indiscernibles, are numerically identical. No criterion of identity for the φs can be correct if it does not guarantee that satisfaction by φs of its identity condition guarantees complete qualitative similarity.

The fact that there are *true* criteria of identity should be a source of amazement. While Leibniz's Law guarantees identity on the basis of the sharing of all properties, a criterion of identity does so on the basis of the sharing of only some. How does it come about that the mere sharing of some properties can guarantee the sharing of all properties? It cannot be a sheer coincidence; an explanation is required. Why is it that sets having the same membership properties are *ipso facto* guaranteed to share all other properties (e.g., have the same subsets, be admired by the same people)? Why should it be the case, if Davidson were right, that the sharing of causal features by events guarantees the sharing of all features by the events in question?

It might be suggested that these facts are explainable simply by pointing out that the proposed criteria of identity are true. Leibniz's Law is, in a sense, trivial; the indiscernibility of identicals is obvious, and the identity of indiscernibles is similarly obvious if such expressions as 'is identical with x' are taken to express properties. Then, if some objects, x and y, are φs and satisfy the φs' condition of identity, then, according to the φs' criterion of identity, x=y. But then, according to Leibniz's Law, x and y share all properties.

This explanation, however, misses the point, for it begins with the truth of some criterion of identity for the φs. And though I am *not* sceptical about the existence of true criteria of identity,[6] my question concerns how their existence is *possible*! That issue is not addressed in a satisfactory way by pointing out that if the existence of some true criterion of identity is actual it is therefore possible.

Suppose that we have a true criterion of identity for the φs. Then, in conjunction with Leibniz's Law, we can derive the following:

(6) $(x)(y)(\phi x \wedge \phi y \supset (R(x,y) \equiv (F)(Fx \equiv Fy)))$,

where '$R(x,y)$' gives the condition of identity for the φs. And it is the left to right conditional of the consequent of (6) – $R(x,y) \supset$

$(F)(Fx \equiv Fy)$ – that amazes. To make clear what it is I am concerned with here, I shall mention (though not advocate) an explanation in the hope that the mentioning will make it clear what it is I believe needs explanation.

Consider the case of physical objects; and suppose that physical objects are identical just in case they have all the same spatio-temporal features. Now, why should it be the case that if physical objects are alike with respect to their spatio-temporal features, they are guaranteed to be alike with respect to all other features (e.g., colour, taste, etc.)? One proposal for an explanation of this fact might consist in claiming that, in some important sense, the spatio-temporal features of physical objects are *all* the features physical objects really have! The 'other' properties physical objects have are, the proposal might go on to say, 'reducible to' or 'emerge from' or 'are supervenient with respect to' the spatio-temporal properties of physical objects. Thus, once the spatio-temporal properties of a physical object are fixed, all others are as well. Hence, physical objects cannot have their spatio-temporal properties in common and yet differ with respect to any of their other features, for, in some sense, there are no 'other' (independent) features such objects have; sharing spatio-temporal features, for physical objects, just is sharing all features, for, in a sense, the spatio-temporal features are *all* the features which physical objects have. So, if physical objects are alike with respect to their spatio-temporal features, they would have to be alike with respect to *all* their properties, and hence, by the identity of indiscernibles, be identical. (Hence, the requirement on criteria of identity mentioned in section 1.3, that they be stronger than Leibniz's Law, would have to be revised; such criteria would have to 'appear' stronger than Leibniz's Law; though the way in which they would have to appear stronger would still make it the case that a given criteria of identity would not be given for everything.) So, in general, the explanation of why criteria of identity and Leibniz's Law are guaranteed to give the same identity-results is that a criterion of identity for the ϕs just is Leibniz's Law applied to the ϕs, since the properties not specified or determined in the ϕs' condition of identity are properties that are such that all ϕs must be alike with respect to them because all ϕs necessarily lack them.

I hasten to point out that I hold no brief for the just mentioned proposal, though it is an interesting suggestion and it is not blatantly absurd.[7] But it is the sort of suggestion which, if true, would explain what it is that needs explanation. In presenting it, I wished only to make it plain that there is something that requires explanation. Unfortunately, I have nothing further to add to the discussion of this issue of how true criteria of identity are possible, and I leave it in its present state. However, this issue is a good introduction to the next matter to be discussed, for it raises the point that a criterion of identity for φs cannot give the same results as Leibniz's Law accidentally.

1.5   *It is necessarily so*

Even if if were true, as a matter of fact, that no two physical objects ever had, has, or will have the same colour, we would not find the following acceptable as a criterion of identity for physical objects:

(7)   (x)(y)(x is a physical object ∧ y is a physical object ⊃
      (x=y ≡ x and y have the same colour)).

We would not accept it, for the claim, even if true, would be true only *contingently*; distinct physical objects could have the same colour. We require that an acceptable criterion of identity should be necessarily true. Part of the reason for this requirement has to do with the fact that satisfaction of the condition of identity must guarantee complete similarity. 'Must guarantee', because it should not be possible for a true criterion of identity for φs and Leibniz's Law to yield inconsistent results concerning which φs are identical. And this guarantee must be grounded in the fact that the entities satisfying the condition of identity in a criterion of identity for φs are *φs*. That is, we cannot have got the criterion of identity for objects sharing an essence, φ, correct unless the fact that objects are φs makes it the case that they are alike with respect to certain properties (the ones indicated by the φs' identity condition) if and only if they are alike with respect to all properties. If so, then the connection between the satisfaction of the antecedent of a criterion of identity for the φs and the satisfaction of its consequent cannot be accidental. Thus, a criterion of identity must have this form:

(8) $\Box(x)(y)(\phi x \land \phi y \supset (x=y \equiv R(x,y))).$[8]

But how is the necessity of the connection between objects' being
ϕs and their being identical if and only if they satisfy the
criterion's identity condition to be guaranteed? I am afraid that I
do not have an answer that is either complete or fully satisfying;
but perhaps what I shall say can serve as a helpful beginning.

The predicates replacing 'ϕ' in a criterion of identity express
essences of the entities that are ϕs; 'is a set', 'is a physical object'
and 'is an event' are, I imagine, plausible examples. But what is it
to be a set, or a physical object, or an event? To be an entity
having such an essence is to be an object of a certain sort. If an
object's being of such a sort implies that the object also has
certain other features, then a claim saying that if an object is of
such a sort, then it has those other features as well, is necessarily
true. Thus, 'if anything is a physical object, it has a spatio-
temporal history', for example, is necessarily true, and does say
something, in its consequent, about what it is to be a physical
object; and the fact that that claim is necessarily true is, at least,
partly responsible for the claim's being informative about what it
is to be a physical object. (Though clearly, not every necessary
conditional whose antecedent is 'x is a physical object' will be
informative about that.)

So, it does seem plausible to think that the requirement that a
criterion of identity be necessary can be met by its being the case
that the fact that the objects in question belong to the sort in
question is importantly and necessarily connected with the fact
that such objects are identical just in case they share certain
properties. And the fact that the connection is necessary can be
guaranteed by guaranteeing that the properties to be shared by
ϕs, according to a criterion of identity for the ϕs, in order for the
ϕs in question to be identical, be properties importantly and
necessarily connected with properties which would be mentioned
in correct answers to the question, What is it to be a ϕ? That is,
for example, it is at least in part because we think that to be a set
is just to be a thing with members that we think that sameness of
members is a necessary and sufficient condition for the identity of
sets. It is at least in part because we are inclined to think that
physical objects are impenetrable occupiers of spatio-temporal
locations that we take sameness of spatio-temporal properties

as ensuring identity for physical objects. In short, the condition of identity must draw upon, in some important way, the very conceptual resources employed in saying what it is to be an entity belonging to the sort for which the criterion of identity having that identity condition is being offered. In so far, then, as a criterion of identity meets this requirement there is, I believe, an important sense in which a criterion of identity for φs will articulate our beliefs about what it is to be a φ; such a criterion will tell us what kind of thing a φ is. And if a criterion of identity does tell us that, if it is 'essence-articulating', it will satisfy the requirement that it be a necessary truth.

1.6 *Non-vacuousness*

One of the tasks with which the discovering and formulating of criteria of identity is being associated is that of finding out what the different kinds of entity are. And the conditions of identity specified in such criteria are selected in accordance with their ability to say something important about what it is to be entities of the kinds for which the criteria are being given. There is thus something to be said in favour of insisting that a criterion of identity be given for only one kind of entity at a time. There is not much to be said in favour of giving a criterion of identity for the entities that have the property of being either a physical object or a set as an essence. For that would suggest that the physical objects and the sets constitute in some important sense a kind of thing. And to the extent that we see intuitively, even if not more deeply, that such a suggestion is fundamentally wrong-headed, we should take steps to guard against it. What would guard against it would be some further condition on criteria of identity whose being met would make it impossible for there to be a criterion of identity for groups whose members are 'too diverse' to constitute a kind.

It is obvious that if we can provide a criterion of identity for the physical objects and one for the sets, we can provide a formula, in the style of (8), for the entities sharing the essence of being either a physical object or a set:[9]

(9) $\Box(x)(y)(x$ is a physical object or a set $\wedge$ y is a physical object or a set $\supset (x = y \equiv (R(x,y) \vee R'(x,y))))$,

32

where 'R(x,y)' and 'R'(x,y)', respectively, give conditions of identity for physical objects and sets.[10] But surely, there just is no kind of entity, in any metaphysically interesting sense, whose nature is to be either impenetrable or membered. But how do we turn this fact into a further restriction on claims of the form (8) qualifying as criteria of identity?

As a first attempt, one might, by focusing on the look of (9), suggest that the true kinds are just those whose members share an essence and for which there is a criterion of identity whose identity condition is *non-disjunctive*. An identity condition will be disjunctive, and hence unsuitable, just in case it has the form

(10) $R(x,y) \lor R'(x,y) \lor \ldots \lor R''^{\cdots'}(x,y)$,

where each disjunct in (10) is a condition of identity for a group of objects that share an essence and form a proper subgroup of the things for which (10) is the disjunctive condition of identity. However, this proposal cannot be satisfactory. The restriction it proposes is syntactic, and rules out certain candidates, e.g., (9), for criteria of identity on the basis of grammatical form. And one suspects that one can produce identity conditions that do not appear disjunctive but accomplish what disjunctive ones do; and there will be some that look disjunctive but which should not be disqualified. In the case at hand, since no physical object has members (in the requisite sense) and no set has a spatio-temporal history,[11] it is easy to give a criterion of identity for the physical objects and the sets whose identity condition is non-disjunctive:

(11) $\square$(x)(y)(x is a physical object or a set $\land$ y is a physical object or a set $\supset$ (x=y $\equiv$ x and y have the same members and the same spatio-temporal history)).

(11) is true, since (a) all physical objects have the same members (none) but only the identical ones have the same spatio-temporal history, (b) all sets have the same spatio-temporal history but only the identical ones have the same members, and (c) no set can be identical with any physical object, since each physical object has some spatio-temporal history and no set does. This syntactic suggestion will not do the job of providing a restriction on criteria of identity which when met will ensure that there is a match of criteria of identity and the groups we intuitively regard as constituting interesting kinds of things.

However, the failure of that proposal provides a clue to what the right restriction is. That clue is seen by noticing that (11) leads to no untoward consequences, *vis-à-vis* which sets and physical objects are identical, because the conjunct in (11)'s condition of identity concerning sameness of members is satisfied by physical objects *vacuously* and the conjunct concerning spatio-temporal sameness is satisfied by sets *vacuously*. We will be well on our way to a correct restriction if we can eliminate vacuously satisfiable parts of identity conditions.

The second clue to what the right restriction is is obtained by noticing the relationship between a given identity criterion's condition of identity and the properties (that things belonging to the relevant kinds have) the having of which ensures that the things in question satisfy the condition. In a criterion of identity for the φs, identical φs must satisfy 'R(x,y)', the φs' condition of identity. 'R(x,y)' specifies a relation only identical φs can bear to 'each other'; the relation is that of likeness with respect to certain properties. But, the individual φs do not have the property of likeness with respect to certain features. The individual φs have certain properties and because of the mutual possession of such properties, 'pairs' of individual φs satisfy 'R(x,y)'. For example, the usual criterion of identity for physical objects does not specify a particular spatio-temporal history which identical physical objects must share; it says that, whatever such history a given physical object has, any physical object with the same such history is identical with it.

The φs' condition of identity picks out a kind (or kinds) of property, such that φs alike with respect to the properties of that kind (or those kinds) are the same φ. That is, the identity condition specifies a property (or properties) of properties, e.g., being a spatio-temporal property, such that identical φs must be alike with respect to the possession and non-possession of all properties having that property (those properties) of properties. Identical physical objects must be alike with respect to all properties that are spatio-temporal properties. Since a property of properties determines a class of properties having that property, I shall appropriate a term from another context and say that any such property of properties is a 'determinable' and that the properties falling under a determinable are 'determinate' properties. A condition of identity for the φs specifies one or

34

more determinables such that identical φs are alike with respect to all determinates falling under those determinables.

In the case of (11), two determinables are specified: membership properties and spatio-temporal properties. But things that are either physical objects or sets and that are identical according to (11) are always alike with respect to the 'genuine' possession and non-possession of determinates falling under one of those determinables and alike with respect to the 'vacuous' possession and non-possession of determinates falling under the other determinable. To aid, then, in ensuring that the entities for which a given criterion of identity is given truly constitute a single, genuine kind, we should insist that such a criterion's condition of identity specify only determinables such that it makes *non-vacuous* sense to say of any entity belonging to the kind for which the criterion is given that it has or lacks at least one determinate from each of those determinables. (It must be kept in mind that my pen vacuously lacks members, while the empty set non-vacuously lacks members.) And (11) does not satisfy this requirement. A criterion of identity may not, in its condition of identity, specify any vacuous determinables. It may not specify any determinable that is not such that for every entity for which it is given it makes non-vacuous sense to attribute to such an entity determinates falling under that determinable. Thus, an identity condition specifies a number of determinables such that φs x and y that are alike with respect to the determinates, F, falling under those determinables are identical. So, the schema for a criterion of identity is this:

$$(12) \quad \Box(x)(y)(\phi x \land \phi y \supset (x=y \equiv (F)(F\epsilon D\phi \supset (Fx \equiv Fy)))),$$

where Dφ is a subclass of determinables such that anything that is a φ can non-vacuously have determinates falling under them all.

In Chapter I, section 3.2, I suggested that it would be a mistake to think of the abstract entities, when among them are properties, propostions and sets, as constituting a metaphysically interesting kind. To rule out the abstract entities, as well as other groups that are too large, I required that the kinds be classes of things that share an essence and for which there is a criterion of identity. This latest condition on criteria of identity does help to rule out those groups that are too large. For it seems clear that, for example, the determinates falling under the determinable 'membership property' will apply or fail to apply to properties only in a vacuous way. And there do not appear to be any determinables which are such that it makes non-vacuous sense to attribute any of the determinates falling under them to all of the abstract entities, and such that they could be used to formulate a correct criterion of identity for the abstract entities.

I hasten to add that I have no theory about when the attribution of a property to an entity is vacuous. All vacuous attributions seem to be necessary falsehoods; the view about 'category errors', according to which vacuous attributions are meaningless, is one to which I do not subscribe. But not all necessary falsehoods involve vacuous attribution; 'the empty set has my pen as a member', though necessarily false, involves no vacuous attribution, for the empty set is of a *sort* of thing to which membership properties apply non-vacuously. I fear that there is no systematic way to distinguish vacuous from non-vacuous attributions that is wholly independent of deciding which groups of entities are too large to form kinds.

1.7 *Partial exclusivity*

To rule out potential criteria of identity that would make it appear, for example, that physical objects and sets belong to the same kind, we require that all of the entities for which a particular criterion of identity is given non-vacuously possess determinates falling under each determinable specified in the condition of identity in the criterion of identity for the kind in question. But, while this requirement does help to ensure that the objects satisfying a given identity condition belong to what is intuitively recognizable as a single, distinct kind, it won't do the whole job. Suppose that each entity other than a physical object has an individual essence, that is, a property (a) which it has in every possible world in which it exists, and (b) which is such that any object having it in any possible world is that entity. Since the property of being other than a physical object is an essence not possessed by everything, nothing said so far stands in the way of the following as a criterion of identity for the non-physical things:

(13) $\Box$(x)(y)(x is other than a physical object $\wedge$ y is other than a physical object $\supset$ (x=y $\equiv$ x and y have the same individual essence)).[12]

36

To the extent that we think that there is more than one kind of thing whose members have individual essences, we should reject (13) as a criterion of identity, despite the fact that it does make non-vacuous sense to attribute to any entity for which (13) is given a determinate falling under the determinable, 'individual essence', specified by (13)'s identity condition.

We cannot, for purposes of overcoming this problem and ruling out the likes of (13), insist that *each* determinable in a criterion of identity be such that its determinates apply non-vacuously *only* to the entities for which the criterion is given. For suppose that there are kinds, the φs and the ψs, that are both importantly different enough to warrant not giving a criterion of identity that applies to the two, and importantly, say, spatio-temporal. The latter fact suggests that in the two criteria of identity, the one for the φs and the other for the ψs, the determinable 'spatio-temporal property' will be specified. Thus, though the identity conditions for one group will specify some further determinable(s), not specified in that for the other, it will not be the case that *each* of the determinables specified by the identity criterion for the φs is such that its determinates apply non-vacuously to φs exclusively; the determinates falling under 'spatio-temporal property' will apply non-vacuously to the ψs as well.[13]

While this suggestion is incorrect, it is on the right track. The correct restriction is obvious. We need only insist on *partial exclusivity*. That is, for each kind, there must be *at least one* determinable, specified by the identity condition in the criterion of identity for the members of that kind, such that it does not make non-vacuous sense to say of any object not of that kind that it has or lacks a determinate falling under that determinable. Thus, to the extent that we see that there really are distinct kinds whose members have individual essences, we can reject (13); and we can reject it as a criterion of identity for the abstract things (in so far as among them are propositions, sets and properties).

It should now be clear, if it were not clear earlier, that criteria of identity cannot be used to define, *ex nihilo*, so to speak, the kinds of thing. For we must already have some clues as to which the kinds are and which groups are too large to be kinds in order to judge whether the conditions of non-vacuousness and partial exclusivity, placed on potential criteria of identity for candidates for kinds, are being met. What the idea of a criterion of identity does do, however, is force us to deal with certain issues concerning the candidates for kinds and to articulate in a precise way our intuitions about what being a member of a certain kind consists in.

1.8 *Minimality*

If a criterion of identity for the φs is to be used to say, in a precise way, something important about what it is to be a φ, then there is a further constraint to be placed on its condition of identity: we should insist that it be *minimal*. That is, the condition of identity should specify the *smallest* number of determinables such that the sharing by φs of the determinates falling under them is necessary and sufficient to ensure numerical identity. Otherwise, we run the risk of useless, though non-vacuous, and possibly misleading conditions of identity. For example, the following is true:

(14) $\Box(x)(y)(x$ is a set $\wedge$ y is a set $\supset (x=y \equiv x$ and y have the same members and are liked by the same people$))$.

However, given the purposes for which a criterion of identity is offered, (14) suggests that it is part of the very idea of a set that sets are liked by people; and that is not so. To rule out such candidates, it is required that a criterion of identity be *minimal*.

It must be pointed out, however, that the criteria of identity for those kinds that are species of metaphysical categories will fail to satisfy either the condition of partial exclusivity or the minimality condition. What should the criterion of identity be for the three-membered sets, for example? I should think that it would be either

(15) $\Box(x)(y)(x$ is a three-membered set $\wedge$ y is a three-membered set $\supset (x=y \equiv (x$ and y are three-membered $\wedge (z)(z\varepsilon x \equiv z\varepsilon y))))$,

or

(16) $\Box(x)(y)(x$ is a three-membered set $\wedge$ y is a three-membered set $\supset (x=y \equiv (z)(z\varepsilon x \equiv z\varepsilon y)))$.

But (15) is clearly not minimal; we could do without the clause, 'x and y are three-membered', even though that clause is, intuitively, not irrelevant in the way 'x and y are liked by the same people' is. And (16) is not partially exclusive; (16)'s condition of identity works just as well for the four-membered sets and for all the sets. However, this is as it should be. One of the tasks to be performed by criteria of identity is that of getting hold of the idea of a kind of thing; that some kinds, like the three-membered sets and the apples, are species of broader kinds is an important fact about such kinds. And we should expect that the only kinds for which criteria of identity, whose identity conditions are partially exclusive and minimal (as well as non-vacuous), can be given are the kinds that are metaphysical categories. For such kinds are not species of broader kinds. In so far as our interests, *qua* metaphysicians, are with the broadest kinds of entity, and not with their species, our interest in criteria of identity should be focused on those criteria that are partially exclusive and minimal. For in such cases, a criterion of identity will indeed tell us something important about what it is to belong to the metaphysical category for which the criterion of identity is given.

1.9 *What is it to be a ϕ*

A criterion of identity for the members of a metaphysical category is a necessarily true principle that provides, for a class of entities sharing an essence, ϕ, a non-vacuous, partially exclusive, and minimal condition that is necessary and sufficient for the identity of the entities, the ϕs, belonging to that category. By being necessarily true (in a certain way), if true at all, such principles provide vehicles for dividing the universe's entities into categories and for articulating something important about what it is to be a member of such a category. For if such a principle is to be necessarily true, then, since its antecedent specifies a kind, its consequent, in virtue of the constraints placed on its identity condition, must say something important about what it is to be of that category: if certain entities are ϕs and there is a criterion of identity for the ϕs, then those entities are identical if and only if they satisfy the ϕs' identity condition.

But it now also seems that something even stronger than that can be said about the relation between objects' being ϕs and their satisfying a certain condition if and only if they are identical.

What is clear so far is that if objects, x and y, are ɸs, then they are identical if and only if R(x,y), where 'R(x,y)' is the ɸs' condition of identity. What now emerges, however, is the idea that if that condition specifies determinables such that *only* ɸs can non-vacuously have determinates falling under *all* of them, then entities that satisfy that condition must not only be identical if they are ɸs, *they must also be ɸs.*

Consider the usual criterion of identity for sets:

(17) □(x)(y)(x is a set ∧ y is a set ⊃ ((x=y) ≡ (z)(zεx≡ zεy))).

The converse of (17) is, of course, false, for objects that are not sets can vacuously satisfy (17)'s consequent. But (17) can be turned into a true bi-conditional by adding a clause ruling out vacuous satisfaction of its consequent. If any things satisfy the condition of identity for sets, either by having the same members or by being the empty set, and are identical by dint of such satisfaction, then those things are sets. Thus,

(18) □(x)(y)(x is a set ∧ y is a set ≡ [x=y ≡ (z)(zεx ≡ zεy) ∧ (∃u)(uεx ∨ Nx) ∧ (∃v)(vεy ∨ Ny)],

where 'N' means 'is the empty set'.

But there is something odd about (18); the clause giving the condition of identity for sets is unnecessary; (18) would be true without it. Thus, simplifying a bit,

(19) □(x)(x is a set ≡ ((∃u)(uεx) ∨ Nx)).

The condition of identity in a criterion of identity for the ɸs specifies a number of determinables such that ɸs are alike with respect to the determinates falling under those determinable if and only if they are identical. Let us say that an object is 'R-ish' (or 'R-al' or 'R-ed') just in case it has, non-vacuously, properties falling under each of the determinables specified by the condition of identity, R(x,y), in some criterion of identity, where that identity condition is non-vacuous, partially exclusive and minimal. Thus, the pen with which I am writing is 'spatio-temporal'; and the set of tables and the empty set are 'membered' (but the Rotary Club is not). And to say, for example, that physical objects, x and y, are spatio-temporal in the same way is to say that x and y have the same spatio-temporal properties, and, given

40

the usual criterion of identity for physical objects, that they are identical.

Objects that are not sets cannot be membered; they neither have members, in the requisite sense, nor are they the empty set. And nothing but a physical object can be, in the requisite sense, spatio-temporal. For if x and y were spatio-temporal in the same way (non-vacuously), they would be physical objects (identical ones, according to the usual criterion of identity). So,

(20) $\Box(x)(\phi x \equiv x$ is R-ish),

where x is R-ish if and only if x non-vacuously has properties from each of the determinables specified by the non-vacuous, partially exclusive, and minimal condition of identity in the criterion of identity for the ϕs. To be a ϕ is to be R-ish, where it is the case that ϕs are identical if and only if they are R-ish in the same way. Thus, for each metaphysical category, there are determinables such that (a) the non-vacuous sharing by things of that category of determinates falling under them is necessary and sufficient for the identity of those things, and (b) the non-vacuous having of determinates falling under them all by any thing is necessary and sufficient for being of that category. The conceptual resources employed in the giving of a criterion of identity for the objects belonging to a given metaphysical category are the same as those employed in saying what it is to belong to that category. A criterion of identity, then, does not merely provide a vehicle for saying something important about the entities that belong to the category for which that criterion is given; it also supplies the conceptual resources for articulating a principle that says directly and precisely what it is to belong to that category.

1.10   *Non-circularity*

When Donald Davidson offered sameness of causes and effects as a condition of identity for events,[15] among the criticisms was a charge of 'circularity'. The ground for that charge was that, since at least some causes and effects are events, Davidson's proposed condition involved identities between events. In this section, I want to survey briefly some ways in which a proposed criterion of identity may be said to be circular and to see whether a criterion's being circular in any of those ways can be said to be a defect and a reason for rejecting it.[16]

(a) Before one can make sense of identity statements involving φs, one must have a principle by which one can tell when one has one or more than one φ. That is what a criterion of identity for φs is supposed to tell us. Thus, if in the condition of identity for the φs there appear open identity sentences the satisfaction of which requires that they be satisfied by φs, one has already presupposed a criterion of identity for the φs. Thus, a criterion with such an identity condition is either circular, requiring its own truth in order to be intelligible, or regressive, requiring the existence of another criterion of identity for the φs in order to make sense of the identity condition in the first.

This complaint is ill-founded. First, a criterion of identity cannot give a general method of telling when we have one or more than one φ. Suppose we have a criterion of identity for mountains. The concept 'mountain' is vague in at least the sense that there is no clear way of dividing cases into those where we have a single mountain with two peaks separated by a saddle and those where we have two, single-peaked mountains separated by a valley. The criterion of identity, however, will not touch this issue. In an application of that criterion to a particular case, the values of the variables must already be given, and they had better be individual mountains. Once those values are given, it can't then be asked whether mountain x is a mountain or a pair of mountains separated by a valley. In so far as anything that is a mountain is not a pair of mountains, a criterion of identity for mountains will have nothing to say about pairs of mountains. Of course, a criterion of identity for the φs will give conditions under which we have one or two φs, since, if x and y are φs, satisfaction of the φs' identity condition implies that we are dealing with one φ and non-satisfaction implies that we are dealing with two. But the usual criterion of identity for physical objects does not tell us where one physical object leaves off and another begins, or whether a chair, for example, is a 'single' physical object or is really six (four legs, a back and a seat). So, even if making sense of open identity sentences to be satisfied by φs required a principle telling us how to count φs, that principle would not be a criterion of identity for the φs.

Second, every criterion of identity contains, just before its condition of identity, an open identity sentence to be satisfied by entities belonging to the kind for which the criterion is given. If 'x=y', when it is to be satisfied by φs, is unintelligible when it appears in the condition of identity for the φs, it should be no less unintelligible when it appears elsewhere in the φs' criterion of identity. A proper complaint concerning circularity has not yet been identified.

(b) A second circularity complaint may hold that it is quantification over φs that requires a criterion of identity for the φs. To allow the variables of quantification to have φs as values is to admit that there are φs; and we cannot make such an admission unless we have a criterion of identity for the φs.[17]

Though there is something right here that I shall later discuss, the objection as stated is not correct, for every criterion of identity, regardless of what its identity condition is like, involves quantification over the entities for which the criterion is given; the antecedent of such a criterion is 'x and y are φs'. The quantifiers, in criteria of identity, are 'unrestricted'. Of course, if the quantifiers involved were restricted, so that the values of their variables were objects only of a certain kind, then the sensible use of those quantifiers requires that they have ranges. But so long as there is anything at all, there are values for the variables of unrestricted quantification.

In a similar vein, if a criterion of identity for the φs constituted a *definition* of 'x=y', when applied to φs, or of 'x is the same φ as y', one could understand the view that the φs' condition of identity cannot contain '=' flanked by terms for φs. For it would then be the case that the definiens contained the definiendum. But no such definitions are offered by a criterion of identity. At best, a criterion of identity leads, in the case of a metaphysical category, to a definition of what it is to be a φ. Thus, such a criterion presupposes already understood and quite general notions of numerical identity and quantification; no special understanding is required in order to understand their use in criteria of identity.

(c) An epistemic version of the circularity complaint suggests that a proposed criterion of identity would be defectively circular if in trying to determine whether certain φs are identical we were always forced by the φs' criterion of identity to decide whether certain other φs are identical. For example, to determine whether events e and e' are identical, the causal criterion directs us to see whether every event that is a cause of e is identical with some event that is a cause of e' (and *vice versa*). But if a criterion of identity is to enable us to deal with the general epistemic issue concerning how to tell when ϕs are identical, we cannot be directed to check on the identity of ϕs.[18] Indeed, in the case of the causal criterion, e=e' only if they have the same causes; but those causes are the same only if they have the same effects, and that is so only if e=e'.

It is not clear how seriously one should take this version of the circularity complaint. A criterion of identity must, of course, have some epistemic import. Having been provided with descriptions of some ϕs, the ϕs' identity criterion specifies a condition the satisfaction of which is necessary and sufficient for the truth of the claim that those descriptions apply to the same ϕ. But a criterion of identity for the ϕs cannot be seen as providing a general method for determining the truth of any identity statement whatsoever involving ϕs.[19] Second, and more importantly, if the causal criterion is defective for this epistemic reason, then the usual criterion of identity for physical objects is probably defective in the same way. We are told, in trying to determine whether x and y are identical physical objects, to determine whether or not every placetime occupied by x is occupied by y and *vice versa*. But it is not clear that there is any way of identifying placetimes except by reference to the physical objects occupying those or nearby placetimes. We might identify placetimes by references to the events occurring at or near them; but we might have to identify events in part by reference to the physical objects that are those events' subjects. Though it may get wider, the circle will be unbroken. It may well be that all criteria of identity, if taken to give directions for solving epistemic problems concerning the identity of members of the kinds for which they are given, give directions that ultimately involve considerations concerning objects belonging to the kinds for which they are given. Epistemic circularity isn't, I think, the real problem.

(d) If some principles contending for status as criteria of identity suffer from a metaphysically unsatisfactory circularity, the unsatisfactoriness may consist in this. One of the purposes I hoped would be served by what I have to say in this chapter and in the previous one is that of advocating the idea that it is not merely nice, when defending the claim that there are entities belonging to a certain kind, to have a criterion of identity for those entities. It is rather, as I shall suggest explicitly in the next section, that our ability to give such a criterion is a crucial part of any metaphysically serious reason for thinking that there are such entities. And that is so because such a criterion articulates our considered opinions of what it is to be an entity of that kind. Indeed, I have argued above that, although a criterion of identity for the objects sharing an essence, φ, is not itself a definition of what it is to be a φ, it does lead directly to a principle of the form (20), which does give, in the case where the φs constitute a metaphysical category, a necessary and sufficient condition for being a φ. And that condition draws on the very concepts used to give the necessary and sufficient condition for the identity of φs. To the extent, then, that the connection between a condition of identity for the φs and a condition for being a φ is as close as I have suggested, it is clear that the identity condition for the φs should not make use of the concept of a φ. For that condition's conceptual resources will be used to formulate a principle of the form (20) which says what it is to be a φ. Since that latter principle is to give us the desired understanding of what it is to be a φ, our understanding of that principle cannot depend on our already understanding what it is to be a φ. Thus, a principle of the form (20), in saying what it is to be a φ, cannot make use, on the right-hand side of its bi-conditional, of the concept of a φ. If it does, it is plainly circular. But the only place in which the concept of a φ could make an appearance there is in the articulation of what it is to be 'R-ish'; thus, on pain of circularity, what does the articulating in the principle saying what it is to be a φ cannot employ the concept of a φ. But if so, then, since what replaces 'R(x,y)' in the φs' criterion of identity is just 'x and y are R-ish in the same way', that criterion's condition of identity cannot employ the concept of a φ either. The reason, then, why the φs' criterion of identity may not be circular, in the sense of employing the concept of a φ in its identity condition, is that, if it were, its corresponding principle, giving necessary and sufficient conditions for being a φ, would be clearly and objectionably circular. A criterion of identity must not be, in this sense, circular.[20]

2 THE SIGNIFICANCE ISSUE AGAIN

The conclusion of an existence argument asserts the existence of entities of a certain sort (e.g., eruptions, colours). The significance argument involves a movement from species to genus, claiming as obvious that entities of a certain sort also belong to another, more inclusive sort (e.g., events, properties). Assuming the latter inference to be sound, of what significance is its conclusion?

The foes of φs can still work for a kind of victory, by arguing that the φs are just ψs and that everyone has already agreed that there are ψs; so nothing new has been discovered, in the sense that no new category of entity has been shown to be non-empty in showing that there are φs. A conclusion of 'taxonomic', but not of 'ontological' significance, has been reached by the friends of φs.

An existential proof for the existence of φs, then, will be ontologically (and not merely taxonomically) significant, if the φs do constitute a new metaphysical category of existent, one which is distinct and disjoint from every other already recognized category of thing. The true friends of φs, of course, have that in mind when they offer existential proofs; they believe that the φs constitute a distinct metaphysical category. But how is that belief to be defended? Given our discussion of existential proofs and criteria of identity, the answer seems obvious. The friends of φs must show that the φs constitute a kind of entity, whose members share an essence and for which there is a criterion of identity, and which is such that there is no wider kind (for whose members there exists a criterion of identity) that properly includes it. In producing the criterion of identity for those φs, the friends of φs will also be providing the materials for a principle articulating what it is to be a φ. The principle can then be compared with the corresponding principles for the already recognized kinds. In so far, then, as the condition of identity for the φs is different from the conditions of identity for the already recognized kinds, the friends of φs have established that the φs constitute a metaphysical category of existent distinct from the already recognized categories. And that will answer the question of the ontological significance of the claim which is the conclusion of the relevant existential proof, the claim that there are φs.

The possession of a criterion of identity for the φs is not mere icing on the cake; it's not merely nice to have such a criterion for the entities one believes to exist. For the giving of a criterion of identity for the φs involves not just giving an answer to the question, When are φs identical?, or even just giving an answer to the question, What is it to be a φ?. It is also additional evidence in favour of the claim that there are φs. A criterion of identity, by giving conditions under which φs are identical, captures and articulates the essence of what it is to be a φ; that is why we can produce, from a criterion of identity, a principle of the form (20). So, to lack a criterion of identity for the φs is to lack a clear idea of what it is to be a φ; for to be a φ is just for there to be a certain condition of identity. So, if we do not have a criterion of identity for the φs, we do not know in any clear and precise way that we are dealing, when thinking about the φs, with a kind of entity at all. And thus, to lack a criterion of identity for the φs is, in a way, to fail to know the first thing one ought to know about an entity whose existence is in question, namely what kind of thing it is.

Our lacking such a criterion for the φs might indicate any of several possibilities. Perhaps it is the case that there could not be any such things as φs; such entities could not have an essence, and there would, thus, be nothing to articulate about those alleged entities in a criterion of identity. Or perhaps the φs do not form a kind, in the sense that the φs belong to different kinds; and, of course, one cannot give a criterion of identity for the φs, if some φs were sets and others were physical objects, for example.[21] Or perhaps, we might suspect that there are φs, but have not yet put our fingers on what it is to be a φ, and so have no clear reason to think that the φs form a kind. In that case, we would not yet have anything to articulate in a criterion of identity. (A fourth possibility is that we haven't been clever enough. In this case, we might have very good evidence for the claim that there are φs and that they form a kind; and we might know just what the essence of that kind is. It's just that we've not been smart, diligent, or clever enough to hit on just the right way to express what we know in a criterion of identity. This possibility is metaphysically uninteresting, though when we have a case of this, as opposed to a case of the third possibility, may be hard to determine.)

In each of these three sorts of cases, we just do not know

enough, we do not know the sorts of things we need to know, about the ɸs to justify serious metaphysical talk of them. So, in advance of having a criterion of identity for the ɸs, one has a right to be sceptical of them and suspicious of their existence. No entity without identity.[22]

Thus, if we are to accept *events* as entities constituting a metaphysical category of existent, we must, at least, be satisfied that a criterion of identity for events can be given that captures and articulates an essence of events not shared by the members of any other kind that we take to be a distinct category of thing. That criterion must be necessary, non-vacuous, partially exclusive, minimal and non-circular; and it must lead to a principle articulating what it is to be an event. All this is what we take sameness of members to do for sets and what spatio-temporal sameness is supposed to do for physical objects. And we can be satisfied with no less for events. For if we fail to do the same for events, we fail to understand just what kind of thing an event is and fail to provide a crucial reason for thinking that there are such things as events.

A criterion of identity for events is, of course, not all there is to a theory about events. And the search for one isn't always the right place to begin the search for a theory about events. But the search for a theory about what events are and the search for a criterion of identity for events are so intimately connected that one cannot be said to be involved in the one unless one is involved in the other. In the next chapter, I shall have a look at three conceptions of events, in part for the purpose of demonstrating the intimacy of that connection.

III

SOME THEORIES OF EVENTS

1 INTRODUCTION

There is a close relation between a theory about the entities belonging to a given metaphysical category and a criterion of identity for those entities. A criterion of identity should be a central part of any such theory, in part because such a criterion, by satisfying the constraints imposed in Chapter II, will employ the concepts in terms of which we can say what it is to be an entity belonging to that category.

In this chapter, I will take a brief look at three views about events that have figured prominently in the recent literature on events. I want to see how the conceptions of events expressed in those views connect with proposals for a criterion of identity for events; the connections should be close. Each of the conceptions of events I discuss in this chapter should, I believe, be rejected. But I do not intend to be thorough in giving reasons for this belief; I do not intend to review the criticisms of these views that have found their way into print. I intend for the most part only to indicate what has moved me to search for another solution to the problems of discovering what it is to be an event and what it takes for events to be identical. I expect neither the adherents nor the opponents of these views to accept these criticisms as decisive. Indeed, I am not convinced that there is anything that counts as decisive criticism in philosophy. What there is, at best, is inductive evaluation of the relative strengths and weaknesses of theories with their accompanying 'refutations' of their rivals. For just this metaphilosophical reason, I was reluctant even to write this chapter, for criticism, when written down, looks as if it is intended by its author as decisive, and I have no such intentions. But it is also for the sake of that reason that I felt it necessary to write this chapter: so that my views about events, together with what I say about my view's rivals, can be seen alongside other views. Their refutations of my views will, of course, be forthcoming.

Each of the views I shall discuss, namely Kim's, Brand's and Davidson's, is rejected by me for roughly the same reason. Each view points out some interesting and important feature of events, and then, taking that feature to be the crucial one to be exploited in a theory about what it is to be an event, formulates a criterion of identity that is appropriately related to the view that events have that feature. My complaint in each case, however, is that the feature exploited isn't crucial enough. The three theories seem to be derived in the sense that what degree of plausibility and appeal they have seems to stem from some other theory exploiting some other, deeper feature of events that explains why events might be what Kim, Brand and Davidson say they are. And that other theory is the one that, I believe, expresses the truth about what events really and at base are.[1]

2   EVENTS AS EXPLICANDA

In a number of papers, Jaegwon Kim has advanced a view about events that has come to be known as the 'property exemplification' view of events.[2] While there is a sense in which that title of Kim's view is apt, there is an important sense in which it is not, for it masks, I believe, the basic motivation for his view. The fundamental clues to understanding what Kim thinks it is to be an event are to be found by concentrating on some issues concerning the concept of *explanation*. At least that is how I shall reconstruct Kim's view.

2.1   *The existence condition*

The explanation-relation holds between what explains (the explicans) and what is explained (the explicandum). For Kim, that relation is, among other things, *deductive*; a necessary condition for any explicans to explain any explicandum is that the former entail the latter.[3] Since entailment relations hold between 'propositional' entities, such things as propositions, statements, or sentences (it does not matter which, for my purposes), what gets explained is the truth of some claim: we explain why the bridge collapsed, why the sky is blue. Generally, what gets explained is a claim that attributes a property to some object. In the case of empirical explanation, the property is one the object in question need not have had. On the other hand, Kim also sees that we speak naturally of explaining avalanches, the sinking of the Titanic, etc. Broadly speaking, explanations are of *events*.[4] Kim, however, rightly wants to insist that events are *not* claims, they are not propositional.[5] So, one question Kim can be seen as posing for himself is this: How is it possible for explanations to be both of truths and of occurrences, when no truth occurs and no occurrence is true? One might avoid this question either by giving up the idea that 'x explains y' is an open question whose substituends for 'y' are sentential or by giving up the idea that when we explain, say, the sinking of the Titanic, we are explaining some event. But neither alternative is appealing; and Kim wants to hold both that the explicanda of explanations are individual events and that the substituends in 'x explains y' are propositional. How is it possible to hold both these ideas consistently? The solution, according to Kim, is that there must be a relation holding between individual events and claims such that to explain the truth of some empirical claim is to explain the occurrence of an event. It must, then, be the case that certain (empirical) claims refer to or describe individual events. So, when an explicans explains the truth of some claim, p, there is a unique event, e, which is the explicandum of that explanation, an event which is uniquely related to p and which is what p refers to or describes. The event, e, must be the *only* event so related to p, for if not, then in explaining the truth of p, there would be no event such that the explanation shows why *it* occurred. Now, the claims whose truth gets explained are ones, according to Kim, that attribute a property to an object; they are of the form 'x has (or exemplifies) F'. If such a claim is to be about, or refer to, or describe some unique thing to be explained, that thing should just be x's having (or exemplifying) of F. Since an object may exemplify a certain property more than once, Kim thinks we can guarantee the required uniqueness of the explicandum by attaching a temporal modifier. Thus, events are the exemplifications by objects of properties at times; and the claims whose truth is to be explained and that refer to or describe events are ones that attribute properties to objects at times. So, more or less, whenever there is a true claim of the form 'x exemplifies F at t' that is a proper target for an empirical, deductive explanation, there is a unique event, referred to or described by that claim, that is x's exemplification of F at t. This is Kim's 'existence condition' for events.[6] So when we have found some claims concerning initial conditions and laws which together entail that the Titanic sank on April 14, 1912, we have explained the event that was the Titanic's sinking on April 14, 1912. Events are, on Kim's view, property-exemplifications; but they are that because they are the descripta of claims attributing properties to objects at times, claims that are the targets of explanations. Events, on Kim's view, are property-exemplifications because they are explicanda. To be an event, on Kim's view, is to be an entity that gets explained. Since an event is related in a certain way to one of the relata (a claim) of an explanation, events come to be property-exemplifications.

Events are said, on this view, to be *exemplifications* of properties by objects at times; and this is unfortunate. Consider an event, e, that is a rock's falling at some time, t. What property is e an exemplification of? It might appear that it is an exemplification of the property of falling; but this must be wrong. What exemplifies a property is a thing that has it. The rock's falling, however, does not have the property of falling; the rock has, and hence exemplifies, that property. The event, however, has, and hence exemplifies, the property of *being a falling*. Events are not exemplifications of properties that objects have at times; they are, rather, the *exemplifyings* of properties that objects have at times. If some object, x (other than an event) exemplifies a property, F, at t, and hence is an exemplification of F at t, then no event exemplifies F at t or is an exemplification of F at t. However, according to the existence condition, some event is an exemplifying of F (by x at t), and is an exemplification of the property of being an F-ing. This confusion between exemplifyings and exemplifications is encouraged by Kim's calling

F, when x's F-ing at t is an event, the 'constitutive property' of an event. For it is natural to infer, from the fact that F is the constitutive property of an event, that F is a property of an event. But this inference is unintended and unwarranted. A constitutive property of an event is not a property of an event; it is a property the exemplifying, not the exemplification, of which is an event.[7] Similarly, such properties are also often called 'generic events'; but this too is misleading. Generic events are not events that are generic, any more than types of cars are cars that are types (though a prototype of a car is a car that is a prototype). What are called generic events are not properties of events; they are properties of objects the exemplifyings of which by those objects are events.

2.2 *The identity condition*

The second fact about explanations that helps to generate Kim's view of events is the fact that they are not truth-functional. The fact that Socrates drank hemlock, together with a law relating hemlock drinking and death, explains why Socrates died. But it does not explain why Xantippe became a widow or why Nixon resigned, despite the fact that Socrates died if and only if Xantippe became a widow and despite the fact that Socrates died if and only if Nixon resigned. The truth-values of explanations are not necessarily preserved under substitution of materially equivalent terms referring to their explicanda.

On several standard views, there is no 'real' phenomenon of opacity; there is no real failure to preserve truth-value under substitution of contained materially equivalent sentences or co-referential terms. Opacity is just a sign of bad semantics, a sign of uncritical acceptance of surface grammar as logical form.[8] On such views, all the usual rules of truth-functionality and substitution of co-referential terms really do work without exception, once we see that such rules only apply to claims' true constituents. A view of this sort is, I believe, at the back of Kim's thinking about explanations. Once explanations are cast in their proper form, it will be correct, Kim thinks, to infer, from the fact that x explains y but does not explain z, that $y \neq z$.[9] Now, if we think of the substituends for 'y' and 'z' as terms designating truth-values, this leads to trouble, for x could explain y and not z even though y and z designate the same truth-value. But Kim believes that certain claims, the targets of empirical, deductive explanations, refer to or describe individual events. And it is clear to Kim that materially equivalent claims do not necessarily refer to or describe the same event.[10]

So Kim's view must be that if event e and event e′ are the same event, then any explanation that explains e explains e′ and *vice versa*. (So, here's a criterion of identity for events: if x and y are events, then x=y if and only if x and y are explained by all the same explanations. But, like the view that events are explicanda, this view suggests the view that Kim 'officially' holds.) Otherwise, explanations are not 'really' transparent. But then the claims whose truth is explained and that describe identical events cannot just be materially equivalent; they must, in order to be describing the same event (since events are the exemplifyings by objects of properties at times) attribute to the same objects the same properties at the same times. That is, it seems clear to Kim that if one claim attributes to x the property F at t and another attributes to x′ F′ at t′, then the facts explaining why the former claim is true do not explain why the latter is true, if x ≠ x′, or F ≠ F′, or t ≠ t′. But if so, then the events those claims describe can't be the same event, for whatever explains an event explains any event identical with it. Thus, if what refer to or describe the explicanda of explanations are claims attributing empirical properties to objects at times, then identical events must be exemplifications (exemplifyings, really) by the same objects of the same properties at the same times. And this is Kim's criterion of identity for events,[11] as generated from views about explanations according to which events are the true explicanda of explanations, and according to which explanations, so understood, suffer from no lack of truth-functionality. This is the view of events as explicanda, from which we can generate the so-called property-exemplification view of events.

Suppose that an event, e, is x's exemplifying of F at t, and that an event, e_2, is x's exemplifying of G at t, where F and G are distinct properties. Despite the fact that Kim's criterion of identity for events says that events are identical only if they are exemplifyings of the same property, that condition does *not* imply that e_1 and e_2 are distinct events. Nothing in that condition or in Kim's existence condition for events says that e_1 could not, in addition to being an exemplifying of F, be an exemplifying of G, and that e_2 could not, in addition to being an exemplifying of G, be an exemplifying of F. And if those were the facts, then e_1 and e_2 would be exemplifyings of the same properties by the same objects at the same times, and hence would be, according to Kim's criterion, identical. But, on Kim's view, e_1 and e_2 cannot be identical; and why this is so can be seen if we look to what I regard as the deeper foundations of Kim's property exemplification view. It is obvious that a certain explanation, E, will explain x's exemplifying of F but will fail to explain x's exemplifying of G, if F and G are distinct. But, on Kim's view, explanations are such that if an explanation explains an event, e, but not an event, e', then $e \neq e'$. That is Kim's point in having explanations be both of truths and of the events those truths refer to or describe. The result of this is that an event can be an exemplifying of only one property. E_1 could not be both an exemplifying of F and an exemplifying of G, if F and G are distinct, for those exemplifyings will not be explained by the same things. (Of course, an event may be x's exemplifying of the (complex) property of being F and G at t; but that event can't be e_1 since there will be explanations of e_1 that are not explanations of it.) So, for each event, there is exactly one property (simple or complex) of which it is an exemplifying. An event may exemplify many different properties, but can be an exemplifying of only one in the sense that, for each event, there is only one property, F, such that that event is an F-ing.

Kim's view has somtimes been criticized for denying certain claims of event identity that seem clearly true.[12] These denials, of such claims as that a certain shooting is a killing, however, are *not* consequences of the idea that identical events must be exemplifyings of the same properties. For if events are exemplifyings at all, that idea is obviously correct. The denials follow from that idea together with the idea that an event can be an exemplifying of only one property. For given that latter idea, then if an event is a shooting it cannot also be a killing, since the property of being a shooting and that of being a killing are distinct. But that latter idea is a consequence, not of the view that events are exemplifyings of properties by objects at times, but of the view that events are explicanda, a view from which Kim's property-exemplifying account is ultimately derived. So those denials of event identity might be avoided without giving up the idea that events are exemplifyings of properties by objects at times, if that idea can be detached from those considerations that seem to motivate Kim's version of that idea and derived from other facts about events. What this shows, I think, is that the fact that events are exemplifyings of properties isn't the crucial fact about events to be exploited in giving a theory about events; it is something to be derived from a theory about what events really are. Indeed, the account of events I shall be advocating is one from which a version of the property-exemplification account of events can be derived; but that version will be motivated by and derived from considerations quite different from those driving Kim's version, and will, as a result, fail to have some of the consequences for event identity that Kim's view of events as explicanda has. I am not inclined, however, to advocate one view of events over anther just on the basis of their respective consequences for event identity. My complaint against Kim's view of events as explicanda is that it misses the concrete particularity that Kim rightly believes is a feature of events. And that feature of events is missed because events, on Kim's view, really are states of affairs.

2.3 *Discussion*

Kim imposes few restrictions on the sorts of properties the exemplifyings of which are, according to him, events. The range of permissible properties is broad enough to allow not only a thing's turning red at a certain time but also a thing's being red at a time to be an event.[13] One might object that the distinction between things that occur (events, in a narrow sense relative to Kim's view) and things that obtain (states of affairs) is blurred in Kim's theory. That, however, is not the source of my difficulty with Kim's view. After all, there is no way to determine, in advance of giving a theory, which groups of entities constitute metaphysical categories. We have no grounds, summed up by the claim that events (in the narrow sense) occur and states of affairs obtain, for insisting that Kim's theory is a theory about entities that do not share an essence and a criterion of identity and that are included in no larger group whose members share an essence and a criterion of identity. Indeed, Kim does give reasons for thinking that the things that occur and those that obtain do constitute a category. All and only such entities are, according to Kim, exemplifyings of empirical properties by objects at times and targets of empirical, deductive explanation. If Kim's events come in species not yet distinguished in his theory, then perhaps the theory is not yet complete; but it does not follow that it is mistaken.

What does disturb about the grouping of things that occur and those that obtain together is this. When an object has any property, F, it is at that time in the state of being F. If that object has F at any other time or if some other object at any time has F, such an object is in the same state, *viz.* of being F. A state of affairs is just an object's being in a certain state at a certain time. And it is the states of affairs that are the things that seem to fit what Kim's theory says of both things that obtain and things that occur; it is the states of affairs, and not the things that occur, that seem to be related to propositional items in the way demanded by Kim's view. We would have a reason to construe events, the things that occur, as belonging to the same kind as the states of affairs, if we had a reason to believe that, in an empirical, deductive explanation of the truth of some proposition that is made true by the occurrence of some event, the occurrence of some individual event is not only explained but is also referred to or described by the proposition entailed by the explanans. But for there to be such a reason, there would have to be a reason for believing that sentences of the form 'x exemplifies F at t' do in fact refer to or describe just one event at most (just as it refers to or describes just one state of affairs, if it refers to or describes states of affairs at all). If that were so, then since sentences of that form are what are entailed, according to Kim, in deductive explanations of events, differences in what propositions are expressed by such sentences will be matched by differences in what events those sentences refer to or describe. However, it seems clear that sentences of that form do not refer to or describe at most one event; such sentences are 'general' with respect to the events that make them true.[14] Multiple exemplifyings of the same property by the same object may occur simultaneously. The earth may quake twice at the same time; and each quaking will make true the sentence 'the earth quaked at noon on October 4, 1984'. But there is no unique event that makes that sentence true. Geology may some day be able to predict when an earthquake will occur. But if the prediction, following from some data and some laws, is of the form 'the earth will quake at noon', a form instances of which refer to or describe events, on Kim's view, it will fail to predict the occurrence of any individual earthquake. That is, no earthquake will be such that some geologist predicted *its* occurrence, though any earthquake then occurring makes true the prediction that *an* earthquake will then occur.

Suppose that John punched someone at noon. Then, on Kim's view, John exemplifies the property of punching someone at noon; so, by the existence condition, there is an event, John's punching of someone at noon. The proposition that John punched someone at noon, however, may be made true by the occurrence of any event that is a punching of someone by John at that time. But it is hard to see how Kim's view can accommodate that fact. For it is clear that if John punched Jones at noon, he punched someone then, and if he also punched Smith then, he punched someone then (the former with a left hook, the latter with a right cross).

John's punching of someone at noon, John's punching of Jones at noon, and John's punching of Smith at noon must be distinct events on Kim's view, because the properties of punching Smith, punching Jones, and punching someone are clearly distinct properties (if Smith and Jones are distinct). (It doesn't matter, in this context, if the punching of Smith and the punching of Jones are construed as 'dyadic', that is, as exemplifyings by a pair of objects of a relational property.) But what, then, are we to make of the event, John's punching of someone at noon? The problem standing in the way of making something of this event is this. It is clear that necessarily that event occurs if John's punching of Smith occurs; for if John punches Smith he punches someone. How is this entailment to be explained?

Consider an ordinary case of entailment. It is necessarily true that if there is an object that is both red and round, then there is an object that is red; 'there is a red, round thing' entails 'there is a red thing'. Now, suppose the former sentence is made true by the existence of some entity, x. If the latter sentence is not also made true by that *same* entity, but by some other, distinct entity, y, it is hard to see why the truth of the former should guarantee the truth of the latter. That is, what explains why the former entails the latter is that whatever entity makes the former true must be a thing that is red and round; such an entity cannot fail to be red (given the fact that it's red and round), and thus cannot fail to make the latter sentence true as well. Imagine that there is only one thing that is both red and round and only one thing that is red. Surely, first of all, those entities must be the very same entity; and second, if, *per impossible*, they were distinct, it would be completely mysterious why a sentence made true by the first of those entities should guarantee the truth of a sentence made true by the second.

I suppose that 'John punched someone at noon' might be understood as 'there is someone, x, such that John punched x at noon', and it is entailed straightforwardly by 'John punched Smith at noon'. But on Kim's view, the former describes an event that is distinct from that described by 'John punched Smith at noon'. That is, the event whose occurrence makes 'John punched Smith at noon' true is, according to Kim, not the event whose occurrence makes true 'John punched someone at noon', however construed or rewritten. So, why should the entailment between the two hold? There must be a story which can be told that shows there to be a connection, other than the 'identity'-connection, between John's punching of Smith and his punching of someone.[15] However, it is not clear that any story can really be satisfactory. For no matter what its details, it will insist that John's punching of someone at noon is distinct from John's punching of Smith.

Suppose we have an account of why it must be that if John punches Smith at noon, then he punches someone at noon; and in that account, John's punching of someone at noon is distinct from his punching of Smith at noon. Presumably, an account of the same sort will be given in explanation of the fact that if John punches Jones at noon, he punches someone at noon; and that account will have John's punching of Jones at noon be distinct from his punching of someone at noon. Now, we have an event, e_1, John's punching of someone at noon, which must occur if John punches Smith at noon, and an event, e_2, John's punching of someone at noon, which must occur if John punches Jones at noon. What is the relationship between e_1 and e_2? Since e_1 and e_2 are both exemplifyings of the property of punching someone by the same individual at the same time, e_1 and e_2 should be, according to Kim, the *same* event. But can this be? E_1 is an event that occurs simply because John punches Smith at noon. Even if he doesn't punch Jones at noon, but still punches Smith, he still punches someone. Similarly, even if John doesn't punch Smith, but still punches Jones, e_2 occurs. However, this should not convince us so quickly that e_1 and e_2 are distinct. That e_2 would still have occurred even if John had punched Jones, but not Smith, does not imply that e_2 would not have occurred if John had not punched Jones, but had punched Smith. It could be held, on the contrary, that since, if John punched either Smith or Jones or both at noon, then John punches someone at noon, his punching of someone at noon, that is, e_1, that is, e_2, would occur. In short, John's punching of someone at noon is simply overdetermined. John's punching of Smith and his punching of Jones are each sufficient and sufficient jointly to 'generate' the *one* event that was his punching of someone.[16] However, I am inclined to regard this approach as wrong-headed, if what one is seeking is a theory that construes events as particulars.

We are being asked to believe that there is one, individual, particular occurrence, John's punching of someone at noon, that would have occurred if John had punched only Smith, and that that very event did occur when John simultaneously punched Smith with a left hook and Jones with a right cross. Just what individual event is this? There seems to be no event answering to this decription. The situation seems similar to the following. Consider Grover Cleveland's successor's being inaugurated. Is this an event that occurs twice? It might seem as if it should, since Grover Cleveland's two terms in office were followed by someone's succeeding him to the Presidency. But, it can't really be the case that some *one* event occurred twice, once because Benjamin Harrison gets inaugurated and once because William McKinley gets inaugurated. That event, on Kim's view, is neither identical with Harrison's nor with McKinley's getting inaugurated. But, what event was it? It could not have been the inaugurating of the one and only person who succeeded Cleveland, for there was no such person. Similarly, each of the two, distinct, simultaneous events, John's punching of Jones and his punching of Smith, made it the case that John's punching of someone occurred. But it can't really be the case that the same event is made to occur by the occurrence of each of those punchings, regardless of which one occurs or if both do.

What seems clear is that events are here being treated, by Kim, as if they were states of affairs, or whatever the entities are that 'correspond' to true empirical sentences or propositions. Since both e_1 and e_2 are referred to by the same proposition, 'John punched someone at noon', and since any explanation that explains the proposition referring to e_1 explains the proposition referring to e_2, e_1 and e_2 must be the same event. But, it seems to me that if events were truly concrete particulars, e_1 and e_2 would have to be distinct. That is, John's punching of Jones at noon must *be* a punching of someone, and so must his punching of Smith. But, since the punching of Jones and the punching of Smith are distinct, so must be the punchings of someone. And even if one were to hold that the punching of Jones and the punching of someone were not identical, but bore some 'generational' relation, it ought to turn out that the punching of someone that is generated from the punching of Jones is distinct from the punching of someone that is generated from the punching of Smith. And this should be the case not only on grounds of common sense, but also on grounds that should be congenial to one who takes events to be explicanda. For any explanation of the occurrence of John's punching of someone, the one which results from his punching of Jones, must surely either make reference to or depend somehow on the fact that John punched Jones; it need not rely at all on the fact that he punched Smith. Thus, an explanation of e_1 must surely be different from an explanation of e_2. But not if all that is being explained is the fact that John punched someone at noon, for such an explanation may well bypass all reference to particular victims. We can explain that just in terms of John's making contact with one of his fists with someone or other.

It is not the idea of events as exemplifyings of properties that forces Kim's view to miss the concrete particularity of events; it is the idea of events as explicanda that does that. For that idea ties events to the proposition-like entities entailed in empirical, deductive explanations. And thus, it is not surprising that Kim's views concerning which events are identical should parallel the sorts of results we expect when we ask which sentences express the same propositions (or which state of affairs–describing sentences describe the same states of affairs). But since a given proposition attributing a property to an object at a time can be made true by the occurrence of more than one event, treating events as explicanda forces one to construe many events as one, as in the case of John's punching of someone at noon. Kim's view forces us to think that there is an event that is John's punching of someone at noon, whereas there is, in the case described, no such event; there were two events, each of which was a punching of someone by John at noon. On Kim's view, events get treated as if they were *types* of events, and not as individual, concrete occurrences; and there is at most one type of event, 'John's punching of someone at noon'. Once this collapsing of events of the same type, where types are determined by the constituent objects, properties and times, is achieved, the 'multiplication' of events ensues, since, on the view of events as explicanda, no event can be an exemplifying of more than one property.

What is thought to be crucial about events, in Kim's view, is that they are targets for explanation. But states of affairs also get explained. And when the events and states of affairs are grouped together and it is said that explicanda are referred to or described by what is entailed in empirical, deductive explanations, pressure is exerted on the concept of an event to accommodate it to a certain view about explanations. What is squeezed out of the concept of an event by that pressure is that events, the things that occur, involve change. For more than one change can result in the obtaining of a given state of affairs. By my lights, Kim's version of the property-exemplifying view of events does not express what is at the heart of the concept of an event in Kim's eyes; it is motivated by a view of events as explicanda, a view that detaches events from the concept of change. If some version of the property-exemplifying view of events is correct, it too will be derived from more basic considerations about what events really are. But those other considerations must not lose sight of the particularity and concreteness of events. They will, I believe and hope to show, have to take seriously the idea that events are changes.

3 EVENTS AS ALMOST
SPATIO-TEMPORAL PARTICULARS

What is meant when it is claimed that events are 'particulars'? One reasonable thing to take that claim as denying is that they are 'universals'. And one way to mark out, roughly, the contrast between particulars and universals is to say that universals, but not particulars, *recur*. As that notion applies to the contrast between properties and physical objects, properties may be said to be universals in the sense that the colour that is the colour of my car is the very same thing that is the colour of my hat; that is, that colour is wholly in my car and in my hat, and in every other thing that has that colour. Physical objects do not, in this sense, recur in that no physical object can be wholly in more than one place at a time; physical objects are spatio-temporal particulars. Properties are universals in that a property may be in more than one place (i.e., may be a property of objects occupying distinct places) at the same time. Events may then be said to be particulars, if they do not, in this sense, recur, that is, if no event is such that it wholly occurs at more than one place at a time. A different notion of recurrence is operative when it is said that events do not recur in the sense that no event occurs more than once (anywhere). It is in this latter sense of recurrence that Chisholm says that events recur;[17] and it is this sense of recurrence which Brand[18] gives an analysis of in order to deny that events literally recur.[19]

To say then that events are particulars is to say, at least in part, that events have spatio-temporal features much like, in some respects, those possessed by physical objects. But how much like physical objects are events in this regard? That both events and physical objects have spatial and temporal locations seems evident, though there may be, as will be discussed (in Chapter V, sections 3 and 4), difficulties in specifying those locations for events. Despite those difficulties, however, it still seems, at first glance, true to say that events, construed as concrete particulars, do have spatio-temporal locations, and so do physical objects. And it is this idea, that physical objects and events are fundamentally spatio-temporal entities, that is the driving force behind Myles Brand's views on events.[20]

Now, in the case of physical objects, the fact that they have spatio-temporal locations is a part of a leading idea concerning what it is to be a physical object; to be a physical object is, at least in part, to be a thing that occupies places at times. The other part of that leading idea is that physical objects occupy their spatio-temporal locations exclusively; not more than one physical object can be in a given place at the same time. This is the idea that physical objects are impenetrable, that they are full or exclusive occupiers of the places they occupy. And it is this idea that leads to the usual criterion of identity for physical objects: physical objects are identical if and only if they have the same spatio-temporal locations.

On the assumption that physical objects are impenetrable – that no more than one physical object can be at a given place at a time – and that that idea is crucial to our understanding of what it is to be a physical object, we may then ask whether impenetrability is a crucial part of the idea of an event. It is Brand's view that events are not impenetrable, that more than one event can occur at the same place simultaneously.[21] And what I am here interested in is the view that, while physical objects and events are dissimilar with respect to impenetrability, they are alike with respect to being spatio-temporal, and the view that just as the spatio-temporality of physical objects is crucial to what it is to be a physical object, the spatio-temporality of events is crucial to what it is to be an event.

If events are to be like physical objects, in that spatio-temporality is to be the core of the idea of what it is to be such an entity, then the criterion of identity for events should draw on the idea of spatio-temporality, just as the criterion of identity for physical objects draws on that idea. But, of course, events and physical objects must draw on that idea in different ways. So, Brand's suggestion is that, while physical objects are identical if and only if they have the same spatio-temporal locations, events are identical if and only if they *necessarily* have the same spatio-temporal locations.[22] The motive behind this criterion is, I presume, this. Since events are particulars, according to Brand, they have spatio-temporal locations, just as physical objects do, though distinct events can have the same spatio-temporal location. However, distinct events, say, e and e', are events that, presumably, are not logically required to be such that e occurs if and only if e' occurs. So, if e and e' are distinct and yet occur at the same time and place, then it is possible for them to have times and places of occurrence that are different. This is so for it would be possible for e to occur and e′ not, in which case e would have a spatio-temporal location not had by e′ (since e′ would have none). If, however, physical objects o and o′ exist at the same place and time, then it is not possible for them to have spatio-temporal locations that are different from each other's, since if they have the same spatio-temporal location then they are, according to the usual criterion of identity for physical objects, identical. If so, then it is not possible for o to exist and o′ not, and not possible for o to have a spatio-temporal location different from o″'s. But, if events e and e′ are such that in every possible world e occurs if and only if e′ does and they have the same spatio-temporal locations, this can be only because, according to Brand, they are the same event. Thus, identical events are those that necessarily have the same place and time of occurrence.

3.1 *Discussion*

How is this criterion of identity intended by Brand to work in particular cases? Let us consider one of Brand's cases:[23] consider the event, e, Nixon's resigning, and the event, e′, the 37th President's resigning. At first blush, it seems as if the criterion implies that e and e′ are distinct events, a most unwelcome consequence. It is, after all, possible that Nixon was not the 37th but the 38th President, because Humphrey won in 1968, making him the 37th President; but he resigned, and Nixon succeeded him, becoming the 38th President; and he resigned too. So, in a possible world in which these things came to pass, there would have been an event, Nixon's resigning, and an event, the 37th President's resigning. And these events would be distinct, since they occurred at different times, the former in 1974, the latter in 1971. Thus, the actual events, e and e′ must be distinct since they, Nixon's resigning and the 37th President's resigning, do not have the same spatio-temporal location in every possible world. But, e and e′ should be the same event, since, regardless of what might have happened, Nixon was the 37th President; so the resigning of the former should be the resigning of the latter.

Brand is, of course, sensitive to this intuition, and has no desire to make e and e' distinct.[24] He diagnoses the problem as arising because of the fact that 'the 37th President' is a definite description whose referent may be different in different possible worlds, while 'Nixon' is a name which designates the same entity in all possible worlds, *viz.* Nixon (even though 'Nixon' may be used in different worlds to designate different individuals). Thus, since 'the 37th President' designates different individuals in different possible worlds, 'the 37th President's resigning' will designate different events in different possible worlds, e.g., the resigning of Nixon, the resigning of Humphrey, etc. And it is clearly the case that whether or not Nixon's resigning and the 37th President's resigning are identical should not depend on whether in some possible world Humphrey is the 37th President and resigns and his resigning and Nixon's (in that world) have the same spatio-temporal location.

Brand's remedy is to ensure that the terms which appear in event descriptions are either rigid designators or, if not, are replaced by rigid designators of the entities they in fact designate.[25] And this strategy is employed not only for the terms designating the subjects of events, but also for the terms designating any other entity (property, time, etc.) appearing in the event descriptions in question. Thus, in the case of e and e', we will replace 'the 37th President' by a term rigidly designating the 37th President, that is, Nixon, and leave rigid 'Nixon' alone. Thus, e and e' would seem to be identical for each is the resigning of the one and only person who in fact was the 37th President, that is, Richard Nixon.

But, it is clear that the device of rigidifying all the terms in event descriptions before applying Brand's criterion will not turn the trick. The reason it won't is that rigidifying each of the terms in an event description does not necessarily turn the event description into a rigid designator of the event actually described. Consider Caesar's death; the description 'Caesar's death' seems to be a definite description of that event. On the assumption that each person suffers only one death, that description will pick out at most one event in each possible world. But it would pick out Caesar's actual death in the actual world, his death due to old age in another possible world, his death due to a fall from a chariot in another, and so on. And these deaths seem clearly to be distinct; a death consisting, in part, in a loss of blood through an unnatural opening, a death consisting, in part, of a hardening of the arteries, and a death consisting, in part, of a cerebral haemorrhage seem clearly to be distinct. This despite the fact that each term in 'Caesar's death' is a rigid designator of the entity it in fact designates. But then it is not at all clear why Brand's rigidifying tactic is at all relevant to the identity of events. We ask whether some event described as a's φing is identical with an event described as b's ψing. Now even after making rigid each rigidifiable expression in those descriptions, we do not necessarily obtain descriptions designating the same events in every possible world, even if they designate the same event in the actual world. But why should the identity of a's φing and b's ψing depend on the spatio-temporal sameness of events that are identical with neither a's φing nor b's ψing?

In any case, the drive to rigidify terms in descriptions of events before applying Brand's criterion is ill-motivated. After all, the criterion says that events are identical if and only if they necessarily have the same spatio-temporal location. It does not say that identical events are designated by terms that in all possible worlds designate events having the same spatio-temporal location. Nixon's resigning and the 37th President's resigning, so described and unrigidified, can only be thought to be distinct according to Brand's criterion if one is prepared to substitute definite descriptions in modal contexts. Thus, Brand's rigidifying tactic is unnecessary.[26] So, let us turn our attention to the criterion itself and what it says about events.

3.2 *Species of spatio-temporal particular*

Brand's condition of identity for events is necessary sameness of spatio-temporal location. Brand intends us to notice, of course, that physical objects as well as events satisfy this condition. After all, if o and o' are identical physical objects, then in every possible world in which o exists o' exists as well, and in all such worlds o and o' have the same spatio-temporal location, since o and o' are identical in every possible world if identical in any possible world. However, we are not to conclude from this fact – that both events and physical objects are identical if and only if they necessarily have the same spatio-temporal location – that events just are physical objects (or *vice versa*). The reason for this is that a proper criterion of identity should, as Brand suggests,[27] make use of the fewest number of determinables the sharing of the determinates falling under which is both necessary and sufficient for identity. So, while the condition of sharing all actual and possible spatio-temporal locations is, according to Brand, a minimal condition of identity for events, it is not a minimal condition of identity for physical objects; a more minimal one – sameness of actual spatio-temporal locations – will work for physical objects. However, there are two things about this I find troublesome. The first has to do with the fact that Brand thinks of his condition of identity for events as one that does in fact work for physical objects (even though it is not a minimal condition of identity for physical objects). And the second has to do with the possibility that Brand is right about that.

Brand's view seems intended to give us the following picture. There is a group of entities, the spatio-temporal things, and the events and the physical objects constitute species of spatio-temporal thing. Those spatio-temporal things that are physical objects are identical just in case they have the same actual spatio-temporal location; and those that are events are identical just in case they have the same possible as well as actual spatio-temporal locations. Perhaps the spatio-temporal things are too diverse to constitute a metaphysical category; but still, it is maintained, there is something that ties all the spatio-temporal things together into one supercategorical kind, *viz*. things of that kind are spatio-temporal.

But a different picture can also be drawn. There is a kind of thing, the spatio-temporal particulars, *all* of which are events; and it is true of members of that kind that they are identical if and only if they necessarily have the same spatio-temporal location. It turns out, however, that a certain species of that kind, the physical objects, are such that identical ones can satisfy that identity condition just by having the same actual spatio-temporal location; physical objects, by satisfying the condition of having the same actual spatio-temporal locations, are guaranteed to satisfy the condition of having the same actual and possible spatio-temporal locations. The situation is reminiscent of the relation between ordinary criteria of identity and Leibniz's Law. Leibniz's Law says that existent things are identical if and only if

68

they share all properties. A criterion of identity for some kind of thing, however, will say that members of that kind are identical if and only if they share all properties of a certain sort; and it must be the case that the sharing of all properties of that sort guarantees the sharing of all properties. Now, such a relationship between an ordinary criterion of identity and Leibniz's Law shows, of course, that the members of the kind for which the ordinary criterion of identity is given constitute a species of the existent things. Similarly, it seems, in so far as satisfaction by physical objects of their criterion of identity guarantees their satisfaction of the criterion of identity for events, the physical objects constitute a species of event. Every physical object is an event, though not every event is a physical object.[28] What Brand seems to have wanted was that the events and physical objects should constitute species of spatio-temporal thing. But this different, and I suspect unwanted, picture emerges.

Though I think that it is the second picture of the relation between events and physical objects, and not the first, that is the one to draw on the basis of Brand's view, both pictures irk. And they irk because they both suppose that the condition of necessary sameness of spatio-temporal location is one that not only is a necessary and sufficient condition for the identity of events but also is a necessary and sufficient (though non-minimal) condition for the identity of physical objects. I want to explain why this supposition is a cause for concern.

Why is it thought that necessary sameness of spatio-temporal location is a necessary and sufficient condition for the identity of physical objects as well as events? Presumably, it is because physical objects that in fact have the same actual spatio-temporal location necessarily have the same spatio-temporal location (for identical things are necessarily identical). So, while necessary sameness of spatio-temporal location cannot be the identity condition in the physical objects' criterion of identity, for it is not minimal, it does appear to Brand that it is a condition under which both events and physical objects are identical. But this is, I suggest, fundamentally misleading since the way in which events have spatio-temporal locations is importantly different from the way in which physical objects have spatio-temporal locations.[29]

Physical objects *persist* through time. And the idea of persistence is such that if a thing persists, say, from a time, t, to a time, t', then at any time between t and t' during which it exists it has *all* of its parts. This is just the idea that physical objects do not have temporal parts (indeed, by my lights, the lacking of temporal parts by a thing is a necessary condition for it to be the subject of an event). So, to say of a physical object that it exists at t and at other times as well is not to imply that there are parts of that thing that are missing at t; though t may not be an interval of long enough duration to include the whole of a thing's existence, all of the thing exists at t. Events, however, bear a different relation to time. If we suppose that some event, e, begins to occur at t and ends at t', then it is correct (simplifying somewhat) to say that e occurred at the interval t-t'. But, though it will be correct to say with respect to some time, t*, that is only a part of that interval, that e is occurring at t*, it is not correct to say that e occurs at t*. That is, events do not persist; events have temporal parts. Thus, it seems misleading to say that both events and physical objects have temporal locations. Though it is true to say that physical objects have temporal locations, that is, times at which they exist, and it is true to say that events have temporal locations, that is, times of occurrence, it is a mistake to think that physical objects and events have temporal locations in the same sense. For if a physical object exists during an interval of time, it also exists at moments in that interval; but if an event occurs during an interval of time, it does not occur at moments in that interval (though it is occurring then).

Physical objects have location in space. They have such locations because they take up space. Physical objects, being made of matter, occupy their locations, and thus fill up the space they occupy. This is why physical objects are the 'exclusive' occupants of the space they occupy, in the sense that more than one physical object cannot occupy the same space simultaneously. Events, however, are not enformed matter (or enmattered forms), and have locations in space only in virtue of the spatial locations of the objects they are changes in. Events, then, do not, in the sense in which physical objects do, occupy the locations in space that are the places at which they occur. Of course, it is, in part, for the reason that events do not occupy their spatial locations that more than one event can occur in the same location simultaneously.[30] But that very reason also shows why it is misleading to say that events are like physical objects in having

70

spatial locations. It is not as if events and physical objects have spatial locations, though it turns out that physical objects occupy theirs to the exclusion of other physical objects, while events do not occupy theirs to the exclusion of other events. Events do not occupy the places at which they occur at all. They do not have their spatial locations by occupying them; if they did, they would be as impenetrable as physical objects.

All this leads me to lodge two complaints against Brand's criterion of identity for events. Neither, however, concerns its truth. That necessary sameness of spatio-temporal location is necessary for the identity of events is obvious; identical events occur in all the same possible worlds and must, in each such world, occur at the same time and place. To show that the condition is not sufficient, it would have to be shown that it is possible for there to be distinct events that occur in all the same possible worlds and have in those worlds the same spatio-temporal locations; that this is possible seems unlikely. So, there may be no obviously false event identity claims following from Brand's criterion.

My first complaint has to do with the criterion's motivation. Brand's motive in proposing necessary sameness of spatio-temporal location seems to be that events are like physical objects in being occupiers of places at times, though unlike them with respect to the possibility of multiple occupancy. In emphasizing events' similarity to physical objects, Brand expresses his commitment to the concreteness of events. But this seems the wrong way to express that commitment. For events and physical objects are unlike in the very respect to which Brand appeals. It is not as if events lack spatio-temporal location; it is rather that it is misleading to say that they are in that respect similar to physical objects. The concreteness of events could be better stressed by pressing the idea that events and physical objects are different with respect to multiple occupancy. And this leads to my second complaint.

It is, of course, part of the very idea of a physical object that physical objects occupy their spatial locations. And that is what, in part, leads to the usual criterion of identity for them. But the fact that events have, in some sense, spatio-temporal locations cannot lead directly to a criterion of identity that performs the function of saying what, at base, it is to be an event, because the facts about the relations between events and places and times cannot be the 'fundamental' facts about events. Those facts seem to me to be derived from other, more basic considerations, considerations concerning the relation between events and the objects they are changes in. After all, that it is true that more than one event can occur in a given place simultaneously is to be derived, in part, from seeing that events do not occupy the places at which they occur, but get their spatial locations from the locations of the objects changes in which are those events. And it is this idea, that events are changes in physical objects, that grounds the idea that events are concrete particulars. It will be from such considerations, concerning the relation between events and the objects they are changes in, that such facts about, say, multiple occupancy, are to be derived, for it is such considerations that embody the idea of an event, the idea to be captured by a criterion of identity for events. So, while Brand's proposed criterion of identity might express a truth, the truth it might express seems to me to be derived and not part of the very idea of an event that a criterion of identity for events should capture and articulate.[31]

4   EVENTS AS CAUSES AND EFFECTS

In his paper, 'Causal relations',[32] Donald Davidson sketches what is in effect an existential proof of the existence of events; the premises of this proof are singular causal statements. And in 'The logical form of action sentences',[33] there is also an existential proof of the existence of actions, which Davidson takes to be a species of event; and the action sentences that appear as premises are ones involving 'causal verbs' (e.g., 'Jones buttered the toast').[34] In addition, Davidson emphasizes that many of the singular terms that purport to describe events do so in terms of those events' causes and/or effects; 'Jones's blowing up of the library' describes an action in terms of one of its effects, while 'Smith's doing what he always wanted to do' describes one in terms of one of its causes.[35]

The concept of causation, then, figures rather prominently in Davidson's discussions of events and actions.[36] Indeed, there seems to be, in 'Causal relations', a suggestion that it is not merely the case that some causes and effects are events, but that *all* causes and effects are events, that only events can be causes and effects. Now I am not interested here in the exegetical issue of whether or not Davidson actually said that the properties of being a cause and being an effect are exclusively properties of events. What I am interested in is the fact that that idea is not implausible and can be defended against putative counter-examples, cases that appear to show that conditions (e.g., a structural weakness of a bridge) can have effects (e.g., the bridge's collapse), that dispositions (e.g., the solubility of salt) can be causes (of, e.g., the salt's dissolving) and that states (e.g., a chair's being red) can be effects. I think that these challenges to the view that only events can be causes and effects (while conditions, dispositions and states are not events) can be met. What was caused was not the chair's being red, but the chair's coming to be red; the chair's being red is the state with which its coming to be red terminated. And the bridge's structural weakness did not cause the bridge's collapse; the structural weakness was merely something that made it possible for some event, e.g., a truck's going over the bridge, to cause the collapse. My aim here is not, however, to carry out this defence of the claim that only events are causes and effects. It is rather to point out that such a defence, if successful, would show that that claim constituted an important conceptual truth about events. And thus, the claim that only events can be causes and effects might serve as the leading idea in a theory about what it is to be an event; the properties of being a cause and being an effect, inasmuch as they are had exclusively by events, would seem to be good candidates for properties in terms of which to express the very idea of an event. To be an event is to be a thing having a place as a link in the chain of causes and effects. And thus, paralleling the connection between the idea that to be a set is to be a thing having members and the claim that identical sets have the same members, and in general the connection between claims about what it is to belong to a certain category and a criterion of identity for the members of that category, it seems natural to conjecture that identical events must fit into the network of causes and effects in the same way. That is, events are identical if and only if they have the same causes and effects. And this is the criterion of identity for events offered by Davidson in 'The individuation of events'.[37]

4.1   *The strongest condition*

One requirement placed on an acceptable criterion of identity is
that its identity condition specify the fewest determinables the
sharing of determinates falling under which by entities belonging
to the kind for which the criterion is given is necessary and
sufficient for the identity of those entities. In so far as events
have both causes and effects, it is clear that sameness of causes
and sameness of effects are each necessary for the identity of
events. But is either of these conditions sufficient by itself? Is
Davidson's condition the strongest one that can be given? If
sameness of causes is alone sufficient for the identity of events,
then it will follow that events having the same causes perforce
have the same effects; and if sameness of effects is alone
sufficient, then events having the same effects must have the
same causes.

But it seems that the antecedents of these last two conditionals
are false. A case of a single particle that undergoes fission,
whereupon each of its two parts moves off in a different
direction, seems to be a case of distinct events having all the
same causes. The distinct events, *viz.* the right half's moving
along the path it takes and the left half's moving along the path it
takes, seem to have as their sole immediate cause the fission of
the particle; and all of the causes of the fission will be remote
causes of both of the movings of the two halves after the fission.
Similarly, it seems that a case of fusion will provide a case of
distinct events having all the same effects; we can imagine a case
where two motions of distinct particles result in a colliding and a
fusing. So, it seems that neither sameness of causes nor sameness
of effects will provide a sufficient condition for the identity of
events. And so, on that score, it is not the case that Davidson's
criterion of identity for events is not the strongest causal criterion
that can be given.

However, there are other grounds for suspecting that if
Davidson's criterion of identity for events is correct, then a
stronger condition of identity for events can be given. Davidson's
proposal is that identical events must be alike with respect to *all*
their causes and *all* their effects. Now, while it may be that causal
chains are temporally continuous, that is, that there are no
temporal gaps between causes and effects, it seems clear that no

causal chain is 'dense'; that is, it is not the case that, between any two events, e_1 and e_2, such that e_1 is a cause of e_2, there is always some other event e', such that e_1 is a cause of e' and e' is a cause of e_2. So, we can distinguish between the remote and the immediate causes and effects of an event. The immediate causes of an event, e, are just those events that are causes of e and that are such that there is no event e' that is both caused by them or by any of them and is also a cause of e. And the immediate effects of an event, e, are those events that are effects of e but not effects of any event that is an effect of e.

Davidson's causal criterion of identity for events is not the strongest such condition that could be given, for it seems that events that are alike with respect to their immediate causes must also be alike with respect to their remote causes (hence, since all causes of events are either immediate or remote, the events will have all the same causes), and events alike with respect to their immediate effects must also be alike with respect to their remote effects. Suppose that e and e' have the same immediate causes, $e_1, \ldots, e_n$; and suppose that there is an event, e^*, which is a remote cause of e. If e^* is a remote cause of e, then it is either a remote or an immediate cause of at least one of e's immediate causes. But if e^* is that, then it is also a remote or immediate cause of at least one of e''s immediate causes, for e and e' have the same immediate causes. If so, then e^* must be a remote cause of e' as well. A similar argument will show that events cannot differ with respect to their remote effects unless they also differ with respect to their immediate effects. Thus, if Davidson's condition, sameness of all causes and effects, is a necessary and sufficient condition of identity for events, then a stronger condition can be given: events are identical if and only if they have the same immediate causes and immediate effects.

Two points are worth noting. First, on similar grounds, if it should turn out that two distinct physical objects cannot occupy the same place simultaneously, then the usual condition of identity for physical objects, sameness of *all* spatio-temporal locations, is not strong enough. A stronger one can be formulated: sameness of any spatio-temporal location. The second point concerns both of these strengthened conditions of identity. The idea behind insisting that a criterion of identity be the strongest possible one was to help ensure that irrelevant determinables not be employed; this would help to ensure that a criterion of identity would lead to a principle saying what it was to be an entity of the kind for which the criterion is given. It should be noted that, if correct, neither the weaker criterion for physical objects nor the weaker causal criterion for events fails to do this; no real irrelevancies get introduced (such as being liked by the same short people). So, in an important sense, no *serious* complaint of non-minimality can be lodged against either.

4.2   *Objections*

Is Davidson's criterion of identity for events true? Myles Brand has argued that it is not by arguing that a case of a particle's undergoing fission followed later by its fissioned parts' fusing would be a counterexample, a case of distinct events, namely the motion of one of the particle's parts between the fission and the fusion and the motion of the other part between the fission and the fusion, that have all the same causes and effets. This is so, apparently, because those two motions have the same immediate cause, the fission, and because the fusing of the parts is the immediate effect of their colliding, which is the immediate joint effect of the two motions.[38]

Another, perhaps clearer, source of difficulty for the causal criterion has also been proposed by Brand. It follows from the causal criterion that there could be at most one event that is, to use Brand's phrase, 'ineffectual', that is, that lacks both causes and effects. For all ineffectual events would trivially have all the same causes and effects, and would thus, on Davidson's criterion, be identical.[39] In addition, the criterion implies that there cannot be two events that have the same effects but are both causeless and that there cannot be two events that have the same causes but are both effectless. But if there could be one event that had no causes or effects, there seems to be no reason why there could not be more than one. In addition, we have already seen that two distinct events can have all the same causes; the causal criterion entails that, if distinct, at most one of those events is effectless. Two distinct events can have all the same effects; the causal criterion entails that, if distinct, at most one of those events is causeless.

This is a great deal of baggage for the causal criterion of

identity to carry about. Weight, however, is not the issue. What is at issue is that it seems that in order to defend that criterion against this objection, it would have to be shown either (a) that it is necessarily true that every event has both a cause and an effect, or (b) that there could not be (for reasons independent of the causal criterion) more than one ineffectual event, more than one causeless event with certain effects, and more than one effectless event with certain causes. At first glance, at least, (b) seems indefensible. Defending (a), in support of the causal criterion, seems a more plausible route to take, though I am inclined to think (a) false. However, regardless of the outcome of either of these defences of the causal criterion, it seems to me that the giving of those defences will show that the causal criterion is not what we are looking for in a criterion of identity for events.

What I mean by this last remark is this. It seems clear that any serious attempt, whether successful or not, to show that necessarily every event has a cause and an effect will have to appeal to at least some of the same intuitions and data that would be appealed to in the discussion of the view that only events are causes and effects. And both discussions will, eventually, have to deal with the question, In virtue of what are events causes and effects? That at least some, if not all, causes and effects are events is a fact that requires explanation. It calls for explanation, not because it is surprising or implausible, but because, even if obvious, it seems derived. There must be some reason why it is that events are links in causal chains, and that reason must be what we are looking for. For it seems that whatever it is that explains why events play the role in causation that they do in fact play (whatever that role is) will do so only by explaining what it is to be an event. There must be something about what events are in virtue of which they are causes and effects, something more fundamental than the fact that they are the relata of causal relations. Causes make things happen, they are bringings about; that is, effects are changes. And it is hard to see how a change could be brought about except by another change. The idea that events are causes and effects, like the idea that events are spatio-temporal and the idea that events are exemplifyings by objects of properties at times, seems to be an idea that is, while true, to be seen to be true by seeing that events are changes. It is, I believe, only by following out the idea that events are changes that we have any hope of explaining the relationship between events and the concept of causation, between events and space and time, and between events and objects and the properties they exemplify at times. And it is only by following out that idea that we have, I believe, any hope of explaining what it is to be an event. And it is this latter task that I want to accomplish.[40] I want to see what kind of theory about events emerges when one follows out the idea that events are changes. If that idea about what events at base really are is right, then we should expect a criterion of identity for events not to make use of concepts whose analysis would ultimately depend, at least in part, on the concept of change, but on the very idea of change itself and on those concepts in terms of which we can understand that idea.

IV
CHANGE

1 INTRODUCTION

Since I intend to propose a theory of events that tries to take seriously the idea that the concept of change is at the very core of the concept of an event, it is important that something be said at this stage about the concept of change. So, the subject of this chapter is the concept of change. The questions and puzzles arising out of the phenomenon of change are as old, at least, as western philosophy; and they continue to torment and perplex. Relief need not, I hope, consist in complete solution; that may be too much to ask, inasmuch as the concept of change may lie too near the centre of the conceptual apparatus we bring to our sensory and intellectual experience. When a concept occupying such a position is called into question, it may be that too much else is thereby called into question as well; there may not be much left to take for granted on which to anchor critical thinking. Since not everything can be up for grabs at once, a discussion of the concept of change is bound to display a bias with respect to certain philosophical views that are controversial and less fundamental than views on the concept of change itself.

My strategy in this discussion will be to start with what seems to me to be the only simple, straightforward and intuitive criterion that attempts to give necessary and sufficient conditions for its being the case that some object has changed. This is the Ancient Criterion of Change (the ACC, for short). I will then raise some (but surely not all) of the questions it engenders and see how the ACC can be made to deal with them. If the result is a defensible version of the ACC, that would be nice; but it would be enough, I hope, if it could be seen how the truth of the ACC hangs on what is said about the issues it raises (and *vice versa*). Since I regard the ACC as fundamentally plausible, it will be tempting, when testing it in hard cases, to hold fast to it and adjust intuitions to suit. While this is not an altogether satisfactory way to proceed, it is not at all clear to me that we would know what to think about change, if we thought that the ACC had to be completely rejected. One can only hope that that criterion will require at most modest revision, and that it can in the main be relied on to predict fairly accurately what our intuitions concerning change are and should be. As a last introductory remark, it should be noted that, since this discussion of the concept of change serves as a prolegomenon to a discussion of the concept of an event, it should be the case that what is said about change not be guided by considerations concerning events. I have found it nearly impossible to fulfil that obligation. I only hope that too many questions haven't been begged and that the considerations concerning events that have crept into the discussion of change are so obviously correct that any reasonable theory of events would have to include them, and that any criterion of change would lead to them.

2   THE ANCIENT CRITERION OF CHANGE

What could be more intuitively clear and obvious than that if an object changes there is a difference between what that object is like before it changes and what it is like afterwards? Similarly, if an object is now different in some respect from what it was once like, it must have changed. These remarks seem to articulate something we know, or at any rate think we know, about the very idea of change itself. And I propose to cast these remarks in the form of a criterion, the Ancient Criterion of Change, in the following way:

(ACC)   An object, x, changes if and only if
      (i)   there is a property, P,
      (ii)   there is an object, x,

(iii)   there are distinct times, t and t', and

(iv)   x has P at t and fails to have P at t' (or *vice versa*; the *vice versa* will hereafter be ignored).

The Ancient Criterion is so called by me because it, or something much like it, was a focus of discussions of change by the ancient Greek philosophers.[1] In my discussion of the ACC, and indeed throughout this work, two ontological issues are ignored: the existence of properties and times. I presume that, if there aren't such things, what I say can be reformulated without reference to them; but in this work I shall be ontologically cavalier about the existence of such entities.

Peter Geach gives the title 'The Cambridge Criterion of Change' to what I have called the ACC;[2] he does this, apparently, because he believes that that criterion was the one espoused by McTaggart and Russell. This may, however, be misleading. Whatever else they might have said on the subject, McTaggart and Russell advocated a principle that does not concern when an object changes, but that does concern when a change occurs;[3] I call this principle the 'Cambridge Criterion of Changes' (the CCC):

(CCC)   A change occurs if and only if

      (i)   there are distinct times, t and t',

      (ii)   there is a proposition, S, and

      (iii) S is true at t and false at t'.[4]

It will be useful to make some remarks here about the differences and connections between the ACC and the CCC, for I want to be concerned with the ACC, and it is helpful to see, at the outset, some of the things it does and does not say.

The CCC makes a commitment (if the right-hand side of its biconditional is ever satisfied) to the existence of things that occur, changes. The ACC speaks only of properties, times and things that change (whether changes change is an issue to be taken up later). The existence of changes is a matter of the success or failure of existential proof. So, while an existential proof for the existence of things that occur may be motivated by the fact that objects change according to the ACC, the ACC does not, on its face, entail the existence of things that occur.

The CCC does not, at least apparently, imply that all changes are changes in or of some object; it leaves open the issue of 'subjectless' changes. The ACC, since it does not speak of changes at all, does not address this issue. If, however, on the basis of other considerations it were shown that there are changes only when objects, according to the ACC, change, and if it were also shown that the subjects of those changes were just the objects that change according to the ACC, then the class of entities thus countenanced (changes) would exclude such entities that are *prima facie* not excluded by the CCC (subjectless changes). I, for one, would welcome such demonstrations.[5]

But even if there are changes and all changes are in or of some object, the ACC and the CCC would still differ in that it seems reasonable to suppose that the adherents of the ACC are committed to the idea that the subjects of those changes are just the objects that change. However, though the CCC implies that, if an object changes, a change occurs, the CCC does not require that the change be a change in the object that changes. Suppose, for example, that Jones's nose twitches; there will be a proposition about Jones that is first true and then false. It would be natural to say, on the CCC, that a change has occurred whose subject was Jones. It might, however, be argued that Jones didn't change, his nose did.[6] That the CCC should imply that the subjects of changes should be the things that change was, no doubt, McTaggart's and Russell's intention; Russell does say that a changing thing is the entity picked out by a term in the proposition whose truth-value changes.[7] But there may be more than one such entity, or there may be no such entity.

I now turn my attention back to the Ancient Criterion.

3 SURVIVAL

The ACC requires that for some thing to change, it must exist at at least two times, a time at which it has a property, and a time at which it lacks that property. This is so, because nothing has a property when it doesn't exist and it does not then lack it either. The ACC thus endorses the view that for an object to change it must *survive* the loss of the property it changes with respect to. The thing lacking the property in question must be the thing that earlier had it.

But the ACC does not seem to require that the thing that changes exist *between* the time it has and the time it lacks the property in question. Would we, however, be inclined to say of some object, x, which was, say, red at t and blue at t', that it had changed if it were also the case that there were times between t and t' during which x did not exist? If we do not say that an object under such circumstances has changed, then it appears that there is a difficulty for the ACC, for the ACC will sanction saying of such an object under those circumstances that it changed, when our considered opinion is that it did not.

I am inclined to think that this is by and large a non-problem, though it is an interesting question whether or not objects can go out of existence and then later come back into existence. I think that there are no circumstances under which we would allow that some object could go out of and then come back into existence and yet not allow that the object might have a property before it went out of existence which it lacked after it came back into existence. If one thinks that objects can have a temporally 'gappy' existence and insists that such an object cannot change in so far as it cannot have a property before going out of existence which it lacks after coming back into existence, one is committed then to the idea that the object in question could *never*, at any time after it comes back into existence, lack a property it had before it went out of existence. But it seems plainly unreasonable to insist that temporally gappy objects should be incapable of change after one of its temporal gaps. Worse still, such a suggestion would imply that such an object could not have changed *before* any of its temporal gaps; for in such a case, too, the object would have a property before going out of existence which it lacked after it came back into existence. So it does not seem at all plausible to deny that objects with temporally gappy existence, if there be any such, can change.

But could some object, x, be such that it was, say, red when it went out of existence, and, at the moment it came back into existence, was blue? That is, suppose that x exists continuously from t_1 to t_2, does not exist between t_2 and t_3, and exists continuously from t_3 to t_4; could x be red at t_2 and blue at t_3? If there is a reason why not, it is this. If there were any such situation as described, it seems clearly to be a case of change; x changed colour. But if x doesn't exist between t_2 and t_3, then nothing can happen to it then. For in order for something to happen to an object it must acquire or lose a property; and to do that it must exist. Now it might be said that something did happen to x in that sense: it was red at t_2 and blue at t_3. But, if x did go from being red at t_2 to being blue at t_3, it did not do so during the stretch of time between t_2 to t_3, for it did not then exist.

If we see change as just an object's being in one state (of having a certain property) at one time and its being in a different state at another, then we shall see no problem in the case just described. But if we see the concept of change, as I do, to be such that for an object to change is for it to be 'involved in process', then there can be no such case as the one described above. Change, I would insist, is a dynamic concept. So, if an object, x, changes, say from being F at t to not being F at t', x must be changing between t and t'; and for that x must exist between t and t'. Now, of course, a process of change can be interrupted; but it cannot be completely interrupted, consisting only of the thing's being in its initial and its terminal states. In order for an object to change it must not only survive the change, it must also persist during it, though perhaps not necessarily at every moment between the time of its being in its 'initial' state and the time of its being in its 'terminal' state. It must exist at all the times during which it is changing.

4   PERSISTENCE IS NOT A CHANGE

The Ancient Criterion, as it stands, places no restrictions on which properties the having and then lacking of which by some object signal that that object has changed. Some problems arise at least in part from this lack of restriction.

Consider the property of being in existence for exactly twenty-five minutes. An object can have and then lack that property just by lasting longer, by persisting. But I take it to be obvious that no object changes merely in virtue of its being the case that it persists. Persisting is a paradigmatic case of not changing. In light of what was said earlier, it might be suggested that nothing changes unless it persists; but persistence itself is not a change. So, the ACC requires qualification.

It seems that when an object persists it changes certain relations that it bears to times. The object was, at the time it had the property of having existed for exactly twenty-five minutes, 'coincident with' a certain instant of time; after that, it was coincident with other, later times. The persistence of an object, then, can perhaps be thought of as consisting in its successively bearing a coincidence-relation to a sequence of times. It seems sufficient, for the purpose of so qualifying the ACC that it does not entail that an object changes just because it persists, to insist that the properties, the having and then lacking of which by an object signal that that object has changed according to the ACC, not include relational properties whose only significant relata are the allegedly changing thing and times.[8] My conjecture is that by ruling out properties relating only changing things and times, only persistence but no genuine case of change gets ruled out. And so I shall presume this qualification to be understood henceforth.

5 COMING AND GOING

Because the Ancient Criterion implies that things that change survive the loss of the property they change with respect to, a problem for that criterion arises when one considers the coming into existence and the going out of existence of objects. A problem arises because, when an object comes into existence at, say, t', it does not acquire a property it lacked at some earlier time, t (nor does it lack a property at t' that it had at t). And this is so, for it did not exist at t; and thus, at t, it neither lacked nor had any of the properties it has at t'. Similar things should be said in the case where an object goes out of existence. According to the ACC, then, no thing that comes into or goes out of existence changes when it comes into or goes out of existence. Or, in the language of things that occur, going out of and coming into existence are not changes a thing undergoes when it goes out of or comes into existence. And I agree; yet, it might be said, what more obvious sort of change can there be?

One suggestion for dealing with this issue starts by agreeing that, when an object comes into existence, it is not that object that changes; the thing that changes is some other thing (similarly for the case of an object's going out of existence). This may be motivated by the idea that if the object that comes to be were the thing that changes, the likely choice of a property for it to lack and then have would be that of existence. And even if existence is a property, nothing lacks it and so nothing acquires it. But surely something changes when a thing comes into (or goes out of) existence! What is the thing that changes? Whatever it is, it must be distinct from the thing that comes into (or goes out of) existence, and it must exist both before and after the thing in question comes into (or goes out of) existence.

The Universe might be proposed as the object in question; on this proposal, it is the Universe that changes when, say, the Eiffel Tower comes into existence, by failing to have and then later acquiring the property of containing the Eiffel Tower. There are the following two objections to this proposal. First, it is not clear that the Universe is a thing. Second, even if it were taken to be a thing that changes when the Eiffel Tower comes into existence, it does seem that the heart of the matter will have been missed. It will also be missed by taking some smaller thing, like the earth, as the thing that changes by lacking and then having the property of having the Eiffel Tower on it. One can, if pressed, agree that when an object comes into or goes out of existence, the Universe (and the earth) will have changed and be different from what it was once like. That fact notwithstanding, it seems clear that such a thing has changed, when the Eiffel Tower comes to be, only because some *portion* of it has changed (though that portion, for the reasons given, cannot be the Eiffel Tower). If so, then there must be some object, which is both part of the Universe and distinct from the Eiffel Tower, that changes and is such that because it changes the Eiffel Tower comes to be. But there seems to be no such object available, though the ACC requires there to be one, if some thing changes when a thing comes or ceases to be. Perhaps, the ACC is simply incapable of dealing with generation and destruction; by insisting on the survival of changing things, the ACC, it might be argued, is equipped to deal only with changes in things, alterations. And no object alters by coming into or going out of existence; it becomes or ceases to be a thing that can alter.

However, it is not clear that such pessimism towards the Ancient Criterion is fully warranted. First, it seems clear that the

ACC is incapable of dealing with creation *ex nihilo* and destruction *in nihilo*. If objects really change, when they come to be *ex nihilo* and cease to be *in nihilo*, then, of course, the ACC has nothing to say, for in such cases, we do appear to have an object's having properties at one time that it neither has nor lacks at another. On the other hand, however, it's not clear that any object does change when there is creation *ex nihilo* or destruction *in nihilo*. Second, it is not clear that we can make good sense of the idea of such comings and ceasings to be. And third, at best we have only a minor failure of the ACC.

The usual things that come and cease to be are things having parts and do not come to be from or cease to be into nothing. For such an object, say, a table, coming into existence is largely a matter of assemblage and arrangement of parts; and going out of existence is largely a matter of disassemblage, re- or disarrangement of parts. We can say of such an object that it does not change when it comes into or goes out of existence. What does change are that object's parts; those parts may change in many ways, but typically they change with respect to the relations they bear to each other.[9] And if they too have parts, those parts do not change when and if they come or cease to be; what does change is their parts. And so on.

Two possibilities loom. The first is that this process of division of objects into their parts, with a concomitant analysis of their comings into and goings out of existence in terms of changes in their parts, comes to end with atoms, objects that have no parts that are themselves objects. In that case, either atoms are eternal or come into existence *ex nihilo* and go out of existence *in nihilo*. In the latter case, the ACC simply cannot cope with these comings and ceasings to be. The second possibility is that there are no atoms; in that case, all comings and ceasings to be can be handled in the same way: the object coming into or going out of existence does not change, its parts change. I am not much attracted to the idea that there are no atoms; and though that point figures importantly in Chapter VI, I have nothing of interest to say in defense of my atomism.

With respect to both these possibilities, there is the following point to be raised. We started with the suggestion that when x, an object with parts, comes into (or goes out of) existence, since it can't be x that has changed, and since we were inclined to think

that when an object comes into (or goes out of) existence some
thing changes, we must find some object to have and then lack a
property. But what could this other object be? The two
possibilities raised seemed to suggest that that other object is the
parts of x. Is there, however, such an object? There *are*, of
course, the parts of x; but there *isn't* the parts of x! There is such
a thing as the set of x's parts; but the set of x's parts is not the
thing that changes when x comes into (or goes out of) existence.
There are heaps and bunches of things that are x's parts. But
neither a bunch nor a heap is a thing; they are things. So, the
heap or bunch of collection of x's parts cannot be *the thing* that
changes when x comes into (or goes out of) existence. So, there
does not seem to be any thing that is such that, when some object
comes into (or goes out of) existence, that thing changes. There
are, of course, thing*s* that change when x comes into (or goes out
of) existence. Things that are to become x's parts change, by
changing the relations they bear to each other, when x comes into
existence; and things that were x's last parts change when x goes
out of existence. But when an object with parts comes into or
goes out of existence, there is no single thing such that a change
in it is what the object's coming into or going out of existence
consists in. If this is correct, then the ACC is not threatened by
the inability to find a thing that changes when an object comes or
ceases to be; there is no such thing to find. Neither coming nor
ceasing to be, in these cases, is a change in any thing; there are,
however, things such that, when they change in certain ways,
some other thing comes or ceases to be.

Some things are made of stuff or matter (clay, water, etc.).
Now, a clay statue does not come into existence *ex nihilo*, nor
need we see its coming to be as a matter of arrangement or re-
arrangement of its parts. Rather, it is a matter of changes in its
matter (or in its surrounding matter). However, as in the case of
objects with parts, there is no such thing such that a change in it
is what the statue's coming into (or going out of) existence consists
in. It is (typically) the clay of which the statue is made that
changes. It does not seem to be the case that it is, for example, any
lump of clay that, say, first has the property of being moderately
amorphous and then has the property of being shaped like
Napoleon. The statue that now exists is not identical with any
thing that was moderately amorphous. Were this not so, we

would be forced to say that the statue existed whenever that lump did, however amorphous that lump was. Indeed, matter does not have a shape. Matter makes up things that have shape. In any case, like the parts of which a thing is made, the matter of a thing is not a thing; it is best thought of as a plurality, as things.[10] Thus, when a thing made of matter comes into or goes out of existence, there is no thing that changes, no thing whose change is what the thing's coming or ceasing to be consists in. There are things that change, however; and because they do, some thing comes into or goes out of existence.

Several paragraphs back, when the issue of whether all objects with parts were such that their parts had parts was raised, two possibilities were mentioned. First, that eventually we get to atoms; second, that there are no atoms, that all objects have parts. In the second case, coming and ceasing to be are always a matter of changes in the parts; in the first case, atoms are either eternal or there is a problem for the ACC due to creation *ex nihilo* and destruction *in nihilo*. Is there now a third possibility? Might there be atoms, having no things as parts, but that are made of matter? In such a case, atoms could come and cease to be without doing so *ex* and *in nihilo*; and their doing so would be a matter of changes in the stuff of which they were made. Of course, we are now faced with the comings and goings of matter. For matter, like things, does not change when it comes or ceases to be, since it does not survive. Coming into and going out of existence for matter must give way to changes in things. What, however, do we end with: partless and matterless things that are either eternal or come and go *ex* and *in nihilo*, or partless things made of matter? And in the latter case, is that stuff (*prima materia*) eternal?[11] Or do we not come to an end at all? In any case, I wish to point out two things before leaving this dreadful topic. First, in either of the first two possibilities, we do eventually get to first *things*, atoms. Second, the ACC is incapable of dealing with creation *ex nihilo* and destruction *in nihilo*, if it is the case that if anything so comes or ceases to be, then some thing changes.[12]

6 WHAT'S THE MATTER WITH SUBSTANTIAL CHANGE?

A subject related to the one just discussed is the subject of substantial change. The cases typically cited as putative cases of substantial change are ones involving caterpillars' becoming butterflies, tadpoles' becoming frogs, scarves' turning into sweaters, princes' being turned into frogs, and so on. All these cases appear to involve an object's changing in such a way that it comes to belong to a kind distinct from the kind to which it once belonged. So, an object changes substantially if and only if it goes from having a property, the having of which makes it the case that it belongs to a kind, K, to lacking that property and acquiring another property, the having of which makes it the case that it belongs to another kind, K'.

The properties the having of which makes it the case that objects belong to the kinds they do seem to be essences. It appears obvious that the property of being a caterpillar is a property had necessarily by any thing that has it at all. If so, then no object changes when it changes substantially, for no object survives the loss of an essence. On the other hand, however, though no prince becomes a frog (witches' incantations notwithstanding), tadpoles do become frogs and caterpillars become butterflies.

If there is some entity that changes when a caterpillar becomes a butterfly, then, in so far as the property of being a caterpillar is an essence of caterpillars (and not butterflies) and that of being a butterfly is an essence of butterflies (and not caterpillars), it is not the caterpillar that so changes, nor is it the butterfly. Caterpillars cannot change into butterflies, in the sense that there is no thing, x, such that at one time x is a caterpillar and at a later time x is a butterfly. Yet, caterpillars become butterflies. We have an apparent contradiction.

There is no thing that is at one time a caterpillar and is later a butterfly, only on condition that the property of being a caterpillar is a property of caterpillars and not butterflies. But this condition might be denied by saying that the kinds determined by the properties of being a butterfly and being a caterpillar are not disjoint. It might be suggested that caterpillars are just young butterflies and butterflies mature caterpillars, that the property of being a caterpillar is one had by certain insects in early stages. On this suggestion, the properties of being a caterpillar and being a butterfly are related in the way the property of being an adolescent and that of being an adult are; growing up is not a substantial change. On this suggestion, then, there is a thing that changes when a caterpillar becomes a butterfly; it is a certain insect, the caterpillar.[13]

Suggestions of this sort may be plausible in certain cases. No one thinks that I became a thing of a different kind when I became an adult; nothing remotely like substantial change is thought to be involved. But I am strongly inclined to think that one cannot take this line with the stories in which princes are turned into frogs; there, there is a clear suggestion that 'real' substantial change is involved. We are not inclined to say that there is a kind, the royal-amphibians, early stages of members of which are princes and later stages frogs. And, returning to actual cases, I think that this adolescent-adult line cannot be taken with the transformation of caterpillars into butterflies, and scarves into sweaters. In these cases, the caterpillars and scarves do belong to kinds, determined by essences, to which the butterflies and sweaters do not belong. If so, then no thing is first a caterpillar and then a butterfly, or first a scarf and then a sweater. But caterpillars become butterflies, scarves become sweaters, and tables become chairs. What is it, then, that changes when one thing becomes another?

If not the caterpillar or the butterfly, could the object that changes when some particular caterpillar becomes a butterfly be some insect? No. For some insect to be the thing that changes, it would have to be such that it was first accidentally a caterpillar and then accidentally a butterfly. But first, if the caterpillars form a kind, then everything having the property of being a caterpillar has that property essentially. And second, even if the insect that changes has that property accidentally, then since anything having that property is a caterpillar, if there were a single caterpillar in a bottle, there would be *two* caterpillars: the one that was a caterpillar essentially (the caterpillar) and the one that was a caterpillar accidentally (the insect). And, for the same reason, since every caterpillar is an insect, there would be two insects in the bottle. But this is absurd.

The upshot of this is that if there is a thing that survives and changes, when a caterpillar becomes a butterfly, that thing cannot have the properties in virtue of which caterpillars are caterpillars and butterflies butterflies. The properties of the changing thing must be such that their being had by that thing makes it the case that there is some other, distinct thing that has the property of being a caterpillar. And later, the changing thing has other properties the having of which makes it the case that there is some third thing that has the property of being a butterfly. My inclination here, however, is to think that there is no such thing that survives and changes when one thing becomes another. What survives and changes is matter. But since matter is best thought of as a plurality, a change in matter is best thought of as a plurality of changes. That is, in cases when one thing becomes another thing, no thing changes. Things change, and the things that change are the things that constitute the matter of the thing that 'becomes' another.

7 RELATIONAL CHANGE

The issue of relational change is another issue arising from the fact that the Ancient Criterion makes no restrictions concerning the properties the having and then lacking of which by an object imply that that object changes. This lack of restriction, in the present instance, seems to lead to certain consequences that have sometimes been reported with displeasure. Geach, for example, says that, on the ACC, Socrates would change when Theaetetus grows taller, that things would change posthumously, and that numbers would change.[14] Plato was aware of the same point and seems to have been moderately appalled.[15] And Terence Paul Smith asserts that, if the ACC were true, 'we shall never be able to say of anything that it has *not* changed . . . it is (surely?) as certain as anything can be that Socrates is not changed by our schoolboy's coming to admire him'.[16] McTaggart, however, did not seem bothered; he says simply that 'if anything changes, then all other things change with it. For its change must change some of their relations to it, and so their relational properties'.[17] Do these consequences really follow. For the most part, they do.

Suppose that some object, x, changes, according to the ACC, during some interval of time, t. There is some property, P (say, that of being red), and x has P at the beginning of t, t_b, and lacks P at the end of t, t_e. Now it does seem obvious that every object, y, that exists throughout t and is distinct from x is such that there is some relation, R, that y bears to x and to x alone throughout t. If so, there is a property, Q, the property of being related by R to a thing having P, that y has at t_b and lacks at t_e. Therefore, according to the ACC, y changes. Thus, generalizing, if during any period of time any object changes, then everything existing during that time changes as well. And if at every moment something or other is changing, then at every moment everything is changing.[18]

The claim that objects change posthumously does not follow from anything in this derivation; to show that claim true, one must add the assumption that objects have properties at times at which they do not exist. And by adding the further assumption that objects can bear relations to other things at times at which those other things do not exist, one can conclude that if any object that ever existed ever changed, then every object is, whenever it exists, constantly changing. Thus, some of the consequences objected to by Geach and Smith are not consequences of the ACC alone, but require assumptions I have earlier rejected. Still, isn't it objectionable enough that when anything changes all contemporaneously existing objects change simultaneously?

To object to that conclusion, one need not claim that there are times at which some objects are, but some objects are not, changing, or that there are times at which some objects are changing and other times when they are not. We might not ever be able to say such things, for it might be that, given the facts, everything just is constantly changing. The objection that may be made, however, is that there are properties the having and then lacking of which by an object do *not*, the ACC notwithstanding, imply that the object has changed.

Suppose that some object, x, is being heated; at t_1 it is 100°F and at t_2 it is 110°F; and suppose that from t_1 to t_2 x is exactly m meters due south of some object, y. Thus, at t_1 y has the property (Q) of being exactly m meters due north of an object that is 100°F, and at t_2 y lacks that property. The objection is that, though between t_1 and t_2 y may well be changing (it might be turning green), it is not the case that it is changing by dint of having and then lacking Q. Things do not change simply because they bear relations to things that change. But the ACC forces us to say that things do so change, for it does not distinguish between those properties the having and then lacking of which signal 'real' or 'non-relational' change from those the having and then lacking of which by an object signal only that some *other* object has really changed. Some further condition must be added to the ACC to rule out cases where objects change 'bogusly', or as I shall say, 'relationally'.[19] Objects that change relationally, the objection contends, do not *ipso facto* change.

But does Socrates really not change just because Theaetetus grows taller or that an object does not change just because another moves away from it? That such things change under such circumstances does not on reflection seem so unacceptable as the objection would make it appear. The derivation above does not, after all, imply that each object is constantly losing or gaining parts, changing colour, or moving, etc. The properties the having and then lacking of which by objects raise this issue are, in an important sense, relational; objects that change in this way do so only because they are related to objects that 'really' change. Those properties include the properties of being a widow, being an uncle, being convicted of a crime, being divorced, being admired by someone, being shot at, etc. And we do, in fact, speak of objects as changing when they have and then lack such properties (or *vice versa*): people change their marital status when they get divorced, and people do become uncles, get shot at, and get convicted.[20] Perhaps what irks about change with respect to such properties is that the objects allegedly so changing do not seem *altered*,[21] they do not seem to be different as a result. But after all, they are different in a sense, a relational sense.

The point about alteration is that though one might say that objects that change relationally are, in a sense, different before and after they so change, they have not *undergone* or *suffered* any change; nothing thereby happened *to* them. The undergoing and suffering was done by and happened to the objects that changed non-rationally, the objects a real change in which brought it about that others changed relationally (for no object changes relationally unless others change non-relationally).

When x goes from being 100°F to being 110°F, we may be

inclined to say that some change has occurred, that there was a heating (of x). But, when y goes from being exactly m metres due north of a 100°F object to not being that (because x is no longer 100°F), we are not inclined to say that by that very fact there was a change that occurred in y. So long as we speak only of things that change, there is really no harm in saying that objects change relationally; so long as we can add 'relationally' after 'change' in the appropriate places, we are not likely to mislead. All that is meant is that an object bears a relation to something that is 'really' changing. The concern is that it might be the case that when objects change, there are occurrences that are the changes in those objects. And it is the spectre of a universe filled with relational changes (as well as non-relational changes, that is, events) that some may find disturbing. So, our concerns are two in number. First, are there things that occur, relational changes, which occur when objects change relationally, in addition, as an existential proof would have it, to events, which occur when objects change 'really'? And second, is there a way to distinguish, from among all the cases in which an object changes, those in which an object changes 'relationally'? I shall consider the second question first.

7.1 *Distinguishing relational and non-relational change*

There is a need to be able to tell, in any case in which an object changes, whether that object changes relationally or non-relationally. By my lights, such a distinguishing principle is not needed in order to know when the ACC applies, for, as I have suggested, I think that there is a sense of 'change' in which objects change both when they change relationally and when they change non-relationally. There are, however, two reasons for providing such a distinguishing principle. First, when an object changes from, say, being red to being blue, it *alters*; but I do not alter when I become an uncle. It is important to have a clear sense of when it is the case that an object alters and when not. To put this point another way, there are at least two ways in which an object can fail to alter: by not changing at all and by changing only relationally. To the extent that we think that, when anything changes, something makes that happen, but nothing need happen for a thing not to change at all, and since it is clear that when a thing changes relationally something makes that happen, it would be good to know which 'non-alterations' are brought about and which are not. And second, not everyone will find my defence of the idea that when an object changes relationally it changes *simpliciter* especially convincing. So it would be good to know which alleged cases of change to be suspicious of. That is, if one's view is that to say of an object that it changes is in part to deny that it changes only relationally, then one will want to formulate a criterion of change (or a revision of the ACC) that rules cases of relational change out. So, one will be forced to make the sort of distinction I want to make anyway, though it will be deployed differently.

In trying to make the distinction, Smith tries to exploit the relational character of the properties the having and then lacking of which signal relational change. He formulates a version of the ACC in terms of predicates:

> An object, x, changes if and only if there are distinct times, t and t′, and a predicate, F, such that F is true of x at t and false of x at t′.

He then defines 'F is a non-relational predicate' as: 'F is a predicate which does not contain any y such that yRx for any R'.[22] Smith claims that the ACC, so reformulated, provides a necessary and sufficient condition for an object to have changed when the Fs are restricted to non-relational predicates. In the case of non-spatial relational predicates, the best we can do, Smith says, is to conclude that one or the other of the objects related by R changes; and in the case of spatial relational predicates, he thinks that no version of the ACC works at all.[23] We'll come back to these points.

It seems, however, that this linguistic method of distinguishing relational from non-relational change just won't do. There are non-relational predicates standing for properties change with respect to which is clearly relational: 'is a widow' and 'is an uncle', for example. And there are predicates qualifying, on Smith's definition, as relational that stand for properties change with respect to which is clearly non-relational: for example, 'is red and is either married or not married to y'. There is just no match between relational predicates and cases where an object changes relationally in the way suggested by Smith's attempt.

The key to distinguishing cases in which an object changes relationally from those in which an object changes non-relationally is the oft-made comment that an object cannot change relationally unless some object simultaneously changes non-relationally. Given that Xantippe was married to Socrates and to no one else at the time he died, she cannot become a widow unless and until he dies; a defendant can't become a convicted felon unless and until the jury renders its verdict. An object can change relationally only if and when it is related to an object that changes non-relationally. (Actually, an object can change relationally due to another object's changing relationally; I became an uncle due to my brother's becoming a father. Still, these 'chains of determination' must eventually end with some object that changes non-relationally.) Any principle doing the desired work must, I think, exploit this 'dependent' character of relational change. My proposal is this:

(R) An object, x, in going from having to lacking a property, P, at an interval of time, t, changes relationally if and only if
  (i) x, in going from having to lacking P at t, changes (according to ACC), and
  (ii) it is not possible that x goes from having to lacking P at t while there is no object, y (distinct from x and any of x's parts), and no property, P′, such that y, by going from having to lacking P′, changes at t.

The parenthetical proviso in (ii) rules out its being the case, for example, that my car changes only relationally when its front bumper gets dented; in such a case, my car clearly changes non-relationally.[24] My contention is that (R) captures the dependent character of relational change and the idea that no object may change non-relationally without its being logically required that some other object (distinct from its parts) change. I want to test (R) and this contention by looking at some cases.

When an object changes by going from being blue to being red, that may require, causally speaking, some other object to change in order to bring it about that the former so changes. But so long as it is logically possible for an object to become red without being caused to do so, it is possible that it becomes red in the absence of any change in any other object. Something, of course, may have to happen to some of its parts; but the proviso in (ii) takes care of that. So, this case is, according to (R), a case of non-relational change, and that seems the right thing to say.

Xantippe's becoming a widow is supposed to be paradigmatically relational; and (R) confirms this. Though it is the case, it is not merely the case, that Xantippe would not have become a widow had Socrates not died.[25] Xantippe could not, in a logical sense, have become a widow unless she had a husband who died. It is not merely a contingent fact that under certain circumstances deaths make some women to become widows, even though it is a contingent fact that those circumstances obtain. (This contrasts with the fact that, under certain circumstances, if a thing is painted red, it will become red, for it is a contingent fact that the laws of nature are what they are.) Since a death logically must occur for anyone to become a widow, and since deaths involve changes in things other than the thing that becomes a widow, Xantippe could not have become a widow, if there were not some other object that changed; for there would then have been no change that could make her a widow. So, when Xantippe became a widow, she thereby changed relationally.[26]

It also seems clear that, if there are events, they can change relationally. A particular eclipse of the sun may start out being my favourite astronomical event, and because, during its late stages, I witness a more spectacular one, it may cease to be my favourite astronomical event. This change in the eclipse involves no alteration in it, but in me; it clearly changes relationally. Indeed, I think it can be argued that whenever an event changes at all, it changes relationally, for I will argue in Chapter V, section 3, that no event can be the subject of a non-relational change; and so, if an event changes, it must change relationally.

And all changes in abstract entities would seem to be relational as well. The non-relational properties that such entities have seem essential to them; and, hence, they could not survive their loss. And all the relations they bear to other abstract things (that do not involve any non-abstract objects) seem essential as well. The only properties that such entities can have and then lack are ones they have in virtue of their relations to concrete things (e.g., being Jones's favourite number) or to other abstract things in virtue of their being related to some concrete thing (e.g., being thought of by Jones while he is also thinking of the empty set).

These cases suggest that an abstract entity can change only if one of the concrete entities to which it is related changes.

7.2 *Motion*

One of my goals in this book is to make a great deal of the idea that the concept of an event is intimately bound up with the concept of change. An event, on my view, turns out to be a non-relational change that consists in some objects' changing non-relationally. Events occur when and only when objects change non-relationally and are the non-relational changes they undergo. So, it is important to me that where there are events, we find something that changes non-relationally. Now it is clear to me that when an object *moves*, there is an event that is that object's moving. So, when an object moves, that object must, according to me, change non-relationally. And this causes difficulty, as I will try to suggest.

Imagine a universe containing just two physical objects, x and y; when x begins to move at t, x and y are m metres apart, and when x stops, at t', they are m+n metres apart. Has any object changed? Now, either y did not change at all or it changed relationally. A good case can be made for the latter alternative, since during the interval from t to t', y had and then lacked the property of being exactly m metres from x; and y could not have so changed (since it was not then moving) had x not moved then. If y changed relationally, then x must have changed non-relationally, since nothing changes relationally unless something else changes non-relationally at the same time, and x is the only other suitable object available. (It can't be that both x and y changed relationally or that x changed relationally and y not at all.) So, I am inclined to believe that when x moved n metres further away from y, x changed in moving and did so non-relationally.[27]

There is this much that can be said in favour of this view. Suppose, in the situation described above, that while x is moving away from y, y is annihilated. In such a situation, I cannot see any reason in favour of saying that when y went out of existence, x would, of necessity, have stopped moving. While it is clear that y would, of necessity, have stopped changing, had x been annihilated, the same just cannot be said of x, had y disappeared. If it can be said that x was moving, and hence changing, when y was there (not doing much of anything, just changing relationally), then it cannot be said that x would have stopped dead in its tracks at the moment y was annihilated. But if x's continuing to be in motion does not depend on y's continued existence, then x's being in motion at all does not depend on any change in y. Thus, x could have moved, and hence changed location, even if x were the universe's only changing thing; x, in moving, changed non-relationally.

However, there are two things to be said against this. The first concerns the properties moving things have and then lack, the having and then lacking of which is that in virtue of which such a thing moves. If, as I would like to maintain, a thing changes when it moves (and does so in accordance with the ACC), there must be properties such a thing has and then lacks. Clearly, the properties must be ones the having of which by an object makes it the case that it has certain spatial locations. If we think of space substantively, as a thing existing independently of being occupied, then the location-properties will be properties like that of being coincident with such-and-such point (or collection of points) of space. If, on the other hand, we think of space, not as an independent existent, but relationally, as a certain set of relations holding among actual (or possible) occupiers, then the location properties will be properties like that of being at such-and-such a distance in so-and-so a direction from some other entity. But in either case, it appears as if location-properties are 'relational' properties, properties things have only in virtue of their relations with other things, either other spatially located objects or space itself (or locations). If that is so, then won't a change by a moving thing with respect to such properties be a relational change, and not a non-relational change as required by the view argued for in the previous paragraph? Indeed, on the substantivalist's view, a moving thing cannot move unless the locations through which it moves change; and those locations change relationally, since they first have and then lack the property of having the moving thing at them; and they could not so change unless some object moved. We seem to have a chain of relational change not grounded in any non-relational change.

The second problem has to do with the 'relativity' of motion, the idea that there are no 'privileged' frames of reference. Of course, once a frame of reference is selected for the specification of the locations of objects at times, the distinction, relative to that frame, between being in motion and being at rest is fixed. But there is no reason to select one frame over any other. Relative to another frame of reference, an object, in motion in the first frame, is at rest, while another object, at rest in the first frame, is in motion. If what I have proposed were correct, then we should say that x would change non-relationally in one frame and relationally in another. This seems similar to suggesting that, relative to one 'frame of reference', Socrates changes non-relationally when he dies while Xantippe changes relationally in becoming a widow; but relative to another, Socrates' change is relational while Xantippe's is non-relational. And this latter is intolerable. So, unless special provision is made for change in location, my suggestion for dividing on an occasion objects into those that non-relationally change spatially (i.e., move) and those that merely relationally so change seems doomed.

Perhaps what must be said is that special provision should be made in the case of motion. Despite what has been said, I am still inclined to the view that objects do change non-relationally when they move, and that there is a difference between moving and merely changing with respect to spatial relations. That objects change when they either move or merely change with respect to their spatial relations is, of course, sanctioned by the ACC; and I am not troubled by this. The problem is to distinguish spatial change due to motion from spatial change due to being spatially related to a moving thing. Perhaps the best that can be done is this. In section 4, above, to rule out persistence as change, the ACC was revised so as to exclude relational properties whose only significant relata (other than the changing thing in question) are times. If we adopt a substantival view of space, we can say that an object moves, and in so doing changes non-relationally, just in case it has and then lacks a relational property whose only significant relata (other than moving things) are places or locations; other spatial changes are relational.

This suggestion, as an addendum to (R), still has the feature that, relative to one frame of reference, an object changes non-relationally (moves) in changing spatially, while relative to another, it changes spatially on that occasion only relationally. The relativity, in the case of motion, of the concepts of relational and non-relational change will simply have to be tolerated along with the relativity of motion itself, on this suggestion. I leave the topic of motion in this not terribly satisfactory state.[28]

7.3 *Relational changes*

Earlier, I mentioned two topics of concern with respect to relational change. One was the problem of distinguishing cases in which an object changes relationally from those in which an object changes non-relationally. The other, to be discussed now, concerns the existence of relational changes. The defenders of the existence of events accept an existential proof of their existence whose principal premises, typically, are claims asserting that some object changes non-relationally (e.g., Jack fell down, Vesuvius erupted). So their view is that if objects change non-relationally, there are changes, events, which are the non-relational changes that objects undergo. But then an argument, whose premise asserts that some objects change relationally, and whose structure is parallel to that in defence of events, may get offered for the existence of entities – relational changes – that occur when things change relationally. The concern is that if successful, that argument would saddle us with accepting the existence of relational changes (e.g., Xantippe's becoming a widow), entities which seem at least as, if not more, suspicious than events. Thus, to avoid having to admit that there are relational changes, we should try to avoid having to admit that objects change relationally.

Can an argument be offered for the existence of relational changes on the basis of the fact that things change relationally? Yes, and it parallels a familiar argument for the existence of events on the basis of the fact that things change non-relationally.[29] Xantippe was Socrates' wife until he died in 399 BC; after he died, she was a widow. In becoming a widow, Xantippe changed relationally due to Socrates' dying; and, we may suppose, Xantippe was at home when she so changed. How is the obvious validity of the inference from 'Xantippe became a widow while at home' to 'Xantippe became a widow' to be explained? It could be argued[30] that to explain this inference we should construe the two statements respectively, as 'There was a change that was a widowing of Xantippe and it occurred at her home' and 'There was a change that was a widowing of Xantippe', where 'is a widowing of' is a relational predicate true of ordered pairs of relational changes and individuals just in case the change is a 'movement' by that individual from lacking to having the property of being the unmarried female survivor of a marriage. And such a change is clearly relational; it could not have occurred unless Socrates died.

However, the merits I take Davidsonian arguments for the existence of non-relational changes (events) to possess are not possessed by the argument just sketched, because, based on the dependent character of relational change, a more ontologically economical semantic analysis of sentences reporting relational change can be offered. The dependency is not mysterious; no object changes relationally unless some object changes non-relationally. Xantippe became a widow because to be a widow is to be the surviving female member of a marriage that ends when the male member dies, and Xantippe's husband, Socrates, died. So, all of the facts about the alleged relational change in Xantippe that was her becoming a widow can be covered simply by reporting the non-relational change in Socrates and by reporting on the marital relation she bore to Socrates. The argument for the existence of relational changes would give 'Xantippe became a widow' the semantic features of 'There was a change that was a widowing of Xantippe'. But the dependence of Xantippe's change on Socrates' death can be more clearly represented, without the implication that there was a change (something that occurred) in Xantippe, even though she changed (relationally), by giving 'Xantippe became a widow' the semantic features of 'there was an event, e, that was a death of Socrates, and Xantippe was married to him up to the time of e, and she survived Socrates'. And all of the adverbial modifiers that might have been attributed to the alleged relational change can be parsed out as attributions of features to the things that changed, both relationally and non-relationally, and to the non-relational changes (events) involved. Thus, so long as we have an ontology of events (non-relational changes), there is an analysis of sentences reporting that things change relationally that does not imply that there are relational changes. Thus, we can say that things do change relationally without being forced to say that there are such things as relational changes. The only changes there are are the non-relational ones, the events. And we can distinguish the cases in which an object changes relationally from those in which an object changes non-relationally (except, perhaps, in the case of motion). And hence we can tell when it is the case that when an object changes, there is a change that object undergoes – only in cases in which an object changes non-relationally. The only changes there are are the ones that are an object's changing non-relationally. And those changes are the events.

8 STATIC AND OTHER PROPERTIES

I want now to make some distinctions among properties for the purpose of further clarifying and refining the Ancient Criterion of Change. Some properties are such that their being possessed at some particular time by an object does *not* imply that that object has changed, is changing, or will change. I call such properties 'static' properties, and among such properties are the property of being blue, that of weighing ten pounds, and that of being located at place p_1. An object that has at some time a static property P is at that time in the state of being P. It seems clearly to be the case that whenever any object changes, that object has and then lacks some static property; and the ACC can be amended to reflect this point.

Some other properties are such that, if an object has such a property at some instant of time, that object is changing at that instant. Being a presently shrinking thing, being a thing having instantaneous velocity v, and being a thing that is turning green are properties of this sort and can be called 'instantaneous dynamic' properties. Clearly, if an object has an instantaneous dynamic property at some instant, t, then there must be an *interval* of time, which includes t, during which that object has and then lacks some relevant static property. If, for example, some thing, x, has at t the property of being a shrinking thing, then there will be a time, t', before t, when x has the property of having a certain size, and a time, t'', after t, when x lacks that property and has the property of having another, smaller size. Unless that is so, x cannot be said to be shrinking at t. It can thus been seen that while an object can be changing at an instant, an object cannot change at an instant. At no instant can an object have and then lack a property. But at an instant an object can be changing, can be in the process of having and lacking a property, by having an instantaneous dynamic property.

There is, it should be noted, a difference between the property of being blue and that of remaining blue. Though both can be possessed at an instant, an object's having the former is independent of what properties it has at surrounding times. An object's remaining blue, however, is not so independent, in that for an object to remain blue at t, it must be blue at times surrounding t. Similarly, an object that has the property of being at place p_1 at t may well be moving at t; but not if at t it has the property of remaining at p_1.[31]

If an object has some instantaneous dynamic property at an instant t, then it will also have at an *interval*, t', which includes t, a property I shall call a 'dynamic' property, the possession of which at that interval by the object implies that at that interval the object is changing from having to lacking a static property. Indeed, the dynamic property just is the property of first having and then lacking a (or having another) static property. It is a property such that at instants, in the interval during which the object has that dynamic property, the object has some instantaneous dynamic property (or properties). The property of reading a book from cover to cover is a dynamic property had by the reader at an interval of time that includes at least the time at which he starts to read the book and the time he finishes. At no instant or proper part of that interval, however, is it true that the reader has the property of reading the book from cover to cover, though the property of being in the process of reading the book from cover to cover is an instantaneous dynamic property the reader has at each instant, and collection thereof, in that interval.

So when it is said that an object has or exemplifies some dynamic property at a time, t, that time must be an interval of time, not an instant. Change takes time. Of course, an object can have a static property or an instantaneous dynamic property at successive instants, and, hence, over an interval; an object can be blue for a year, and an object can have an instantaneous acceleration of 32 ft./sec.^{2} for the entire time it takes to fall to earth. As a result, some expressions for properties may be ambiguous with respect to its picking out a dynamic or an instantaneous dynamic property. For example, the verb 'to rot' may be like that. It has a dynamic sense in which it picks out a property of, say, a log that it would have over the whole interval of time at which the log is rotting, *viz*. the property of going from being wholly unrotten to being completely rotten. But it also has an instantaneous dynamic sense in which it picks out a property applicable to the log at each instant during which it is rotting. And its applying to the log at each such instant would imply that at different surrounding instants it had different rot-related static properties. Of course the fact that the log has the dynamic property of rotting is not independent of the fact that at instants in the interval of the rotting the log has the instantaneous property of rotting (of being in the process of rotting in the dynamic sense).[32]

I have now said most of what I have to say about the conditions under which an object changes. Some of what I have said is obvious, some of it plainly unsatisfactory, and much hasn't been said at all. Still, the Ancient Criterion of Change seems not to have fared too badly. So far, the only needed modifications have to do with restricting the range of properties, which are such that when an object has and then lacks one of them that object changes, to static properties and to those that do not merely relate changing things to times. And if a narrower notion of change is sought, one that does not have things change when they merely change relationally, (R) (amended to take account of motion) can be appended to the ACC as an exception. And the only clear limitation on the ACC's applicability arises in case things change when they come into existence *ex nihilo* and go out of existence *in nihilo*. Still there is much more to be said about change; but I shall forebear. I want to try constructing a theory of events that takes as its leading idea the claim that events are the changes objects undergo when they change non-relationally. And so, I wanted to say enough about what it is for objects to change in order to give that leading idea some substance. There is, however, one further issue I wish to take up in this chapter.

9 DOES ANYTHING EVER CHANGE?

According to the Ancient Criterion of Change, for something to change it must have a property at one time and it must lack that property at another. But consider the following well-known argument:

(1)   x at t is F
(2)   x at t' (t' ≠ t) is not F
(3)   Therefore, by the indiscernibility of identicals,[33] x at t ≠ x at t'.

According to the ACC, (1) and (2) imply that x has changed. The argument, however, suggests that nothing changes, since change takes time and allegedly results in a thing's lacking a property it once had. Thus, nothing changes, according to this argument, since nothing survives change, and that, because objects cannot have and lack the same property.[34]

It is clear that the argument from (1) and (2) to (3) is a good one for showing that such things, if there were any, as 'x at t', the so-called temporal parts or slices of things, do not change.[35] But the argument isn't a good one for showing that nothing changes, unless there is forthcoming an argument for the claim that apparently enduring things have temporal parts, a claim the argument above presupposes. One reason that might be given for thinking that there are such temporal slices consists in pointing out that the thing that has F at t is qualitatively dissimilar from the one that fails to have F at t'; but of course this involves a confusion that begs the question. The defender of enduring things will point out that the object that at t had F and the one that at t' failed to have F are, indeed, qualitatively alike in that the former lacked F at t' and the latter had F at t. Another explanation might be that a four-dimensional, spacetime view of objects is forced on us by relativistic physics, and that that should make us see objects as related to time and to space analogously; thus, since physical objects have spatial parts, they have temporal parts as well.[36] In any event, I am not especially interested here in how one might defend or oppose the existence of temporal slices of enduring things.[37] What interests me is the idea that a temporal slice theorist might hold that the concept of change can be reconstructed to accommodate temporal slices. The usual idea of change is unavailable to the temporal slice theorist, for temporal slices cannot persist long enough to change; as soon as one loses a property, it ceases to exist. So how is change understood by a temporal slice theorist? Consider the following proposal:

An apparently persisting thing changes if and only if it is a
sequence of temporal slices such that at least two temporal
slices in that sequence differ in some way in addition to their
temporal properties.

So, it is argued, the concept of change can accommodate the idea
that allegedly persisting things are just sequences of temporal
slices; and the idea of actually enduring things is not needed in
order to capture the idea of change.[38]

There are several things that ought to bother one about this
reconstruction. First, no one is inclined to think that some thing
has changed just because Jones at noon is hungry and Smith at 1
p.m. is not (unless Jones = Smith). It cannot be just any
sequence of temporal slices that will constitute a changing thing.
We cannot take seriously the reconstruction of the concept of
change unless it is accompanied by a theory about which
sequences of slices do and which do not constitute apparently
persisting things. But, as Chisholm has persuasively argued, it is
implausible to suppose that such a theory can be given that does
not import the notion of an enduring thing.[39]

A second source of concern about this reconstructed account of
change is this. The treatment, in section 5, of coming into and
going out of existence seems to work nicely, *vis-à-vis* the ACC,
so long as creation *ex nihilo* and destruction *in nihilo* are not
involved. But a temporal slice theorist cannot deal with coming
into and going out of existence in terms of changes in underlying
parts or matter, for that would re-introduce survivable, changeable things. The temporal slice theorist must treat the coming
into and going out of existence of temporal slices as creation *ex
nihilo* and destruction *in nihilo*.

Third, to treat objects as on a par with respect to spatial and
temporal parts, as the reconstructed account would have us do,
would make an apparently persisting, ordinary thing's being
different at different times no more significant, from the point of
view of change, than such a thing's being different at different
places.[40] It would be no more reasonable to think that some thing
had changed on the grounds that it was blue yesterday and red
today than it would be to think that something had changed on
the grounds that its left half is blue and its right half is green. To
think that things change on this reconstructed account is just to

try to take seriously the bad joke of inferring that the stairs move from the fact that they go to the second floor.

A fourth problem is that if the reconstructed account of change is to cope with the idea that physical objects have temporal parts and that nothing literally survives change, then the reconstruction of the concept of change is really, I suspect, fraudulent. We are given a version of the concept of change in terms of non-temporal differences between temporal slices; but the account is an account of *apparent* change. We are given a story about what makes us think that some apparently enduring thing has changed (a story much like a Humean account of identity over time); but no temporal part changes. This is an account of change that I regard as incompatible with the very idea of an event.

To the extent that it offers an account of change at all, the reconstruction offers a 'static' conception of change, a conception that is platonistic (see *Phaedo*, 103d). A motion picture is a series of still photographs (ignore the fact that they are photographs of something) that are flashed before us in such a way that the image of photograph n remains when photograph n+1 is flashed before us. No thing on the film moves or changes; we have rather the replacement of one image by another, slightly different image. Similarly, the static conception sees change as involving nothing more than the replacement of an object in one state by another, distinct object in another, contrary state. Those objects follow one upon the other rapidly; there are no temporal gaps (as there are between the photographs) to notice or fail to notice. The gaps that there are that we do not notice are ontological. The static conception construes change as replacement.

The Ancient Criterion, on the other hand, insisting as it does on objects that survive change, offers a 'dynamic' conception of change. It takes seriously the idea that the thing that was F is the very thing that is no longer F; it takes seriously the idea that a changing thing is involved in a dynamic process. If the static conception can be seen as platonistic, the dynamic conception is aristotelian, for it is the dynamic conception that stands behind Aristotle's talk of change as movement from potentiality to actuality. The static conception can do without, I should think, the concept of an event; it gets by with the notion of a temporal slice, properties of such things, and a story about creation *ex nihilo* and destruction *in nihilo*. But the concept of an event is the concept of a dynamic process of change, the idea of a thing's coming to be different from the way it was. Of course, there is no need for an ontology of events in a world of temporal parts, because, in such a world, nothing ever happens.[41] But if there are good reasons for thinking that there are events, then in so far as events are the changes objects undergo when they change non-relationally, then it is not the static conception of change that is required. It is the dynamic conception that stands behind the very idea of an event. And it is the idea of an event I wish to begin discussing in the next chapter.

V

EVENTS AND CHANGES

1 CHANGE IN A RESPECT

When an object changes, it does not merely come to lack a
property it earlier had. After all, a changing thing does not go
out of existence when it changes; it survives the loss of the
property it earlier had. The lack of the property in question,
then, must consist in its having some other property. What other
property?

Consider an object, x, which went from being navy blue to
being sky blue. Did x change colour? Yes, for there is a colour,
navy blue, it once had and then lacked, and a colour, sky blue, it
once lacked and then had. No, for it remained blue. Such concomitant change and non-change in colour in the same object
does not bother us in the way we would be bothered if it were
claimed that, while x was going from being navy blue to being sky
blue, it remained navy blue (or red). We are not bothered,
because the simultaneous change and non-change in colour does
not truly offend our intuition that, while an object can change in
one respect while remaining unchanged in another, an object
cannot change in one respect while remaining unchanged in the
very same respect.

There is no offence against that intuition, because there is a
looseness in speaking of both the change from navy to sky blue
and the non-change of remaining blue as a change and a non-
change in the same respect, namely colour. Navy blue and sky
blue are, of course, colours; but they are also *shades* of a colour,

111

namely blue. Blue, however, though a colour, is not a shade of any colour. Whether we take, on some particular occasion, navy blue and sky blue as colours or shades of colour is perhaps a contextual matter. What is clear, however, is that we cannot think of navy blue as a colour (as opposed to a shade) on any occasion where blue is being thought of as (another) colour. (Imagine a dispute about the colour of my coat, where one of the disputants insists that it's blue, and the other insists that it's navy. After all, since an object can't have all over two different colours, they can't both be right, can they?) Thus, if navy blue and sky blue are being thought of as shades of colour, then when x changes from being navy blue to sky blue, x changes; but x does not change in the same respect as that in which x, by remaining blue, does not change. If we do think of x as having changed colour when it goes from being navy blue to being sky blue, we cannot deny that x has changed colour on the ground that it was blue all along. That change by an object with respect to its being navy blue and change by an object with respect to its being blue are not to be thought of as changes in the same respect is made clear, further, by the fact that no object changes simply in virtue of the fact that it goes from being navy blue to being blue (or *vice versa*); for there is no such simple fact. Everything that is that shade of blue is blue; so no change is implied.

When we speak of a respect in which a thing changes, we have in mind a group of properties (marked off by a determinable) such that when an object, in changing in that respect, goes from having one to having another property, both those properties belong to that group. There is no respect in which things change to which both blue and navy blue belong, for those properties are not contraries. Change in a respect must involve the having of a property and the subsequent acquiring of another, contrary property. A respect in which things change must be populated by properties guaranteed to be such that, if an object has one and later has another of them, then that object has changed.[1]

This same point is exemplified in the fact that no object can be said, without further comment, to change from being red to being square. The further comment might be, for example, that it is a law of nature that red things are round and blue things square and the object in question changed from being red to being blue. In any case, there must be some explanation that can be given, if sense is to be made of the claim that some thing changed by going from being red to being square. Aristotle makes this same observation in the *Physics* (Book 1, Ch. 5, 188a32-189a10):

> Our first presupposition must be that in nature nothing acts on or is acted on by, any other thing at random, nor may anything come from anything else, unless we mean that it does so in virtue of a concomitant attribute. For how could 'white' come from 'musical', unless 'musical' happened to be an attribute of the non-white or the black. . . . It is clear that our principles must be contraries.

2 QUALITY SPACES

In light of the foregoing, I shall call any set, S, of simple (non-compound), static properties, $\{P_0, P_1, . . ., P_n, . . .\}$, a *quality space* if and only if S meets the following two conditions:

(i)   if at any time, t, any object, x, has $P_i \varepsilon S$, then at t, for any $j \neq i$, it is not the case that x has $P_j \varepsilon S$,

(ii) if any object, x, which has $P_i \varepsilon S$ at any time, t, fails to have P_i at a time t' ($t \neq t'$) (and still exists), then x changes in S (or in respect 'S'), that is, by t', x has, for some $j \neq i$, $P_j \varepsilon S$.[2]

What (i) says is that a quality space consists of mutually exclusive static properties. The import of (ii) is that quality spaces are kinds of properties that are such that, if any object changes by losing a property belonging to a given quality space, it must come to have another property of the same kind. Static properties that objects can have and then lack thus divide into kinds in accordance with the following intuitive principle: P and Q belong to the same kind just in case they are contraries and it makes good sense to suppose that a thing having P comes to have Q. So, a quality space is a set of static properties such that when an object loses one of its properties, one belonging to a given quality space, at least one result is that the object comes to have another property from that same quality space.[3]

An object changes, then, if and only if it first has one and then has another property, where those properties belong to the same quality space (and where the successive havings of them is not what that object's persisting for some period of time consists in). And, though this will require some refinement, an *event* is a 'movement' by an object from the having of one to the having of another property, where those properties belong to the same quality space, and where those properties are such that the object's successive havings of them implies that the object changes non-relationally. That is, events are non-relational changes in objects; when an object changes non-relationally in a certain respect, there is an event that is that object's changing in that respect. An event is a movement by an object through some portion of a quality space.

The question of which properties belong to which quality spaces is one that cannot be answered *a priori*. It can be answered, if it arises at all,[4] only after we observe what the results of various changes that come over objects are; and clearly, observation won't do the job unless it is coloured and shaped by scientific theories telling us how to describe those changes.[5] And even after such questions are answered, it need not be the case that all static properties can be fitted into quality spaces, if those spaces are already partially filled, for they may not meet the condition of mutual exclusivity. Furthermore, in so far as the idea of a quality space is the idea of a respect in which things change, properties that no thing having them can lose do not belong to any quality space (though this does not mean that such properties can be ignored as unimportant). Still, we do have some good, intuitive ideas about which properties belong together; and those ideas, I should think, correspond roughly to our general groupings of properties under determinables.

2.1 *Graphs of changes*

Suppose that the static properties are, to the extent possible, assigned to their 'appropriate' quality spaces. We can then assign to each quality in a given space a number (or numbers), and, as a result, we can represent each member of that quality space as a point on a line (or a plane, if it, so to speak, takes two numbers to 'fix' the position of a property in that space; or a solid, if it takes three). The assignment of numbers to the properties in a given space may be a quite natural one. For example, if we were assigning numbers to 'location' properties (e.g., the property of being located at such-and-such a place), a natural way of doing that would be (in the case of location on a one-dimensional surface) to choose some point as origin and assign to each location property a number corresponding to the distance from the origin an object having that property is. In other cases, the assignment of numbers to the properties in a quality space, with its concomitant representing of those properties as points on a line (or plane, etc.) may not be as natural or seem forced on us. In a quality space, should there be one, populated by properties persons have in so far as they are in certain moods, there may be no natural ordering of those properties that would yield a natural pairing of certain mood-properties with low numbers and others with higher numbers. Indeed, it may well be the case that, for different purposes on different occasions, there are reasons for a 're-ordering' or 're-assigning' of the properties in a given quality space to different numbers. How the properties are matched with numbers is really of no particular importance; the interest in matching properties with numbers and then representing those properties as points on a surface is strictly graphic and illustrative.

Having represented each element in a given quality space as a point on a line (or plane, etc.), we can then represent (in the usual way) times by points on a line. By putting the two representations together, we can represent each change that comes over an object, when it moves from having one to having another property within the quality space to which those properties belong, by a *graph* that plots the movement of that object through that quality space against time. Such a graph will be n+1-dimensional, with one of them the temporal dimension, and the other n representing the number of numbers needed to fix a property's position in its quality space. Such a graph plots a bit of an object's history; it plots which properties, within a given quality space, a given object has at different moments. It is a graph that represents the changes, within a given space, an object undergoes. Thus, for example, the movement by an object, x, during the interval from t_1 to t_2, from p_1 to p_n at a constant velocity (on a one-dimensional surface) could be represented by a graph that looks like this (Figure 5.1), (where n and m are the points assigned, respectively to the property of being located at p_1 and to that of being located at p_2):

115

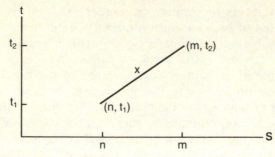

Figure 5.1

2.2 *Continuous and other changes*

It seems reasonable to say that a continuous change by an object,
x, through some portion of a quality space, S, during a period of
time from t_1 to t_2, consists in that object's changing continuously
in S during that period. And for x to change continuously in S
during t_1-t_2, it must be the case that there is no non-instantaneous
and non-disjoint interval, t'-t'', within t_1-t_2, such that x has a
property P (in S) at every instant in that interval. That is, in short
(and ignoring, for simplicity's sake, doubling back), an object
changes continuously when it has a different property (within a
given quality space) at each different instant. An interrupted
change is one that is not continuous in this sense. If the
properties in S can be represented naturally by points on a line
and the properties are suitably assigned to the points on that line,
then the graph of a continuous change will *not* look like this
(Figure 5.2):

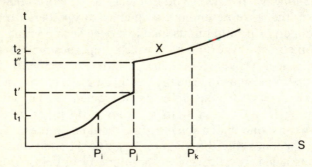

Figure 5.2

116

Events and changes

The reason for this is that the graph shows that, between t' and t'', x remained P_j; x did *not* change continuously throughout the period from t_1 to t_2, for during the interval from t' to t'', x was not changing at all. The change in x taking place from t_1 to t_2 was not, in this sense, continuous; for in order for x's change to be continuous during that period, x must be changing at every moment in that interval. That is, if x changes continuously during a period of time, then at every moment in that interval, x must be changing (though no object changes at an instant – change takes time – an object can at an instant be changing). So, if a person, in changing location, by moving from point A to point B, stops to check the time, that person's movement from A to B is non-continuous. It is, rather, interrupted; the motion is 'temporally gappy'. If the person does not at any time stop, then, even though he or she may change speed or direction, the motion is continuous (that is, uninterrupted).[6]

This contrast between temporally continuous and non-continuous (interrupted, temporally gappy) changes should be distinguished from another contrast. Suppose that a particle, x, is moving along a line from point A to point Z, during the period from t_1 to t_n; and suppose that when x gets to point K it 'jumps' from there to point N without going through the points between K and N. At no time is x located at any of the points between K and N, and there is no temporal gap between x's being at K and its being at N.[7] Now x's change is temporally continuous; x does not linger anywhere, its motion is uninterrupted. There is, however, a sense in which its motion is 'gappy'. It will help to look at a graph of this change, where the location properties are ordered in the normal way:

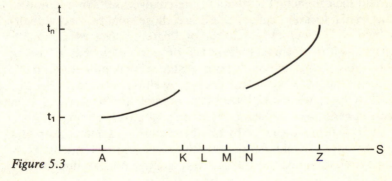

Figure 5.3

117

It is clear that x's motion is not gappy in a temporal sense, for x does not spend any time lingering at any one point; x changes location continuously. But its motion is 'qualitatively' gappy in the sense that there are properties, having to do, in this case, with being located at points between K and N, which x 'ought' to have had, in going from having the property of being at K to having the property of being at N, or would have 'normally' been expected to have had, but did not. This departure from normalcy might be thought to be so severe as to prompt rejection of the case (particles just don't, can't, behave that way). In any event, in so far as we don't reject such cases, it may not be easy to tell when we have such a case. In the case of motion, we already have expectations about which points a particle would normally go through (on a one-dimensional surface) in going from one place to another, and so a clear idea about which motions, should we admit them, are qualitatively gappy. In other cases, where there is no clear sense to be made of the idea that, in quality space S, property Q clearly belongs 'between' properties R and S, then whether a graph gives the impression that the change in question is qualitatively gappy is wholly gratuitous, simply a function of the arbitrary way in which the properties in that space are assigned to points on the line. In such cases, nothing whatever is to be made of the idea of a change in that space being qualitatively gappy; in such a case, that idea is only a reflection of gratuitous features of the graph of the change and not a reflection of any significant feature of the change itself. Still, there will be some quality spaces in which an ordering of their members seems quite appropriate and natural, and in which the appearance of a graph of a change in that space exhibiting qualitative gappiness would indicate actual features of the change itself. In addition to the spatial-location space, there are those quality spaces determined by properties admitting of degrees, such as a 'wealth space', whose members are such properties as that of being incredibly poor, moderately poor, just making it, moderately well-off, well-off, very well-off, extremely well-off, obscenely rich. In such a case, we could imagine a windfall profit accruing to a person resulting in a change that is qualitatively gappy.

It is clear that a change by an object through some portion of a quality space could be both continuous and not qualitatively gappy, continuous and qualitatively gappy, non-continuous and not qualitatively gappy, or non-continuous and qualitatively gappy.

2.3 *Dense and discrete quality spaces*

The two distinctions just made have to do with senses in which an object can be said to change continuously from having one to having another property within a given quality space. The distinction I want to draw here concerns the properties within a given quality space. The properties within a given quality space may be such that there is a sense in which it is correct to say that for any pair of properties in that space there is another property 'between' them. Such a quality space will be said to be *dense*. A quality space whose members are quantitatively measured weight properties (e.g., the property of weighing 2.3 pounds) is a dense quality space; similarly, a spatial-location space is dense. Between any two properties in such a space (e.g., the property of weighing n pounds and the property of weighing m pounds, where $n<m$), there is another property (e.g., the property of weighing $n+\varepsilon$ pounds, where $0<\varepsilon<m-n$). Any quality space not having this feature is a *discrete* space. A quality space whose members are the ordinary colour properties (*viz.* red, blue, etc.) is a discrete space.

If the properties in a dense space are ordered in the natural way (so that they are assigned to points on a line, say, such that the order of the points matches the 'order' of the properties), and if an object changes in that space in a way which is not qualitatively gappy, then the graph of that change will be an unbroken line. However, that line may not be a smooth curve, since the change might be interrupted or there may be sharp turns.

In a discrete space whose properties are naturally orderable, if the properties are assigned points on a line, a graph of an uninterrupted change in that space by an object will be a series of disconnected points, for there won't be as many points to which properties are assigned as there are points on the line. But we could, if we choose, assign to the properties in a discrete quality space not points but intervals of points where the intervals assigned to those properties are contiguous with others; then a change through a discrete space could be graphed by an unbroken line, if the properties are suitably arranged. (Still, in such a case, no significance would be attributed to the character of the line within any interval.)

The distinction between dense and discrete quality spaces cuts across both the distinction between temporally continuous and interrupted changes and the distinction between qualitatively gappy and non-gappy changes. A change in a dense space can be uninterrupted or interrupted, and can be qualitatively gappy or non-gappy. That a spatial-location space is dense does not imply that it is impossible for an object to get from one place to another without going through places in between. If such a jump is impossible, it is so for a reason other than that the spatial-location properties constitute a dense quality space. And a change by an object through some portion of a discrete space can be uninterrupted as well as interrupted.

3 THE SUBJECT AND SPATIAL LOCATION OF AN EVENT

Events are non-relational changes; they are the non-relational movements of objects through quality spaces at times. Events, thus, have subjects. When an object changes (non-relationally) from having a property P_i to having a property P_j at some time, t, there is an event consisting in that object's first having P_i and then having P_j (at t). Thus, the *subject* of that event is just the object that changes, the object whose change is that event. In so far as events are changes in objects, an event is located wherever the object whose change it is is located at the time that object so changes. If some event is some object's changing from being blue to being green at some time, t, that event is located wherever that object is located when at t it changed from being blue to being green. Events have spatial location in virtue of their being changes in things (their subjects) that have spatial location.

However, a problem is raised by the fact that there is, in general, no unique object an event is a change in. The problem arises in cases where a changing thing is part of some other thing. Suppose that my car's windshield changes at some time, t, by cracking. So, there was an event, the windshield's cracking at t. But if the windshield of my car changed, then my car, which had that windshield as a part at the time, also changed then. Of course, it did not change by cracking, but it changed none the less; it had an uncracked windshield before t, and after t, it had a cracked one (the same windshield). In changing this way, my car did not change relationally; there was a non-relational change, a real alteration, in my car.[8] Thus, the following seems obviously true: if e is an event that is a change in an object, x, and e occurs at t, then for any object, y, such that x is a part of y at t, there is an event, e', that is a change in y and occurs at t. I am, however, inclined to think not only that this principle is true but also that something stronger can be said, namely that e=e'. I believe and want to adopt the Principle of Event Enlargement:

(PEE)   Any event which is a change in an object is (is identical with) a change in any other object of which the first is a part.[9]

After all, my car was the subject of an event only because its windshield cracked; nothing else happened to it. What happened to my car was that its windshield cracked. When the roof of my house burns, something happens to my house. It burns, not in the sense that all of it burns, but in the sense that part of it burns. There isn't anything else that the burning of my house (in that sense) could be but the burning of the roof.[10]

The problem for the spatial location of events arising out of PEE is this: if an event occurs at any place occupied (at the time of that event) by the object whose change is that event, then because of PEE a change in any object that is a part of any other object will not have a unique subject. And thus, such an event will have no unique location. If x is a proper part of y, which is, in turn, a proper part of z, then x is a proper part of z. But then any change in x is also a change in y and a change in z, and hence, will occur at the place of x, that of y, and that of z, all distinct locations. If the universe were an object everything is a part of, then all simultaneous events (at least) would have the same spatial location. If we are to be able to talk sensibly about the spatial locations of events, we had better do better than that. For if anything is certain about the spatial location of events it is that the last eruption of Mt St Helens did *not* occur at the same place as did my (simultaneously) sighing with relief as a result of my knowing that I was not then at the location of that eruption.

In so far as the subject of an event is that object a change in which is that event, then there is no such thing as the subject of any event that is a change in any object that is a part of any other object. Such an object, that is, one a change in which is some event, is of course 'involved' in that event, where that notion of involvement can be defined as follows:

If x is any object, e is any event, and t is a time, then x *is involved* in e *at* t if and only if it is the case that (a) if e occurs (or is occurring) at t, then x changes (or is changing) at t, and (b) a change in x at t is identical with e at t.

The reference to times in this definition are there, in part, to deal with the possibility of an event's involving different objects at different times during its occurrence. Also, if x is a changing part of z, and y is an unchanging part of z, then while a change in x is a change in z, and both x and z are involved in that event, y is not involved in that change in z; clause (a) rules y to be uninvolved. From this definition and PEE, it follows that if any object changes non-relationally, then it and any objects of which it is a part are all involved in the event that is that change.

While many objects may be involved in a given event, it seems clear that many of them are irrelevantly involved; my car and my house are irrelevant, respectively, to the windshield's cracking and the roof's burning. They are involved irrelevantly, for the only reason they are involved at all is that they happen to be such that some objects (the windshield and the roof) were parts of them, and it was those latter objects that really changed. Had my car at that time not had that windshield, then the cracking of that windshield would not have been a change in my car. Indeed, under those circumstances, my car would not have changed non-relationally at all.

I propose, then, that the 'real' subjects of events are just those objects whose changes make it the case that there are other objects, of which the former ones are parts, that change in the light of PEE. That is, I propose that the phrase 'the subject of an event' be reserved for the *minimally involved object* that changes, the minimally involved subject of an event. That notion can be defined as follows:

If x is any object, e is any event, and t is a time, then x is the *minimally involved subject* of e *at* t if and only if (a) x is involved in e at t, and (b) x is the *smallest* object which is such that a change in x at t is identical with e at t.[11]

Thus, my windshield is the subject, in this sense, of the cracking; and my roof the subject of the burning, unless only a part of it is burning, in which case the change in the roof has as its true (i.e., minimal) subject that part that is burning.

In the light of this, we can see that an event can have as a location the location of any object a change in which is that event; and an event can have a maximal location, the location of the largest object, if any, a change in a part of which is that event. But what deserves to be called *the* spatial location of an event (at a time) is the location of the event's subject, the smallest object a change in which is that event (at that time).[12] Hereafter, unless I specify otherwise, I shall use the phrases 'the subject of an event' and 'the location of an event' (and their ilk) to refer, respectively, to an event's minimal subject and location.[13]

The impression should not be left that, armed with the definition just given, the locating of events is a simple matter. For one thing, the location of an event whose subject is some object is neither more nor less easily specifiable than is the location of that object itself. Whatever the difficulties in saying where changeable things are are among the difficulties in saying where the changes that come over them are. The principles employed in giving the locations of changeable things may be stringent or loose, and may be dependent in part on the purposes for which the locations of those objects is sought. And any such vagaries will naturally extend to the locations of events.

It might be thought that there are events having disjointed locations. Suppose that a heatwave causes the melting of all the world's snow. If there is such a thing as the world's snow, then its melting surely has a disjointed region of space as its location, since the snow has such a location. However, I am not inclined to think that there is any such thing as the world's snow; and to the extent that there isn't, then its melting does not have a disjointed location, for there is no such event. An event occurs just in case some object changes non-relationally, and is the non-relational change that object thereby undergoes. Each event, then, has some changing thing for its subject. When there is no such thing, there is no event. Thus, if the world's snow is not a thing, but things, then while there will be events that are changes in the things that make up the world's snow, no event is a change in the world's snow; and so we do not have a case yet of an event with a disjointed spatial location.

But there do seem to be objects whose parts are separated from each other (e.g., partly disassembled radios), and in so far as we think of their locations as disjointed, so are their changes' locations. It is not clear, however, that all the cases that seem intuitively like that really are like that. Is it clear that there is an event that is the rolling of the dice across the table, an event whose subject is the disjointed entity, the dice? Perhaps the dice is no thing at all, but two things (one die and another). If so, then no event is a change in the dice, since there is no such thing for any such event to be a change in; there are, however, events that are changes in the dice. (Another possibility: though there is no thing that is the dice, there is an event that is a change in them, an event that is a 'sum' of the rollings of the two dies. I consider this possibility later on.) At any rate, what does seem clear to me is that where it is unreasonable to think that object x and y combine in some way to form some composite thing (e.g., Venus and the dime in my pocket), it is also unreasonable to think that there can be an event having such a pair as its alleged subject, and unreasonable to think that locations need be found for such alleged events.

3.1 *Involved objects*

The previous section was concerned with issues attending the specification of the spatial location of an event once that event's subject, its minimally involved subject, has been determined. But further issues concerning the spatial location of events arise in so far as it may be difficult to determine which objects are the ones involved in a given event. An event's minimal location at a time during which it is occurring is the location at that time of the smallest object a change in which is that event at that time. But which objects are the ones minimally involved? Armed wih the definition of 'minimally involved subject' and some reasonable intuitions, many cases can be sorted out and settled. All sorts of objects, involved and uninvolved, can get mentioned in the course of describing some event. For example, a certain event could be described as the most peculiar event to occur east of Chicago and west of Buffalo on June 14, 1980; what happened was that my pen rose mysteriously off my desk in Detroit. Now, of course, when that event occurred, both Chicago and Buffalo (and every other contemporaneously existing thing) changed *relationally* as a result of that event's occurrence. But clearly, those cities were not involved in my pen's rising; and the definition (and good sense) shows that, since my pen was not (then or ever) a part of either Chicago or Buffalo, and there was no change in either of those cities of which the rising of my pen was a part. One cannot tell, just by looking at a description of an event, what that event's subject, minimal or not, is. But other cases are not so easily settled.

The cases I have in mind as the ones creating problems for specifying which objects are involved in (and therefore, what the spatial locations are of) events are cases stemming from cases usually brought up in connection with *actions* and the *times* of their performance. Now it is a contentious issue whether actions are events, and I do not intend to try settling it here. Nevertheless there are cases of events that are clearly not actions that raise the same issues and problems as those which arise out of consideration of actions. So, it will not hurt to introduce and discuss these matters *via* the action cases. Those cases are typically brought forth for the purpose of discussing certain questions about the *identity* of actions. The connection between that issue and the present one is obvious. Events are changes in objects; it is a property of each event that it has a certain object as subject. Leibniz's Law requires that identical events have the same subject. Thus, our concern over what the subjects and involved objects of certain puzzling cases of events (and actions) are is a concern over a necessary condition for the identity of events (and actions).

The cases in question were brought into prominence by Professor J.J. Thomson, in her seminal paper, 'The time of a killing',[14] and involve actions described in terms of so-called 'causal' verbs. Thomson correctly points out that the problems she generates concerning the time of performance of certain actions can similarly be generated focusing instead on the spatial location of actions (and thus on the issue of which the involved objects are). Here is how the issue concerning spatial location can be generated.

Suppose that Jones kills Smith by shooting him with a pistol; Jones is located at place p_1 when he shoots, and Smith is located at place p_2 when he is hit and dies. There was the action of Jones's shooting, which is located at p_1;[15] there was also Smith's dying, an event occurring at p_2. But there was also Jones's killing of Smith.[16] Where shall it be said that Jones's killing of Smith took place? It might be argued that the location of that killing cannot be p_1 on the grounds that that would suggest that, since only Jones, but not Smith, was located there, Smith was therefore not an object involved in the action that was Jones's killing of him. For the location of an action must include the locations of all the minimally involved objects (at the time they were so involved). And, the argument might continue, Smith was surely involved in the killing, and not irrelevantly, for unless he was the subject of a dying (brought about by Jones's shooting), Jones's killing of him could not have occurred. On one view motivated by such considerations, Smith's dying was an event that was a part of the action that was Jones's killing of him (the shooting by Jones was another part). And surely, the specification of the location of an action must include the spatial location of all its parts. Thus, the location of Jones's killing of Smith must include at least the location of Jones's shooting and that of Smith's dying. (Therefore, on this view, the killing can't be the shooting, for they have different minimally involved objects and, hence, different locations.) However, another view has it that the killing of Smith by Jones was just the shooting (which in turn was just Jones's moving of his body); and thus, the killing was located just where Jones was located at the time he shot Smith, and that, therefore, Smith was not an object involved in the killing. And there are other views as well. So, is Smith involved in the killing or not? Is Smith's location at any time to be included in the location of Jones's killing of Smith?

This same issue can be generated with respect to events that are clearly not actions. Suppose that on some occasion the chiming of a bell (that is, its ringing) shattered a glass located half a mile from the bell. There was an event that was the bell's chiming and one that was the glass's shattering; and their locations are straightforward. But what of the location of the bell's shattering of the glass? Paralleling the views that can be taken in the case of the killing, one view insists on the glass's being involved in the bell's shattering of it and, hence, insists on the glass's location being included in the location of the bell's shattering of the glass; another view would insist that the location of that event include only the location of the bell when it chimed, for the bell was the minimal subject of that event. And there can be other views as well.

I shall be returning to this issue when the parallel issue of the temporal location of events is discussed. I hope to solve both problems at once. But I want now to mention and discuss briefly another issue concerning the spatial location of events.

3.2   *Do events change spatial location?*

The subject of the spatial locations of events should not be left before saying something about whether events change with respect to their spatial location, that is, whether events move. It would seem that there is some reason to think that events do move. After all, if the location of an event is just the location of the object that event is a change in (at the time it is undergoing that change), then when the subject of an event changes location, during the time at which it is the subject of an event, the event it is undergoing should change location as well. As Dretske remarks, the event can't very well be left behind![17] And we do speak of parties as moving indoors, of battles shifting location, and of floating crap games.

What I shall say about this issue is not new. It seems to me that the issue has been largely settled by Dretske, in his paper 'Can events move?' Though I am not inclined to agree with everything Dretske says in that paper, he is surely correct in most of what he says about the issue in question. What I shall do here is, for the most part, merely recapitulate the considerations motivating the view Dretske and I share. And that view is that events do not change with respect to their spatial locations; events do not move.

Physical objects and events have spatial parts. The legs of which my chair is in part constructed are, I presume, spatial parts of that chair; and the locations of those parts are parts of the location of the thing having those parts. The spatial parts of a physical object are just those physical objects of which it is constituted. Similarly, an event may have spatial parts; the things which at a time, t, are the spatial parts of an event are just those events which occur at t and which constitute the event at t. Thus, among the spatial parts of a playing of a symphony by an orchestra are the violinists' playing of the violins, the cellists' playing of the celli, and so on. Indeed, so long as the minimal subject of an event has spatial parts (at the time at which it is the subject of that event), the event that is the change in that object will have spatial parts; and those spatial parts will be the changes in the spatial parts of the event's subject (so long as the changes are among those of which the event is constituted). The locations of the spatial parts of events are just the locations of the spatial parts whose changes they are, and are parts of the location of the event of which they are the spatial parts. (Of course, more than one spatial part of an event may have the same location.)

Physical objects, however, do not have temporal parts. I earlier suggested that the having of temporal parts by physical objects is incompatible with the existence of events which are changes in such objects. And I take that as a *reductio ad absurdum* of the view that physical objects have temporal parts. In any case, it seems clear that if physical objects had temporal parts, then physical objects would not move. For any physical object to move, at least some of its spatial parts must first have one and then have another spatial location. (If all the spatial parts do that, then the object rotates or shifts; if only some do, then it oozes, spreads, grows, or shrinks.) But if physical objects had temporal as well as spatial parts, then no such thing that is at a place p_1, at t_1, would be a thing that is at p_2 at t_2. This is just a special case of the general idea that objects having temporal parts cannot, because they have temporal parts, change. For when an object moves it changes.

But it is obvious that, unlike physical objects, events do have temporal parts.[18] This is so because, while an object can be changing at an instant, there are no instantaneous events. Events are changes in objects, and for an object to change it must first have and then lack a property. Change takes time.[19] Events occur at intervals of time; and at intervals within such intervals events of which an event is composed may occur; and they are the temporal parts of events.

What would it be for an event to move? Presumably, it would be for an event to be such that at least one of its spatial parts is in one place at one time and in another place at another time. But for an event to be (to occur) in one place at one time and in another place at another time, it is not sufficient that it be occurring at one place at one time and occurring at another place at another time (that surely happens). That is analogous to a physical object's being said to move on the grounds that one spatial part of it has one location at one time and another spatial part has another location at a later time. An event may be said to be occurring at moments and intervals of time that are parts of the time at which it occurs; but no event occurs during any proper part of the time at which it occurs. Hence, for any distinct times, t and t' (whether instants or intervals), such that an event is occurring during both, it is not the case that that event occurs at either t or t'. But, if an event moves, it must occur at one place at one time and at another place at another time. And this is impossible. Again, it is possible for an event to be occurring at one place at one time and at another place at another time. But that only implies that some temporal part of it has one while another temporal part has another location. And that is not sufficient for its being the case that an event moves. No event can be said to occur at any place where only some proper temporal or spatial part of it occurs; and no event can be said to occur at any time when only some proper temporal or spatial part of it occurs then.

A physical object can move either because all of it or because some spatial part of it may be wholly in one place at one time and wholly in another place at another time. Since events have temporal parts, however, no event or spatial part of an event can be wholly in one place at one time and in another place at another time. Nothing moves just because one part of it has a location at one time not shared by another part at another time. Events do not move.

In this respect, there is nothing special about movement. We should be able to turn this version of Dretske's argument into a quite general argument against the possibility of an event's being the subject of any event whatsoever. How the argument is to be generalized is fairly obvious. For anything whatever to be the subject of an event, it must have a property at one time which it lacks at another. But it is hard (but not impossible, there is an exception I shall mention) to see how an event could have a property at one time that it lacks at another, despite apparent cases of this, as when we say that the party got boisterous or that the storm became more destructive. But was it really the case that the party lacked the property of being boisterous and then acquired it? The party was not boisterous, only its later parts were. It is no more plausible to say that the party was either boisterous or not if it became boisterous than it is to say that the table is green because its left half is green. We can, I suppose, by saying that the party lacked and then had the property of being boisterous, mean only that its later parts were boisterous. But this is not a case of change. When a physical object changes, it is not the case that some of its earlier parts have a property lacked by some of its later parts, for it has no such parts. Perhaps, the earlier and later parts of that object's 'history' were different; but that does not imply that its history changed. Events are not the subjects of events for the same reason that they do not move; they have temporal parts.

To say, however, that an event cannot be the subject of an event is not to say that an event cannot change; it is only to say that an event cannot change non-relationally. An event could change if there were a property it had and then lacked, the having and then lacking of which was independent, in a sense, of what the event was like at different times. We've run across this idea before. It was argued earlier that physical objects change that way, namely relationally. Events can change relationally, for their so changing does not require that events have and then lack properties the having and then lacking of which would make them subjects of events. A particular performance of Pachelbel's Canon in D might start out being my favourite performance of it; I made a prediction on the basis of the first few measures about what the rest of it would be like and judged it, on that basis, to be my favourite performance. But, things did not turn out as predicted; and so, near the end of that performance, it was not my favourite. Though the performance didn't change non-relationally, it did at one time bear a certain relation to an entity (me) with a certain property and at another time did not. So, the performance changed relationally.[20] But, as I earlier argued, for an entity (of any sort) to change relationally is not for it to be the subject of an event.

4 THE TEMPORAL FEATURES OF EVENTS

Events are changes; they are the (non-relational) movements of objects through quality spaces from the having of one to the having of another property. Since the quality spaces in which a thing changes are populated by contraries, those properties an object has and then acquires, in virtue of which it changes and is the subject of some event, cannot be possessed by the object in question simultaneously. Change takes time. Events thus have temporal features, among which are those having to do with their times of occurrence. This section is devoted to a discussion of some of the temporal features of events.

Among the facts concerning the temporal features of events, construed as the changes objects undergo when they change non-relationally, is the fact that no event is literally repeatable; events do not recur. For an event to recur is for it to occur more than once; that is, an event recurs just in case there are distinct times at which it occurs. Events occur only at intervals of time, and if a certain event begins to occur at t_1 and ends at t_2 (say, without interruption), then that event does not occur either at t_1, or t_2, or at any instant in between, or during any interval properly included in the interval from t_1 to t_2. The event in question may be occurring at such times, but does not occur at such times. No event occurs at any time that does not include all the times at which it is occurring. Hence, for any distinct times, t and t' (be they instants or intervals), it cannot be the case that an event occurs both at t and at t', though it may be occurring at both those times in so far as one part of the event may occur at t and another part at t'.[21] But no event can occur at both those times, since if an event did occur at both t and t', then it would have occurred at a time (*viz.* t) that did not include a time (*viz.* t') during which it was occurring. For an event to recur there would have to be distinct intervals of time such that that event occurs at both those times. That, however, requires that an event occur at a time that does not include all the times at which it is occurring. Therefore, events do not recur.

This fact notwithstanding, we still do say such things as that there was an eruption of Mt St Helens yesterday and the same thing happened again today. Since the things that happen are events, it would appear that in saying such things we imply that events can happen again, that events recur. What is needed, then, is a way of understanding such remarks that is not inconsistent with the fact that events do not recur. That way has been, I believe, supplied by Myles Brand.[22] Briefly, his proposal is to treat claims that apparently say that some event happened more than once in the way one would naturally treat claims apparently saying, for example, that two people own the same car, despite the fact that the cars owned by the two are distinct physical objects. In the latter case, that the two own the same car is to be understood, not as saying that a single car is co-owned, but as saying that the car owned by the one and that owned by the other belong to the same sort. And sameness of sort is to be understood, roughly, as the sharing of properties the knowledge of the possession of which is available in the situation in which the judgement that the two own the same car is made. (The properties in question must not include any that necessarily less than two things can have. Otherwise, no two cars could belong to the same sort, since no two could share the property of being located in a certain place.) Sameness of sort is taken, by Brand, for the purposes of understanding ordinary judgments of the kind considered here, to be a context-dependent notion. And this seems to be correct; I'd be justified in saying that you and I own the same car, if all I knew was that we both owned Fords, but not if I also knew that yours was manufactured in 1982 and mine was manufactured in 1933. Similarly, claims that apparently say of an event that it recurred are to be understood in terms of a context-dependent notion of sharing of certain properties. Brand's account seems to me substantially correct. And I have nothing further to say here about the alleged recurrence of events.

4.1 *When events occur*

Events occur over intervals of time. But if an event occurs over an interval of time, t, it occurs during any interval that includes t (though it does not follow from this that it is occurring at every instant in those larger intervals). So, events have non-minimal times of occurrence, just as they have non-minimal spatial locations. If my heart skipped a beat today, that beat-skipping occurred during April, 1982, during the twentieth century, and so on. Is there anything answering to the idea of the 'minimal' period of time during which an event occurs? I think so, but that notion will not be unproblematic.

Suppose that some object, x, changes from being located at place p_1 to being located at p_2; and suppose, for simplicity's sake, that x so changes just once and does so uninterruptedly and without returning to p_1 before getting to p_2. An interval of time *during* which x's moving from p_1 to p_2 occurs is any non-disjoint interval that includes a time at which x is at p_1 and a time at which x is at p_2. Similarly, making the same simplifying suppositions, if some event is an object's going from having a property P to having a property Q, then an interval of time during which that event occurs is any interval that includes a time when its subject has P and a time when it has Q. Clearly, then, there is no unique period of time during which a given event occurs. We should, of course, be interested in the idea of the *minimal* duration of an event; and that is the idea of an interval of time that is the *shortest* interval during which an event occurs. Such a minimal temporal interval deserves to be called 'the time *at* which an event occurs'.[23] But, as we shall see, this notion is not unproblematic.

Consider, again, x's movement from p_1 to p_2; and suppose that x was at rest at p_1 up to the time of the event in question, and that x comes to rest when it reaches p_2. It seems clear that there was *no* instant of time, t, such that, at every (nearby) instant before t, x was at rest, and such that at t and thereafter (for a while) x was moving. The truth seems to be that there was an instant, t', such that x was at rest at t' (in place p_1) and at every instant thereafter (for a while) x was moving. That is, there is no first moment of motion, only a last moment of rest. Were this not generally so, it would have to be the case that when a thing begins to move, it begins its motion with some definite velocity at a certain moment such that at every (nearby) earlier instant its velocity was zero; and thus, every beginning of motion would involve a discontinuous jump from a velocity of zero to some definite, non-zero velocity, without an acceleration up to that velocity. And that will hardly do as a description of what generally happens. Similarly, there will be no last moment at which x is moving towards p_2, though there will be a first moment at which x is at rest, at which x is at p_2. Otherwise, there would have to be a qualitatively gappy deceleration from some non-zero to a zero velocity.

It should also be noticed that if x moved to p_2, stopped for a while, and then moved again, there would have been a first and a last moment of the 'unchange', of x's being at p_2, but no last moment of its getting to p_2 and no first moment of x's remaining at p_2. The reason for this is that for an object to be remaining at p_2 at a time, t, the object must be at p_2 at t and at times surrounding t. Thus, an object is not remaining at p_2 at the instant it first gets to p_2, though it is then going to remain there. Similar, it is not remaining at p_2 at the time of its last moment of rest.

What I have said here about motion and rest seems to apply quite generally to change. In general, it appears reasonable to say that when any object changes during some interval of time, where its changing is bounded on both temporal sides by no change, there will be a last moment at which the object was not changing, no first moment at which the object started changing, no last moment at which it is still changing, and a first moment at which it is no longer changing.[24]

There appears to be a puzzle in the offing. On the one hand, if asked to specify the shortest interval of time during which x's motion occurs, when the last moment at which x was at p_1 was t_1 and the first moment at which x was at p_2 was t_2, it seems as if we should say that it occurs at the *open* interval t_1-t_2, the interval of time between but not including t_1 and t_2. And the reason for not including t_1 and t_2 is that at those times x was *not* moving. On the other hand, we are interested in the time of the event which is a movement by x *from* the having of the property of being located at p_1 *to* the having of the property of being located at p_2. And surely, the time of that movement should include a time at which it had the former and a time at which it had the latter property. The shortest period of time meeting that condition, however, is the *closed* interval t_1-t_2, an interval that includes both t_1 and t_2. But, surely, x's motion just is the motion from p_1 to p_2. Since the open interval from t_1 to t_2 is shorter than the closed interval from t_1 to t_2, we seem to have one and the same event with different (minimal) times of occurrence, whereas it follows from the indiscernibility of identicals that identical events have the same time of occurrence.

There really is no puzzle here at all. It is clear that x's moving from p_1 to p_2 occurs during the *closed* interval from t_1 to t_2. It does not occur during any shorter interval of time (e.g., the open interval from t_1 to t_2), for any shorter interval would fail to include either times during which x was moving from p_1 to p_2 or times at which x was at p_1 or at p_2. Clearly, the minimal temporal duration of the event cannot fail to include the times of any of the movings that were parts of x's moving from p_1 to p_2. But in addition, it cannot fail to include the last (relevant) time at which x was at p_1 or the first (relevant) time at which it was at p_2. And the reason for this is that the event in question is a movement by x *from* p_1 *to* p_2; the event in question was a change by x from its having the property of being at p_1 to its having the property of being at p_2. The time of that event must include times at which its subject has those properties. So, though the event was uninterrupted, its time of occurrence included two times, t_1 and t_2, when x was not moving. This should not irk, however, since, though x was not moving at t_1 and t_2, neither was it remaining at rest then.[25] (During the open interval between t_1 and t_2, x was moving at every instant therein; it was not then moving from p_1 to p_2, but *between* p_1 and p_2.)

The issues arising for movements through space arise quite generally for events. An event is a (non-relational) change which is an object's 'moving' from the having of one to the having of another property (within a given quality space). So, the time of such an event must include a time at which the subject of the event has the one and a time at which it has the other property. And those times are not, generally, times at which the subject is changing in that quality space (except when the subject was changing in that space immediately before or after the event in question); neither, of course, is the object at those times 'remaining at' those properties. So, the minimal time during which an event, consisting of a movement from the having of P to the having of Q, occurs includes the last time at which its subject has P (during which it may not be changing), the first time at which its subject has a Q (during which it may not be changing) and the open interval between those times (at every moment during which the subject of the event is changing in the respect to which P and Q belong, assuming the change to be uninterrupted). And such an event will occur during any period of time that includes that closed interval.

4.2 *Dense and discrete quality spaces – a problem*

Earlier, I drew a distinction between kinds of quality spaces. The *dense* quality spaces are those whose members are such that, however 'arranged' (i.e., assigned numbers for the purpose of producing graphs of changes), between any two of those properties there is another property. The (minimal) time of occurrence of movements by objects in such spaces is by and large straightforward; such an event occurs at an interval, in the manner described above. The reason the time of occurrence of such events is usually straightforward is that any such event is generally a movement by its subject from the having of one to the having of another property in such a way that in getting from the initial to the terminal state the subject of the event passes through intermediate states. In getting from the having of P_1 to the having of P_n, during the closed interval t_1-t_n, the subject of the event in question generally has, at times between t_1 and t_n, properties in between P_1 and P_n. In such cases there will be a last moment at which the subject of the event has P_1 and a first moment at which it has P_n.

A discrete quality space is a quality space that is not dense; it is a quality space in which it makes sense to suppose that an object moves 'directly' from the having of one to the having of another property in that space, for there are no properties in between. The quality space, if there is one, whose members are the properties things have in virtue of which they have the colour hair they have seems to be a discrete quality space, if we think of those properties as just those of being white-haired, blond, red-haired, etc., without countenancing gradations. It can happen that someone changed from being blond to being red-haired without having to have some other colour hair in the process.

The problem I wish to call attention to does not arise in those cases of change in a discrete quality space where the change is some object's going from the having of one to the having of another property, and where that change involves the object's

136

passing through some other property in the course of getting from its initial to its terminal state. In such cases, the time of such an event is the usual closed interval beginning with the last moment at which the object is in the initial state and ending with the first moment at which the object is in the terminal state.

Now during all such events, there will be times at which the changing thing moves from the having of one to the having of another property *without* having another property in between. There will be a movement by the changing thing from the having of P to the having of Q 'directly'. And it is in the case of such events that a problem for the notion of the time of occurrence of such an event arises. This problem will also arise in cases of movements in dense spaces where, even though the space is dense, a thing changing in that space gets from the having of one to the having of another property directly by skipping over the properties it would normally have to have (e.g., getting from p_1 to p_n, without passing through any intermediate places). The problem in both these sorts of cases is that there seems to be *no* interval of time which could be the time at which such an event occurs; for such an event has *no* minimal duration, only non-minimal durations. How is that possible?[26]

We are considering any case of a non-relational change by an object, x, from having a property P to having a property Q, where there is no property, in the dense or discrete quality space to which both P and Q belong, that x has after it has P but before it has Q. When does such an event occur? Any interval of time that includes a time at which x has P and a time at which x has Q is an interval *during* which that event occurs (assume, for the sake of simplicity, x changed from having P to having Q just once); and there are an infinite number of such non-minimal intervals. But what of the shortest interval during which this event occurs, that is, the interval of time *at* which it occurs? That interval should be one which includes the last moment at which x has P and the first moment at which x has Q (and the times during which x is changing between having P and Q). But if there is a last moment at which x has P, then there is *no* first moment at which x has Q, and if there is a first moment at which x has Q, there there is *no* last moment at which x has P (assuming, as I do, that the times are dense). Suppose that the last moment at which x has P is t and that there is a first moment at which x has Q, say, t'. T' cannot be t, for P and Q are contraries and cannot be had simultaneously by x. Therefore, t' and t are distinct times. But, if distinct, then, since the times are dense, there must be a time, t*, between t and t'. What could x be like at t*? It can't have P then, for t* is later than t, and t is, by hypothesis, the last moment at which x has P. It can't have Q at t*, for t* is earlier than t', and t', by hypothesis, is the first moment at which x has Q. But at t*, x exists and is changing in the quality space to which P and Q belong. So, it must have some property in that space; but, x can't have any other property in that space, since, by hypothesis, x moves from having P to having Q directly. Therefore, on the assumption that t is the last moment at which x has P, it follows that t' cannot be the first moment at which x has Q. But t' is *any* time at which x has Q (after having had P). Therefore, there is no first moment at which x has Q. The times during which x has Q, then, begin with an *open* interval, beginning with the times after t (when x has P). Thus, there is no interval of time that includes a time at which x has P and a time at which x has Q such that no shorter interval includes such times. Therefore, x's change from having P to having Q, when direct, has no minimal duration, and thus, no time of occurence! A precisely parallel argument for the same conclusion can be generated from the assumption that there is a first moment at which x has Q but no last moment at which x has P. But surely, if there are such events, there must be times at which they occur.

Perhaps this is the place where one should be forced to take back the insistence that there are no instantaneous events, and to say that x's going directly from the having of P to the having of Q is an instantaneous event. But what could be meant by saying that? That it occurs at the last moment at which x has P? Hardly, for at that time x is *not* changing; and an event cannot be said to occur wholly at a time during which its subject is not changing. (Similarly for the first moment, if there is one, at which x has Q.) Moreover, we are speaking of change, a movement from the having of one to the having of another property by some object. This notion of change is a dynamic notion, a notion of change as process. No notion of instantaneousness that is not misleadingly so called can apply to such a concept of change. The direct change by x from having P to having Q cannot take place at a durationless instant, for x cannot have both P and Q at such an instant (since they are contraries). Nor can the transition between the having of P and the having of Q be instantaneous, for there is no transition. That is, up until t, x has P, and at *every* moment thereafter (for a while at least), x has Q.

It might be suggested that this problem of the time of occurrence of direct changes is not really a problem arising out of the particular views concerning events and their times of occurrence that I am advocating. It might be suggested that this problem must arise on any theory about events and their times of occurrence for it arises from the density of time, a fact that must be coped with by any theory of events. And the reason that might be offered for this opinion is that the density of *space* causes a parallel problem for physical objects. This should show that both problems arise from features of time and space and not from theories about events and physical objects. The problem for physical objects arising from the density of space is that it apparently can be proved that, our tactile experiences notwithstanding, no physical objects ever touch.

If any two physical objects, O and O′, are to touch, there must be a place, p, where a part, O_1, of O and a part, O'_1, of O′ are in contact. But, if we suppose that O_1 is located at p, then O'_1 can't also be located at p (at the same time), unless $O_1 = O'_1$ (a hypothesis I am ruling out), since distinct physical objects cannot occupy the same place simultaneously. Thus, O'_1, that part of O′ allegedly in contact with O_1, must be located at some place, p′, distinct from p. But since space is dense, there must be places between p and p′ not occupied either by parts of O or by parts of O′. Therefore, since O_1 and O'_1 are not in contact, O and O′ are not touching. Of course, if O_1 occupies a closed set of points and O'_1 occupies an open set of points, then there would be no problem with their being in contact. But, there is no reason to suppose that there is this difference between O_1 and O'_1. Moreover, it is not clear that any physical object occupies an open set of points; it seems more likely that physical objects have closed boundaries and that it is the spaces between them that are constituted by open sets of points. In any case, even if one accepted the idea that O_1's location is a closed set of points while O'_1's is an open one, there would still be the problem of saying *where* O_1 and O'_1 are in contact. To say that they are in contact at p, which is part of O_1's closed boundary, is infelicitous, since neither O'₁ nor any part of it is located there; it is difficult, I think, to say that objects can be in contact at a place where no part of one of them is located.

Now, this suggestion, for saving me from thinking that the problem of the time of occurrence of direct changes is mine and not a general problem, goes on to suggest that the view that no physical objects ever touch is surely false. But its falsity, the suggestion continues, is not the crucial point. The crucial point is that the argument creates a problem because of the density of space and not because of some special view about physical objects. And so it is not my views about events causing the problem of the time of direct changes; it is the density of time, for the problems are perfectly analogous. And whatever it takes to solve the one will solve the other as well.

I suppose that I would be pleased if it were the case, for the reasons given, that the problem of direct changes really is just a special case of a more general problem concerning the density of time. But the fact is that it *is* my problem. And the reason for this is as follows. We can, as a matter of fact, just admit that the argument just sketched does show that physical objects cannot touch (we don't have to take this line, but we *can*). Physical objects cannot touch, though they can get arbitrarily close. This view does sound a bit paradoxical, but it is not obviously absurd. It is a view that can be accepted without having to give up any view whose truth we believe crucial to our understanding of the nature of physical objects or the space they occupy. There must, of course, be an account of tactile sensation that does not rely on actual contact; but, after all, electrons affect each other without being in contact. And, of course, nothing said so far rules out the parts of distinct physical objects from being arranged like the cogs in interlocking gears; and that would explain why, despite the fact that there is always space between objects, we sometimes cannot see the space between them. In short, no conceptual difficulties stand in the way of simply accepting the mildly paradoxical view that physical objects never touch.

Nothing like this is possible, however, in the case of the time of direct changes. Events, on my view, occur at intervals of time; there are no instantaneous events. Therefore, for each event, there must be an interval of time during which it occurs such that it occurs during no shorter interval. But, there are no minimal intervals of time during which direct changes occur. Thus, there are direct changes, but they do not have times of occurence. This view is genuinely impossible. No amount of hand-waving can make it possible for one to say that the view is, though slightly paradoxical, nevertheless true and can be accepted if one is prepared to swallow hard. There is a genuine problem here, and it is of my own making, for it arises out of my insistence that there are no instantaneous events. Now I think that this view is well-motivated, by a dynamic conception of events as changes, and true. But the fact remains that if events could occur instantaneously, there would be no problem of the time of occurrence of direct changes. So, the problem is not due to the density of time; it is due to the denial of the claim that there are events that occur instantaneously.

My proposal for dealing with this problem can be introduced in the following way. The term 'Smith's winning of the race' is ambiguous. In one sense it refers to a non-instantaneous process that begins some time during the race and ends when the race is won; it refers to Smith's doing something (e.g., putting on a burst of speed) that terminates in his being in the state of winning the race. In this sense, 'Smith's winning of the race' refers to an event (if actions are events). In another sense, however, the term refers to something that is instantaneous, something that first obtains at the moment Smith is at the finish line (given that no one gets there before him); it refers, in this sense, to the beginning of Smith's being in the state of having won the race. The question, When did Smith win the race?, when that is a request for a specification of the time at which Smith did something having the result that he wins the race, is to be answered by specifying an interval that includes the time he gets to the finish line and some earlier times as well (at those earlier times he is in the process of winning the race). But, when construed as a request for a specification of the time at which Smith's winning of the race, in the process sense, terminated, it is a request for the time at which the state of his winning of the race first obtained and is to be answered by giving the time at which he got to the finish line. And that time is an instant, one before which he is not yet at the finish line and after which he is beyond it. (Actually, 'his arriving at the finish line' and 'his crossing of the finish line' are ambiguous in the same way.) That is, there is an instant before which Smith has not yet won the race (in the state sense) and after which he has; and that instant is the time at which his winning of the race, in the state sense, first obtains. But that instant is not the time of occurrence of the event that is his winning of the race; it is the time at which that event terminates.

Similarly, 'x's getting to have property Q (from having P)' is ambiguous. In the process sense, it refers to something non-instantaneous, an event that terminates in x's first having Q. In the state sense, it refers to that with which that event terminates, x's first having Q, and the event terminating with x's being in that state terminates at an instant.

The original problem was that the conjunction, of the claim that there are direct changes and the claim that every event has an interval of time for its time of occurrence, appears to be a contradiction. One can restore consistency by rejecting one or both conjuncts. I propose, rather, to accept them both, but suggest that the claims can be understood in such a way that they can be seen as consistent. I wish to hold that no event is instantaneous. However, no direct change is an instantaneous event. 'Direct changes', in so far as they are instantaneous, are not changes. The terms referring to 'direct changes' are ambiguous, however, referring, in their process sense, to non-instantaneous events, and, in their state sense, to the states with which those events terminate.

My proposal consists in part of the conjecture that, when the 'ultimate' quality spaces in which objects change non-relationally are determined, it will be seen (a) that all such spaces are dense, and (b) that no object ever moves in such a space from having one to having any other quality without also having another quality in that space between the having of the former and the having of the latter. That is, all ultimate quality spaces are dense, and all changes in them are dense. If this is so, then it will be possible to maintain that the time of occurrence of every event is an interval.

Part of what I have in mind by calling some quality spaces 'ultimate' and withholding that epithet from others is this. Suppose that some object goes from being red to being blue 'directly' (where the space to which those colours belong is discrete). On my proposal, we should see the situation in the following way. There is an event, the object's going from being red to being blue, and that event terminates instantaneously in the object's first being blue. But that event is not 'ultimately' a change in that discrete colour-space. Rather that event consists in that object's (or its parts') changing in one or more quality spaces; and those other changes, of which the change in colour consists, are dense changes in dense spaces. And so, the time of the change in colour is just the time of occurrence of those dense changes of which the direct change (in the process sense) is composed. (When an object moves from being lighter to being heavier (by gaining weight) in a discrete, comparative-weight space, that change ultimately consists of a dense change in a dense space whose members are real-valued measures of weight.) My suggestion is not that there are no discrete quality spaces or that no object ever goes from having one to having another quality in any dense or discrete quality space without having another quality from the same space in between. The suggestion is rather that such changes consist of other events that are dense changes in dense spaces, and that the time of such an event is the shortest interval during which the dense changes of which the direct change is composed occur. Further, the terms referring to these direct changes are ambiguous, referring in one sense to the non-instantaneous events that are composed of dense changes in dense spaces, and in another to the states with which such events terminate instantaneously. And their referring, in one sense, to those instantaneous states make one infer (fallaciously) that the events to which they refer, in their other sense, are instantaneous events.[27]

In some cases, the existence of just noticeable differences may explain why we think that a change is really direct and not composed of dense changes; we do not see the changes of which a turning blue is composed, due sometimes to the fact that its constituent changes have subjects that are invisible to us. We see the thing to be red at one moment and blue at the 'next', and we take the change to be direct and instantaneous. But, on my proposal, what is instantaneous is not any change, but the obtaining of a state with which some change terminates. So, there are direct changes, but none that are not composed of dense changes in dense quality spaces. And the terms referring to direct changes also ambiguously refer to the states with which direct changes' constituent changes terminate, thus giving the false impression that direct changes are instantaneous events having no minimal times of occurrence. But, like the times of dense changes, the time of a direct change is an interval, the smallest interval during which the dense changes of which it is composed occur.

This proposal does, I believe, solve my problem of the time of direct changes. And it is a solution in the spirit of the dynamic conception of change I have been advocating; it insists that even direct changes involve objects 'in process'. Also, it makes use of an ambiguity similar to one figuring in my discussion, in the next section, of the time and place of a killing. And it makes use of the idea that will have to be exploited, in any case, to get hold of the idea of an 'atomic' event and of the relationship between, for example, a sinking of a ship and the sinkings of its parts. So, there is that much to be said in favour of my conjecture: it meshes comfortably with other things I have wanted, for independent reasons, to say about events, and it appears to solve my problem concerning the time of direct changes. It also strikes me that the general idea behind the conjecture has some intuitive appeal.

On the other hand, I have no direct, independent argument either for the claim that the ultimate quality spaces in which things change non-relationally are dense or for the claim that all changes in such spaces are either dense or composed of dense changes. Moreover, the conjecture takes what I presume is a contentious stand on what appear to be certain matters of fact concerning allegedly discontinuous movements through space and allegedly discontinuous changes of state. I must hold either that there are no such changes or that they are really composed of dense changes in objects related to the allegedly discontinuously changing thing. I must say that I am not terribly troubled by this consequence of my proposal; but that I am not reflects only my scientific biases.

4.3   *The time and place of a killing*

I want now to raise an issue concerning the time at which certain events occur that parallels the issue raised earlier concerning which objects are involved in certain events. The spatial location of an event is just the location (at the time of the event in question) of all the objects minimally involved. Questions then arise about which the objects are that are involved in such events as window shatterings by bell ringings, and actions such as killings performed by shooting.

The time at which an event (or action) occurs is just the time of all those changes that are parts of the event (or action) in question. But the question then arises, Which changes are parts of such events? As before, the cases I have in mind as raising this question are those brought into prominence by Professor J.J. Thomson. In 'The time of a killing', she raises these problems concerning a certain class of actions, actions like killings and meltings. But, it is clear that the same issues arise for events that are clearly not actions. Thomson raises these problems about the time at which certain actions are performed, because that issue affects her principal concern in that paper, the identity of actions. The connection between the temporal issue and the identity issue is obvious: identical actions and events must occur at the same time. So, if such actions as shootings and killings occur at different times, then such actions cannot be identical. Such actions are not identical, if Thomson is right, because there are certain changes that are parts of killings but are not parts of shootings, and those changes occur at times other than the times of shootings; thus, shootings and killings will have different times of occurrence. The parallel and connection between this problem and the one concerning involved objects is obvious: the 'extra' changes that are parts of killings but not of shootings turn out to be changes in objects minimally involved in killings but not in shootings. Here is how the temporal problems arise.

Suppose that the following circumstances obtain: (i) a kills b by shooting him, (ii) a shoots b at t_1, and (iii) b later dies at t_3. Now, while some philosophers[28] have held that a's shooting of b and a's killing of b are one and the same action, and hence have all the same temporal features, Thomson and others[29] have held that the alleged identity of the shooting and the killing runs afoul of the obviously true claim that identical actions must have the same time of occurrence. According to Thomson,[30] at t_2, a time between t_1 and t_3, it is true to say that a's shooting of b has occurred, but false, since at t_2 b is not yet dead, to say that a's killing of b has occurred; this is the 'tense' problem. Further, though a's shooting of b occurred at t_1, a's killing of b did not occur then, since b did not die at t_1; this is the 'date' problem. And lastly, while b's death occurred n hours after a's shooting of him occurred, it did not occur n hours after a's killing of him occurred, since b's death is that event with which the killing terminates; this is the 'temporal order' problem. Thus, the shooting and the killing cannot be identical, since they have different temporal features. And they have different temporal features, for Thomson, because there is at least one change that is a part of the killing but not of the shooting and that occurs at a time distinct from that of the shooting. Any specification of the time of the killing must, therefore, include the time of that change; thus, the killing occurs at a longer interval of time than does the shooting. And that extra change is b's death.

The tense, date and temporal order problems can obviously be raised for events that are clearly not actions. As earlier, the bell chimes and as a result a glass later breaks. What is the relation between the bell's chiming and the bell's shattering of the glass? Some would say that those events are identical. But others, following Thomson, would insist that there is a time at which it is true that the bell's chiming has occurred, but at which it is not true to say that the bell's shattering of the glass has occurred, that the bell's chiming but not its shattering of the glass occurred at a certain time, and that the glass's breaking occurred n seconds after the bell's chiming, but not n seconds after the bell's shattering of the glass. Thus, those events can't be identical. And the reason given for these temporal differences between the chiming and the shattering is that the latter event has as a part a change, the glass's shattering, which is *not* a part of the chiming, and that part occurred at a time distinct from the time of the chiming. Thus, it does not matter whether this problem is discussed in terms of actions or events that are not actions; the issues are the same. So, since the action cases are more familiar, I will discuss the issues in the context of those cases; what will be said will apply in a straightforward way to all the cases of concern here.

Thomson considers salvaging the identity of the shooting and the killing by denying that that identity is inconsistent with the idea that identical actions must occur at the same time. As she points out, one might argue as follows:

After all,. . . once a has shot b (supposing the wound a fatal one. . .), there is nothing further a need do in order to have killed b. And if you had watched a shoot b at t_1, then, even if you saw nothing further of the matter, you could later tell your friends that you had seen a kill b.[31]

The defence of the identity of the killing and the shooting would go on to admit that one is forced to say such things as that a has killed b by t_2, that a killed b at t_1, and that a killed b before b died. However, the defence goes on, though such things might be odd and perhaps misleading, they may nevertheless be true.

Thomson's criticism of this defence[32] is that the view it defends is *so* odd and misleading in what it implies – for example, that people are killed before they die, that someone has already blown up a library that still stands undamaged – that if another view not having such consequences could be found, it surely would be preferable. It is simply not enough to insist 'odd, but true', and to say that we must reconcile ourselves to these implications. And I do not disagree. I would not wish to deny that there is a felt oddity about the identity of the killing and the shooting and its consequences (e.g., that a kills b before b dies); nor would I deny that such things can be misleading. A defence of such claims cannot consist in saying that oddity does not imply falsity or that truth is sometimes stranger than either fiction or philosophy.[33] Nevertheless, I do wish to defend the view that the identity of a's shooting of b and a's killing of b, in the circumstances described, is *not* thrown in doubt by Thomson's argument, and I want to defend the idea that the temporal features of events and actions are consistent with that identity. But, if we are to become reconciled to that and similar identities, the reconciliation must not be achieved just by swallowing hard; what must be reconciled are the facts.

In the 'Individuation of events', Davidson offers us some help in this direction. After suggesting a 'causal' analysis of such sentences as 'a killed b', under which 'to describe an event as a killing is to describe it as an event. . .that caused a death',[34] he suggests that under some circumstances we may know of some event that it was a shooting but not know, due to the remoteness of the effect, that it was a killing; so it may sometimes be misleading to say, before b's death, that a killed him, since that would suggest that we are in a position to know what effect the shooting had. But the issue at hand is not really resolved by Davidson's suggestion, for the issue is whether or not someone who said that would have been speaking *truly*, though misleadingly. Epistemological considerations aside, can we describe an event as one which brought about another if that other has not yet occurred? Davidson insists[35] that we must distinguish such events as Jones's walking of the dog, which is not over until the dog has been walked, and Jones's killing of Smith, which is over when Jones finishes poisoning Smith's tea, even though Smith does not drink the tea until ten minutes later. In the former case, it would be odd and false to say that Jones walked the dog before the dog was walked; but in the latter case, it would be true, though perhaps odd, to say that Jones had killed Smith before Smith died. Now while I am in agreement with the spirit of such claims (though I shall have something to say about the tea-poisoning later), I think we need to see some deeper reason for thinking that killing Smith is not like walking one's dog, in that while the latter (like winning a race) describes Smith's action in terms of a state with which his action terminates, the former describes Smith's action in terms of an effect his action remotely causes. If that can be done, we will be well on our way to explaining how it can be true that a killed b before b died, how it can be that b was killed before b died, and how it can be that a's shooting of b is a's killing of b.

Thomson's objections to the identification of shootings and killings are intended to apply to a broad class of cases, though she finds herself unable to give a systematic criterion which marks off that class.[36] She correctly finds defective the attempt to characterize the cases to which her objections are meant to apply as cases involving 'causal' verbs, where a verb is causal, in a sentence of the form 'x φed y', if the sentence can be rewritten as 'x caused y to be φed'. The attempt fails for the verbs involved in her objections – *viz*. 'kill', 'blow up', 'melt' – are not causal in this sense. If, for example, x coerces z into killing y, then while it is true that x caused y to be killed, it is not true that x killed y, even though x gets y killed.

It seems to me, however, that the causal analysis is not too far from the truth. It is surely true that if x killed y, then x caused y's death. The problem concerns the converse. But it should be noted that the difficulties for the converse arise only when an aspect of 'multiple agency' is introduced into potential counter-examples, that is, only when it is the case that something else must be done (either by x or by another), beyond what x did (e.g., shoot b), in order for the effect (e.g., b's death) to occur, nature not included. Thus, if x plants the bomb under the library, then he does not blow up the library *by* planting the bomb and the question of whether or not the bomb planting is his blowing up of the library does not arise, if x or his co-conspirator must still press a button activating the timing device. In that case, there is a time at which it is true that x has planted the bomb and false that he has blown up the library. But, returning to killings, if x did do something that caused y's death, and if neither x nor anyone else did something, after x did what he did, that causally contributed to y's death, then x killed y. Interesting cases arise when the additional agent happens to be the victim; consider cases of what I call 'suicide traps', where, for example, x poisons y's tea, which has yet to be (but will be) drunk, and where x rigs y's door so that when y opens it y sets off a gun which fires, killing him. Of course, we will want to hold x responsible for y's death in both cases; x did do something that caused y's death. But, though it is true that x killed y, it is so, I think, in an extended sense. For there is an important difference between the suicide traps and the cases which occur in circumstances describable by (i)-(iii). In the latter cases, x kills y *by* shooting him. In the suicide traps, however, x does not kill y either *by* poisoning his tea or *by* rigging his door. The tea-poisoning and the door-rigging are similar to the buying of an airline ticket, in that the buying of the ticket will not result, on its own, in one's getting to one's destination, though it does make it possible for a flying to have that effect; one does not get to one's destination *by* buying a ticket. While one cannot kill someone by rigging his door or by poisoning his tea, such actions do make it possible for other events (namely door-openings and tea-drinkings, respectively) to have that effect; but you can kill someone by shooting him. So, in the suicide traps, it is true that x does something that causally contributes to y's death, and x does kill y. But x kills y in an extended sense, since though there was an event whose occurrence ensures that y will die, that event was y's drinking of the tea or opening of the door; that is, no action of x's was such that *by* performing it, x killed y. (And the same is to be said where the additional agent is neither x nor y.) In the multiple agency cases where the additional agent is x himself, where he does something else after, say, planting the bomb, e.g., setting the timing device, we will, of course, say that x blew up the library; but the action one may be inclined to identify with his blowing up of the library will not be the bomb-planting, but rather the device-setting. The cases in which such identities are apt to be affirmed are just those in which we would use the 'by'-locution, for in those cases, there is no question of multiple agency; and it is only when there is an aspect of multiple agency involved in any case that there is any hesitation (barring Thomson's objections) in asserting the allegedly suspicious identities.

So, once cases of multiple agency are excluded from consideration, it seems that nothing stands in the way of characterizing the expressions, like 'kill', to which Thomson's objections are meant to apply, as 'causal' verbs; and sentences of the form 'x φed y', where 'φ' is replaced by a causal verb, can be treated, in cases where there is no multiple agency, as equivalent to

(1)   x did something that causes y to be φed (or y's being φed).

(This is better than 'x caused y to be φed', since (1) mentions, however, indefinitely, the event (*viz.* what x did) that is said to have caused y's being φed.) The cases to which the tense, date, and temporal order problems are to apply are those in which it is claimed that x φed y, where

(2)   'x φed y' is equivalent (barring multiple agency) to 'x did something which causes y's being φed),
(3)   there are terms of the forms 'x's ψing' and 'x's ψing of y' that purport to refer to 'what x did', and
(4)   it might be claimed that x's ψing (of y)= x's φing (of y).[37]

Thomson's claim is that in such cases the ψing (e.g., a's shooting of b) and the φing (e.g., a's killing of b) cannot be identical. I think they can be, and that there are no temporal (or spatial) problems for this view.

Terms of the form 'y's being φd (by x)' are ambiguous; and I think that disambiguating them helps to straighten out this matter of the temporal (and spatial) location of shootings and killings.

There is a sense of 'y's being φed (by x)' in which it denotes a *non-relational state* of y. The non-relational state of y denoted is one of the states y gets into as a result of something's happening to y, as a result of some event that was the bringing about of some change in y. It is that state of y the obtaining of which makes it true to say, if x brought about the change, that x has φed y. If y does not come to be in the state of having been φed by x, then x has not φed y, and no action of x's (intentional or not) is, counts as, amounts to, terminates in, or level-generates x's φing of y. 'The door's being closed (by Jones)', in this sense, denotes a state of the door which obtains as a result of someone's closing it, and does not obtain (i.e., y is not in that state) until the door is completely closed. It should be noted that for a door to be in the non-relational state of being closed, it is not necessary for it not to have been in that state; it might always have been closed. This contrasts with the state of being killed, for example, since nothing that has never been in the state of being alive can be in that state. So, to say of someone that he is in the state of being killed is to imply that he got to be in the state of being dead by being killed. This distinction among non-relational states, however, is not of particular concern here, since we are worried here about such states construed as the results of events and actions.

The non-relational state sense is not to be confused with what might be called the *process* sense some of these expressions possess. In the process sense of 'the door's being closed (by Jones)', that phrase seems to be related to the sentence 'the door is being closed (by Jones)', and denotes an event (the door's closing), whose subject is the door, and which begins when the door begins to move in the direction of the door frame and ends when the door gets to be in the non-relational state of being closed (by Jones). Now, while the door is in the process of being closed by Jones, Jones may have his hand on the door knob all the while, guiding, so to speak, the door into its frame. In these circumstances, Jones may, during the time at which the door is closing, be said to be in the process of closing the door; and his action may be described as 'his closing of the door' (but only if the door gets closed). If, however, Jones kicks the door, sending it on its way, then during most of the time the door is in the process of closing, it is not the case that Jones is in the process of closing the door. If there ever were such a process involving

Jones, it was not during that period of time (i.e., while the door was in the process of closing) that he was engaged in it. During that period, it would indeed be odd, misleading and false to say that Jones is closing the door; you would not be interrupting some door-closing activity of his, if you asked him for a match while the door was closing. It would not be correct for Jones to answer an inquiry about his activities at the time by saying that he was closing the door. Jones's closing of the door was that action of his that resulted in the door's being in the non-relational state of being closed. And, Jones performed the action having that result when he kicked the door. The answer to the question, When was the door closed by Jones?, when that is a request for a specification of the time at which the door got to be in the non-relational state of being closed (by Jones), is: the time at which the door met its frame. But, when that question is a request for a specification of the time at which Jones did something that had the result that the door got to be in the state of being closed, the answer is: the time at which he kicked it; for the kicking of the door *was* that action of Jones's that had that result.[38]

It is surely odd and false to say, returning to shootings and killings, that b was killed (by a), before b died, if 'b was killed (by a)' is about b's being killed (by a), in the non-relational state sense. For b cannot be in that state until he has died; he cannot be said to be in that state before he dies no matter how certain it is that he will be in that state. But it is neither odd nor false to say that the action a performed, which resulted in b's being in that state, occurred before b's being in that state obtained. The action a performed may be simultaneous with b's being killed (in the process sense) if a kills b by strangling him. But, though it must be the case that b's death and b's being killed (in the sense in which that phrase denotes a state that b is in when he is dead) follow immmediately upon the termination of the process of b's being killed,[39] it need not follow immediately upon a's killing of him, for there may be temporal lag between actions and their remote effects. So, a's action that resulted in b's being killed (in the non-relational state sense) could have preceded b's death and b's being killed (in the non-relational state sense), and it could have been identical with the killing of by by a, since the killing was just the action a performed that had the result that b got (when he died) into the state of being killed. There are, at least, no temporal difficulties standing in the way of making such a claim.

We can even make good sense of what Thomson calls the 'Hollywood' use of language where the victim says, upon being shot, 'you killed me', and the 'bad joke' of claiming that you melted the chocolate at t_1, when what you did at t_1 was flip the switch and when the chocolate's being melted (in the non-relational state sense) did not obtain until t_3.[40] To make such good sense, we must see that there is, in addition to a non-relational state sense and a process sense of expressions of the form 'y's being ϕed (by x)', a *relational state* sense. Just as when Socrates died, Xantippe, *ipso facto*, changed relationally – she became a widow – it is also the case that when, at t_1, a fires the fatal shot, b changes relationally. At t_1 (and at no moment before), b was fired at by a; being fired at (by a) is a relational state of b at t_1, and that is so because a shot at him at t_1. So, we may say that 'b's being shot (by a)', in this sense, refers to a relational state of b, a state which obtains at the time a shoots. And, since the shooting was a fatal one, b's state at the time of his being shot is a state of being fatally shot. That is, b is at t_1 in a relational state produced by an event (a's shooting of b at t_1) that will result in b's being in the non-relational state of being killed; b cannot be in that relational state at t_1, unless he gets to be in that non-relational one. But if, at t_1, b is in the relational state of being fatally shot (by a), then why not say that, at t_1, b is in the relational state of being killed (by a)? Those seem to be the same state. So, it is not at all odd or false to say that b's being killed (in the relational state sense) obtained before b's being killed (in the non-relational state sense) obtained (if, of course, b dies). A's killing of b is an action of a's that (i) terminates at t_1 in a's being in the state of having killed b (when b gets to be in the relational state of being killed, and (ii) causes b's dying (i.e., b's being killed in the process sense), an event that terminates at t_3 in b's being in the non-relational state of being killed (of being dead as a result of a killing).

And yet the oddity felt in saying that a killed b before b dies remains. It remains, I think, because we want to say that a has not killed b until b's being killed in the non-relational state sense has obtained.[41] It is all well enough to say that when a shoots b at t_1, b's being killed (in the relational state sense) has obtained; but b's being killed (in the non-relational state sense) has not. Does not 'a killed b' mean that a did something that result*ed* in b's being killed (in the non-relational sense), and that if b is not in that state at some particular time (no matter what relational state he is in then), then at that time a has not killed b, even though he has shot b? I think that there is reason to believe that this is not necessarily so.

The causal analysis of sentences of the form 'x φed y' (when there is no question of multiple agency) shows that sentences of that form contain, in some sense, *two* verbs governing two sentences: one sentence says that x did something, the other expresses the idea that x's doing something had a certain result (*viz.* that y got to be in the non-relational state of being φed).[42] But why should we think that the tense of the verb 'φ' in 'x φed y' governs both of those sentences, so as to indicate not only that x's doing occurred in the past, but also that y's being in that non-relational state obtained in the past? After all, 'x's φing of y' refers to something x did; and its so referring makes true 'x φed y'. What matters to that term's succeeding in denoting is that y gets to be in the non-relational state of being φed; it should not matter when y gets into that state. We should understand 'x φed y' as 'x did something which causes (at some time or other) b's being φed (in the non-relational state sense)'. The term generated from 'x φed y', namely 'x's φing of y', refers to the event that produced y's being in that state; so there seems to be no reason to think that the time of the result is past, just because the time of the event that produces that result is past. The tense of 'x φed y' seems to me to govern only the verb in the phrase denoting the producing event, not the verb in the phrase having to do with the produced non-relational state. That we must take the tense of the verb in 'x φed y' to govern both verbs is an easily made mistake resulting in a puzzle about how a can kill b before b dies; but it is a mistake that can easily be corrected. It is not, of course, impossible for one to intend the tense of the verb in 'x φed y' to govern both verbs; and, given the epistemological problem of telling what result some action has before the result occurs, it is perhaps not unnatural to take someone who has uttered a sentence of the form 'x φed y' to have intended that. But, it is a mistake, I think, to presume that that must be so. One who says that some event has a certain effect, may be presumed to have information that would justify his making such a claim; but, in order to possess such information it is not necessary for the effect already to have occurred. Sometimes we can go out on speculative limbs with confidence. So, while it may on occasion be misleading to say, before b dies, that a killed b, it need not be false to say it; for what a speaker may mislead an audience about is, perhaps, the quality of his evidence, and not the facts. Thus, I see in the end no clear objections, based on temporal grounds, to the identity of a's shooting of b and his killing of b.[43]

4.4 *When and where certain events occur*

The generalization of the argument just offered and its implications for the time and place at which certain events occur is fairly straightforward. Some claims of the form 'x φed y' seem to report the occurrence of changes, and they do so by describing those changes in terms of some effects those changes have. Thus, 'the bell shattered the glass by chiming' means something like this: there was a chiming, e, whose subject was the bell, and that event (e) has another event, the glass's shattering (which terminates in the glass's being in the non-relational state of being shattered), as an effect. The bell's chiming is the event that sentence is, in some sense, about; and the description 'the bell's shattering of the glass' is a description of that event that describes it in terms of one of its effects. The glass's shattering is *not* something it describes. The bell's shattering of the glass is an event that occurs when the event that caused the glass to shatter occurs, for it was the event that caused the glass to shatter. The glass's shattering was not a part of that event; it was an effect of it. So, the glass was not an object involved in the shattering of it (it was involved in its shattering). Similarly, the victim was not an object involved in the killing of him. And if those objects were not involved, then the times of their changes are not parts of the times at which the events bringing their changes about occurred; and their locations are not parts of the minimal spatial locations of the events that brought about their changes. So, in the case of a's killing of b, the only minimally involved object is a; neither b, nor the gun, nor the bullet are involved. And thus, only the time and place at which a changes in the appropriate ways are the time and place at which the killing of b occurs. Similarly, only the bell is minimally involved in the shattering of the glass; and so, only the time and place of its chiming (the event causing the glass's shattering) are the time and place at which the bell's shattering of the glass occurred.

A description of an event can mislead us about which objects are involved in it, where the event takes place, and when it takes place. For such a description may mention objects that are involved though not minimally so, objects that are not involved at all, and changes that are not parts of the event being described.

VI

EVENTS AS CHANGES

1 SPATIO-TEMPORAL SAMENESS

Despite whatever uncertainties or unclarities there may be concerning the notions of the time and the place of the occurrence of an event, it is clear that occurrence at the same time and at the same place is a necessary condition for the identity of events. This follows straightforwardly from the principle of the indiscernibility of identicals and the fact that events have times and places of occurrence. But is this condition also sufficient for the identity for events? Or can two or more events occur simultaneously in the same place? These questions were broached earlier, in Chapter III's discussion of Brand's view of events. But I want to have another, slightly different look at them here, for I believe that seeing why these questions are to be answered in the way I will suggest at the outset of this chapter helps to motivate what I will later say about the nature of events. And that will supply the conceptual foundations for my proposal concerning the criterion of identity for events.

So, can two or more events occur at the same place at the same time? From a metaphysical point of view, a great deal depends on how this question is answered. If sameness of spatial and temporal features is a necessary and sufficient condition for the identity of events, then, in so far as it is also necessary and sufficient for the identity of physical objects, the apparently two categories of spatio-temporal thing will collapse into one. Cars and the collidings of them and cheques and the signings of them

157

will all belong to the same category. This much is obvious in light of the discussion in Chapter II of the relation between a criterion of identity for objects belonging to a certain category and a claim about what it is to belong to that category. To belong to a certain category is just to be a thing for which there is a certain criterion of identity; the differences between categories are to be found in differences in the criteria of identity for the objects belonging to them. So, if spatio-temporal sameness were the condition of identity for both events and physical objects, then, if in any case some event and some physical object had the same spatial and temporal features, it would follow that that event just is that physical object. Each change in a physical object would be identical with a temporal part of the physical object it is a change in, and each physical object would be identical with some event or sequence of events.[1]

1.1 *Lemmon's criterion*

In his 'Comments on D. Davidson's "The logical form of action sentences" ',[2] E.J. Lemmon suggested spatio-temporal sameness as a condition of identity for events, and saw that that suggestion would result in a collapsing of the categories of events and physical objects into one category of spatio-temporal particulars. Quine is another who takes this view. In *Word and Object*,[3] he writes:

> Physical objects. . .are not to be distinguished from events. . . . Each comprises simply the content, however heterogeneous, of some portion of space-time, however disconnected and gerry-mandered.

And, in 'Things and their place in theories',[4] he continues in the same vein:

> An action or transaction can be identified with the physical objects consisting of the temporal segment or segments of the agent or agents for the duration. Misgivings about this approach to events have been expressed, on the grounds that it does not distinguish two acts that are performed simultaneously, such as walking and chewing gum. But I think that all the distinctions that need to be drawn can be drawn, still, at the

level of general terms. Not all walks are gum chewings, nor *vice versa*, though an occasional one may be.

Quine's reason for taking this view apparently is related to his view of physical objects as composed of temporal slices; and he dismisses the charge that such a view implies that nothing really changes as based on an 'obvious misinterpretation'.[5] As I argued, however, in Chapter IV, section 9, such a dismissal is hasty and incorrect. But the issue here is not whether spatio-temporal sameness is a well-motivated condition of identity for events; the issue is whether it is a correct one.

In his reply to Lemmon, Davidson[6] said that he wasn't sure that Lemmon's view wasn't correct; but he expressed the desire for an argument that would allay suspicion towards that criterion generated by what appear to be counterexamples. If we locate the things that happen to a person, as well as the things he does, at the body of the person, then when Jones thinks of Vienna and catches a cold during the entire period in which he swims the channel, the thinking, the catching and the swimming all seem to occur in the same place simultaneously. If those events are really not three but one, then there had better be an argument for this doctrine of the trinity, in view of the obvious counterintuitiveness involved in saying that those events are identical. And such an argument cannot be the argument, whatever it is, that leads to the Lemmon criterion; it must be a direct argument for the truth of the consequences of that criterion (or the question will be begged).

In 'The individuation of events',[7] Davidson still appears undecided on the issue (though he has, as we saw, a proposal of his own). First, he suggests that Lemmon's condition is *not* sufficient for the identity of events:

> . . .it seems natural to say that two different changes can come over the whole of a substance at the same time. For example, if a metal ball becomes warmer during a certain minute, and during that time rotates through 35 degrees, must we say that these are the same event? It would seem not.[8]

But, then, though he offers no general argument in favour of Lemmon's criterion, Davidson suggests that there may be arguments in that direction for particular cases, arguments of the sort which I said we must offer in counterintuitive cases (like Quine's and the swimming-thinking-cold-catching case). In the warming-rotating case, Davidson offers this argument:

> . . .it might be maintained that the warming of the ball during *m* is identical with the sum of the motions of the particles that constitute the ball during *m*; and so is the rotation.[9]

But Myles Brand, in 'Particulars, events, and actions',[10] offers a reason for thinking that this argument is unpersuasive; he suggests that, while the warming and the rotating are molecular motions, they are not the same molecular motion:

> The molecular motion that appears macroscopically as rotation is different from the molecular motion that appears macroscopically as growing warmer.[11]

What is important here, however, is not whether Brand's reply is correct or whether there is a rejoinder to it. What is important is the fact that the dialectic over such cases can go on interminably, and that that fact, as I hope to show, can be explained.

Why do none of the examples seem to be decisive, in that, for any case supporting either side of the dispute over the Lemmon criterion of event identity, an argument can be constructed to show that the case does not really support that side of the dispute? Even in the case of what I regard as outrageous examples, like the walking/gum-chewing case, which seem obviously, Quine notwithstanding, to refute the Lemmon criterion, it seems to be possible that an argument could be mustered whose conclusion would be that the case *supported* that criterion. Why does it seem that the dialectic over these cases is unending?

In favour of the Lemmon criterion, we seem always to be able to say one of two things when faced with what appear to be two or more events that occur in simultaneously in the same place. We can say that the appearance is mere, and that the apparently distinct events really are identical. Or we can admit that the events really are distinct, but have different locations. It is, we are reminded, simply incorrect to identify the location of an event just by reference to *the* object which changes, for a change in any object is a change in any other object of which the first is a part. The issue is not whether two or more events can occur

160

simultaneously within any region of space (of course they can), but whether or not two or more simultaneous events can have the same minimal location, the same subject. Here, the aim is to retain our intuitions about the identity and distinctness of particular events, while retaining the Lemmon condition as the condition of identity for events. We retain, for example, the distinctness of the cold-catching, the thinking and the swimming, by arguing that not all changes that come over a person have that person's body as their minimal subject and, hence, minimal location. Similarly, it might be argued that a gum-chewing is minimally located at the lower portion of the chewer's head, while his walking has a different minimal location.

However, such a strategy for saving Lemmon's criterion fails to get at the heart of the issue. For we do have these intuitions about the distinctness of thinkings, cold-catchings and swim-mings, and about the distinctness of walkings and gum-chewings; and these intuitions are, I submit, clearly correct, yet *not* grounded in considerations regarding the minimal locations of such events. What may be troubling is that these intuitions may be grounded in considerations expressed in the form of *rhetorical* questions of the sort, How can an event that is an instance of the type 'catching a cold' be identical with an event that is an instance of the type 'thinking of Vienna'? Now, while these intuitions may be correct, we must look for deeper foundations that show why such questions have the answers that they do. And I think that the concept of a quality space in which a thing changes supplies those deeper foundations.

1.2 *Quality spaces and the Lemmon criterion*

A quality space is a set of simple, mutually exclusive, static properties of objects that is such that, when an object changes by ceasing to have one of the properties in that quality space, at least one result of that change is that the object acquires another property from that same space. So, can two or more simulta-neous changes have the same minimal location? It would seem so. For each event, on the picture of events which the discussion of quality spaces in Chapter V, section 2, provided, is a movement by some object during a stretch of time through some portion of a quality space. Though during a particular stretch of time there cannot be more than one movement by any object through each quality space – since no object can possess all over mutually exclusive properties at the same time – there are, so it seems, numerous quality spaces. And there seems to be no reason to suppose that an object cannot possess all over properties belonging to different quality spaces such that it changes in those spaces simultaneously. And hence, there seems to be no reason to suppose that an object cannot be the subject of distinct simultaneous events. But is this clearly true?

Consider a particle that moves continuously during the period of time from t to t' from point p to point p' along a diagonal path (on a two-dimensional surface, for the sake of simplicity). How shall this change in the particle, its moving from p to p', be graphed? There are at least two ways of graphing this change. The first consists in plotting the particle's movement during t-t' through a 'location' space whose members are the properties of being located at such-and-such a point on the two-dimensional surface in which the particle is moving. That is, each property in that space is such that an object has it if and only if it is located at some particular point on that surface. The graph of the particle's movement will be three-dimensional, with moments of time represented on one axis, and the location properties represented on a plane; and it will look like this (Figure 6.1):

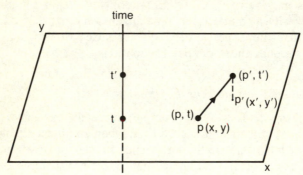

Figure 6.1

However, a second suggestion for graphing the particle's movement construes the properties of being located at the various distances from an origin in (whatever is) the horizontal

162

direction (the properties of having such-and-such a horizontal coordinate) and the properties of being located at various distances from an origin in (whatever is) the vertical direction (the properties of having such-and-such a vertical coordinate) as constituting *different* quality spaces. Here, in order to plot the particle's movement from p to p′ during t-t′, we need two graphs, one plotting the particle's movement through a horizontal-location space and another plotting the particle's movement through a vertical-location space. And the graphs will look like this (Figure 6.2):

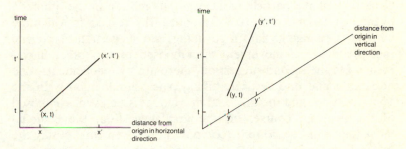

Figure 6.2

What difference do these two ways of graphing the particle's diagonal movement make? Since the intuitive idea of a quality space is the idea of a respect in which things change and since each graph corresponds to a movement through a different quality space, each of the two graphs on the second suggestion is a graph of a distinct change. The second suggestion, then, would have us view the particle's diagonal movement as a *composite* event, consisting of a horizontal movement and a vertical movement, both of which occur at the interval t-t′ and have the particle as minimal subject. The first suggestion, however, since it shows the particle changing location in only one respect, views the particle's movement as, in the requisite sense, non-composite. What appear on the second suggestion as distinct horizontal and vertical movements appear on the first suggestion as no more than *vectors* of a single movement; and vectors of movements are not movements, they are *aspects* of movements. That is, the property of having such-and-such a vertical vector is a property of the particle's movement; it is not a property of the particle. The particle does not move vertically or horizontally; it moves diagonally. The diagonal movement, however, has both a horizontal and a vertical aspect. The second suggestion, then, takes what appear on the first suggestion as vectors or aspects of a movement and construes them as movements; it reconstrues properties of events as properties of the subjects of events. And graphs of events plot properties of things that change, not properties of changes, against time. Thus, the second suggestion takes what the first suggestion takes to be two properties of the particle's movement (concerning its directional aspects) to be two properties of the particle (concerning its motion in the direction of the aspects or vectors of the motion) with respect to which the particle is changing; and in so doing, the suggestion 'discovers' that the diagonal movement is composed of two other movements. On the second suggestion, there are two movements, one horizontal and one vertical, taking place simultaneously in the same location; and the diagonal movement is an event composed of the two. Of course, on the first suggestion, the diagonal movement can be said to be composed of movements: during the first half of the interval t-t', the particle moves halfway from p to p', and covers the rest of the distance in the remaining time. But, the diagonal movement is not, on the first suggestion, composed of horizontal and vertical movements.[12] The diagonal movement has horizontal and vertical vectors; but again, vectors of movements are not movements.

In the case of movement across space, my inclination is to collapse all the location spaces into one, and not to make vectors of movements into movements. The reasons for being so inclined will emerge shortly. But in any event, if one does collapse the location spaces into one, then it will be true to say that each particle can be the subject of only one movement through space at a time.

Consider, now, the case of an adolescent boy. Imagine constructing a graph plotting the lowering of his voice from ages twelve to sixteen, and a graph plotting the growth of facial hair during the same period (and let us not be concerned with the minimal locations and subjects of these changes). It seems reasonable to suppose that the lowering of the boy's voice and the growth of his facial hair are two distinct events the boy undergoes during those years; and the two graphs, plotting his movements through two different quality spaces, reflect that. The maturing of the boy during that period would then be seen as a composite event consisting, in part, of those two changes. However, we can collapse the two quality spaces, and some others, into one *maturation* space. Now, the lowering of the voice and the growth of facial hair would appear, not as distinct changes, not as events of which the boy's maturing is, in part, composed, but as distinct vectors or aspects of the boy's maturation. In this case, my inclination is not to collapse the relevant quality spaces into one maturation space, but to make changes out of vectors of changes (and again, the reasons for this will emerge shortly).

We can now see why the Davidson-Brand debate, over the identity of the warming and the rotating, along with other such debates, can go on indefinitely. An examination of Brand's response shows that he makes movements out of what Davidson's argument for the identity of the warming and the rotating had construed as vectors of movements. Thus, Brand takes Davidson's event, a warming-rotating (an event with a warming and a rotating vector), and divides it into two distinct events, a warming and a rotating. One proposal speaks of different vectors or aspects of a movement, while the other speaks of different movements. Thus, without settling the question of whether the differences between warmings and rotatings are differences in aspects of events or in events, there can be no end to the debate. And apart from independent considerations that determine in general what it is to be a vector of a movement (a feature of events) and what it is to be a movement (a feature of changing things), both approaches seem, ignoring an occasional counter-intuitiveness, pre-analytically legitimate.

The upshot of the foregoing is this. The more divided the properties of changing things into distinct quality spaces, the more distinct changes there can be that can come over the whole of an object simultaneously. The more the properties of things can be compressed into fewer and fewer quality spaces, the fewer the number of distinct simultaneous changes will be to which an object can be subject. If there were only one, universal quality space in which things change, then, and only then, at most one change could come over an object at a time. For in that case, there would only be one respect in which things change. So, the issue of whether or not sameness of spatial and temporal location constitutes an adequate condition of identity for events turns on whether or not there is only one or more than one quality space in which things change. And I cannot see any reason for thinking that there is exactly one such space, exactly one respect in which anything changes when it changes. Thus, I see, in the end, no reason to believe, and lots of reasons to disbelieve, that more than one event cannot occur in the same place simultaneously. The criterion of identity advocated by Lemmon is false.

2   REFINING THE PICTURE

An event is a change in an object; and a change is a 'movement', from the having of one to the having of another property, by an object through some portion of a quality space during an interval of time. In the last section, I suggested, in a rough way, what amounts to a starting point for a criterion of identity for events based on that idea of events as changes. The suggestion was embodied in the idea that since one proposal for graphing a certain event involved the use of two distinct quality spaces, we were construing, on that proposal, that event as really composed of two other, distinct, events. Identical events are the same change; and changes are identical only if they are changes in the same quality space. I would like to make this idea somewhat more precise.

We can begin to refine this picture of the relation between events and quality spaces by asking why we are, in some cases, inclined to make vectors of movements into movements, and, in other cases, inclined to relegate putative movements to the status of a vector. Consider the examples from the previous section. Why does it seem right to collapse all the (directional) location spaces into one location space, so that the diagonal movement of the particle is construed as an event having horizontal and vertical vectors or aspects, and not as an event composed of horizontal and vertical movements? I think that the reason has to do with the fact that we have a physical theory that assigns to space no intrinsic directionality and according to which the forces producing movements of objects are all fundamentally the same and operate in the same way regardless of the direction of the movements they produce. If, on the contrary, for example, the horizontal movements of objects were the results of the impartings of momentum by other objects, but upward vertical movements were the results of the will of God, and downward vertical movements due to the natural tendency of all things to seek to come to rest at the centre of the universe, then it would, I think, be appropriate to say that movements through space were composed of horizontal and vertical movements (some of which possibly null), and we would be justified in dividing the single, multi-dimensional location space into distinct horizontal- and vertical-location spaces. In such a situation, there would be a reason for thinking that horizontal and vertical movements were movements, and hence events, of different kinds, and that diagonal movements were events composed of events of those kinds. But we do not believe anything like this to be true; the sorts of forces which can produce movements in one direction can also produce movements in the other directions as well.[13]

Why does it seem right to divide the single maturation space into several distinct quality spaces, so that the maturing of the boy is seen as an event composed of voice lowerings and hair growings, and not as an event with vocal and hirsute vectors? Again, I think the reason has to do with the fact that we believe that an adequate physiology of adolescence shows that the growth of facial hair can be traced to factors to which the lowering of the voice cannot (and *vice versa*). And such an empirical theory provides a reason for thinking that a boy's maturation is an event composed of other events which are jointly brought about by the conjunction of several different sorts of forces. Such a theory tells us that when a boy matures, he really undergoes a lowering of his voice, etc., etc.[14]

On the basis of these examples, I want to suggest what it is that scientific theories tell us concerning events and quality spaces. Such theories tell us what the ultimate constituents of things are. They tell us what sorts of properties these ultimate objects have in virtue of which things which are composed of them have the properties they have. And they tell us what sorts of changes ultimate objects can undergo in virtue of which things composed of those objects undergo the changes they undergo; and they tell us what those changes in ultimate objects consist in. For example, we are told that water is a bunch of molecules and that a heating of water is an increasing of the mean kinetic energy of those molecules; that the molecules are composed of such-and-such particles and that an increasing of the molecules' mean kinetic energy consists in an increasing of the motion of those particles, and so on. Such an analysis stops when the science in question gets to objects it takes to be such that their changes are not to be construed as composed of changes in other objects of which they are constituted. Scientific theories are, in part, theories about what the ultimate quality spaces are through which ultimate objects move when they change.[15]

I offer now certain definitions, framed in the light of what I take to be the relation between scientific theories and events and quality spaces. These definitions are intended to make more precise the ideas about events I am advocating, and they are motivated by my interest in giving an account of events as changes, that is, as movements by objects in quality spaces at times. Here are the definitions.

(D1)   An object, x, is an *atomic object* for a theory, T, if and only if it is the case, in T, that x exists and there is no object, y, distinct from x, such that y is a part of x.[16]

(D2)   A set, S, is an *atomic quality space* for a theory, T, if and only if S is a dense quality space whose members are qualities that objects that are atomic in T can have (according to T).[17]

(D3)   An event, e, is an *atomic event* for a theory, T, if and only if e is a movement of some object, x, which is atomic according to T, where e consists in x's moving from having P_i to having P_k, at some interval of time, t, where P_i and P_k belong to a quality space, S, that is atomic according to T.

D3 says that an atomic event is a movement by an atomic object in an atomic quality space. D3, however, can only be regarded as a tentative formulation of the idea of an atomic event; it will require revision and complication.

One idea of an atomic entity is the idea of an entity belonging to a certain sort such that no proper part of it is an entity belonging to the same sort; if the Fs have atoms, an atomic F is an F no proper part of which is an F. An atomic physical object is one that has no physical object as a proper part; and an atomic set is, analogously, a set none of whose members is a set. One interesting thing about this idea of an atomic set is that some atomic sets are larger than some non-atomic sets. So, the idea of atomicity is not necessarily the idea of a 'smallest' thing of its kind; it is sometimes the idea of a 'most basic' such thing. We tend to think, in the case of physical objects, of the ideas of a smallest thing and a most basic thing as coinciding. The idea of an atomic event is the idea of an event of which others are composed. However, compromises will have to be made. After all, events have temporal parts, since they are changes and change takes time; and many of the temporal parts of events are events, no matter how short an event's duration is. So, there is no hope of getting hold of the idea of an event none of whose temporal parts are events; atomicity for events cannot be simply a matter of minimality of duration or of a change having no changes as temporal parts. What else figures in may seem a bit arbitrary; still, the idea is to build into the notion of an atomic event as much of the ideas of a smallest and of a most basic event as possible.

The time of occurrence of any event is the shortest interval of time during which it occurs. That time may be disjointed, if, in changing from having P_i to having P_k, an object lingers for a while, not changing at all, in the space to which P_i and P_k belong, at P_j. In the case of a temporally discontinuous change, I am not inclined to think of the involved object's movement as atomic (even if that object and the space in which it is moving are atomic); that event seems rather to be composed of (perhaps atomic) events, one the object's going from having P_i to having P_j, the other the object's going from having P_j to having P_k. For a change in some object in a quality space to be temporally continuous, that object must be changing in that space at every moment in all the open intervals between the beginning and end of that change. Temporally discontinuous changes are not atomic events; and this restriction will be added to D3.

Suppose that a certain event, e, is a movement by an atomic object, x, in a discrete quality space, S, from having P_i to having P_k; and suppose that in so moving, x 'passes through' a property P_j (in S); that is, at some time during e, x has P_j (though it does not linger there). Intuitively, e does not strike one as atomic, but rather as composed of a pair of temporally contiguous, perhaps

169

atomic, events: x's going from having P_i to having P_j, and x's going from having P_j to having P_k. Now, either of those latter events might involve its subjects having an intermediate property; and if so, we would again suspect a failure of atomicity. But in a discrete quality space this must come to an end. There is always a resolution of any change in a discrete space into a sequence of temporal parts, each of which is a direct change; and those direct changes have no temporal parts which are themselves changes in that discrete space. However, that a change in a discrete space has no temporal parts that are changes in the same space should not be taken as a sign that that change is atomic. For, as I have proposed, such an event is composed of dense changes in one or more dense quality spaces. Thus, whether or not a direct change is an atomic event is determined by whether or not the dense changes of which it is composed can be thought of as composing an atomic event. That an event composed of others should turn out to be atomic at all may strike one as odd; but I think that some good sense can be made of this idea, by pointing out which composed events should not be thought of as atomic.

First, an event composed of other events should not be atomic, if the subjects of those other events are not the same. Second, an event should not be atomic if the events of which it is composed are changes in different quality spaces. Thus, no event is atomic, if it is either composed of a change in Venus and a change in Mars (even if Venus and Mars were atomic objects) or composed of a change in shape and a change in colour (if the colours and the shapes form different spaces). Third, an event that contains a 'repetition' should not be taken to be atomic. That is, suppose that an event, e, is a dense, continuous change in an atomic object, x, in a dense space, S, where e consists in x's going from having P_i to having P_k, where x has during the time of e all the properties between P_i and P_k. The event, e, contains a repetition just in case x has during the time of e's occurrence any of the properties between P_i and P_k more than once at distinct times. Thus, if the earth were an atomic object and a three-dimensional location space were an atomic quality space, and if the earth's path around the sun were stationary, then though each orbiting of the earth around the sun might be atomic (though composed), an event composed of two such orbitings would not be, since in such a case the earth would, on two distinct occasions, have the same spatial location.

This is, I think the best that can be done for the idea of atomicity as it applies to events. Given the fact that changes in dense quality spaces have temporal parts which are themselves events, more cannot have been expected.[18] I have tried to be guided by the idea that atomic events should be as short and as uncomplicated as possible, but there are limits to which this idea can be pursued. There will be events composed of other events that, regardless of their length, will have to be taken as atomic; but even though atomic events will have temporal parts that are atomic, I believe that no serious problems will result. Thus, the following is my final version of the definition of an atomic event:

(D3*) An event, e, is an *atomic event* for a theory, T, if and only if
   (i)   e's subject, x, is an object that is atomic according to T,
   (ii) e is x's moving from having P_i to having P_k, at some interval of time, t, where P_i and P_k belong to a dense quality space, S, which is atomic according to T,
   (iii) e is temporally continuous,
   (iv) no event of which e is composed is a change whose minimal subject is distinct from x,
   (v)   no event of which e is composed is a change in a quality space distinct from S, and
   (vi) there is no property, P_j, in S that x has at two or more times during t.

So, for example, a warming of a ball will not be atomic, since it is composed of changes involving different subjects; and my maturing isn't atomic, even if I were an atomic object, since it is composed of my changing in more than one atomic quality space. But an atomic object's moving continuously from one place to another in a straight line could be atomic, even though that event has temporal parts that are atomic events. It is, of course, the case that which the atomic objects, quality spaces and events are will be determined together; the question of which entities satisfy any of the definitions D1, D2, and D3* cannot be settled independently of settling the question of which entities satisfy the others.

171

I now offer a hypothesis about events on the basis of which I intend to discuss descriptions of events and a criterion of identity for events:

(H)   Every event is
    (a)   an atomic event, or
    (b)   an event composed of simultaneous atomic events (a synchronic non-atomic event), or
    (c)   an event composed of a temporal sequence of events each of which is either an atomic event or a synchronic non-atomic event (a diachronic event).[19]

3   DESCRIPTIONS OF EVENTS

Each atomic event is a movement by an atomic object from having one to having another property in a particular atomic quality space (within the limitations imposed by D3*). Now, for each pair of static properties within a given atomic quality space, which are such that, if an atomic object were to move at some interval of time from having the one to having the other, then that change might be an atomic event, then there is a *dynamic* property that the object in question will have at that interval of time. That dynamic property just is the property of moving from having the one to having the other static property. An atomic event, then, is an atomic object's having or exemplifying of such a dynamic property at some interval of time (within the limitations of D3*). Thus, an account of events as exemplifyings of dynamic properties at times, derived from an account of events as changes.

Sometimes there is a verb already in our language that expresses such a dynamic property; but if there isn't, one can always be introduced and defined in terms of the static properties the successive havings of which is what having that dynamic property consists in. The verb 'to rot' might be such a verb were it not for the fact that the things that rot aren't atomic objects. But if there were a true theory in which medium-sized, not-so-dry goods were atomic, it might well qualify as such a verb.[20] A verb or verb phrase will be called an 'atomic event verb' when it means the same as, or is equivalent on the theory T to, 'moves

172

from exemplifying P_i to exemplifying P_k, where P_i and P_k belong to an atomic quality space and it is possible that an atomic object's having the dynamic property that verb expresses at some interval of time is an atomic event (in T).[21]

Such verbs and the dynamic properties of atomic objects they express are associated with properties of atomic events which are *atomic event types*. An event is of the atomic event type 'φing' just in case that event is an atomic event that is its subject's exemplifying of the dynamic property expressed by the verb 'φ', where 'φ' is an atomic event verb. Thus, for example, if the rotting of a log were an atomic event, and 'rot' were an atomic event verb true of the log at the interval of time in which the log was rotting, then the atomic event undergone by the log would be a rotting and would be an event of the atomic event type 'rotting'. For an event to be of the atomic event type which, in a canonical language for the theory T in question, is called a 'φing', it must be an atomic event consisting in some atomic object's exemplifying of the dynamic property expressed by the verb 'φ', where 'φ' is an atomic event verb, at some interval of time t. Each atomic event is an instance of some atomic event type. Since it can be the case that some atomic events are movings from having P_i to having P_j to having P_k, they are also movings from having P_i to having P_k. And it might turn out that 'moves from having P_i to having P_j to having P_k' and 'moves from having P_i to having P_k' are both atomic event verbs; and the property of being a moving from having P_i to having P_j to having P_k and the property of being a moving from having P_i to having P_k might both be atomic event types. Thus, in light of the fact that those are different atomic event types (surely, a sufficient condition for the distinctness of types is distinctness of instances of those types), an atomic event can be an instance of more than one atomic event type. The types of which non-atomic events belong can be derived from the atomic event types to which their atomic constituents belong. If some non-atomic event is composed of an atomic event of type φ followed by an atomic event of type ψ, then that non-atomic is an event of the type 'event composed of an atomic event of type φ followed by an atomic event of type ψ'.

A *canonical description* of an atomic event is a singular term of the form '[x, φ, t]', where 'x' is to be replaced by a name or description of the atomic object that is the (minimal) subject of that atomic event, 't' is to be replaced by a name or description of the (minimal) interval of time at which the event occurs, and 'ϕ' is to be replaced by an atomic event verb that expresses a dynamic property the having or exemplifying of which (by the object referred to by whatever replaces 'x' at the interval referred to by whatever replaces 't') is that atomic event. Such a term may be read as: x's exemplifying of ϕ at t. It must be kept in mind, however, that an atomic event may be referred to by a phrase of the form 'x's exemplifying of ϕ at t' (or 'x's ϕing at t'), where that phrase is *not* canonical. If such a phrase is to be a canonical description of an atomic event, and if it is to be rewritable as '[x, ϕ, t]', 'ϕ' must be an atomic event verb. It should also be kept in mind that an atomic event may have more than one canonical description, for there may be more than one atomic event verb that can replace 'ϕ' in a given case.[22]

The appearance of no canonical description of an atomic event logically ensures that there is an event satisfying it; that is an empirical matter. But it does seem that if there is an atomic event satisfying a particular such description, then there is at most one that does; more of that, however, a bit later. It should also be emphasized that there is no systematic way to generate canonical descriptions of atomic events from sentences, of the form 'x ϕed at t', made true by the occurrence of an atomic event, or from terms of the form 'x's ϕing at t', that in fact refer to atomic events. Such sentences and terms, though they may be made true by or refer to some atomic event, need not speak of that atomic event by employing an atomic event verb. That a description of an atomic event is canonical or not is determined not only by the description's form, but also by its content; the event must be described, in part, by means of an atomic event verb.

The basic idea behind this characterization of the canonical descriptions of atomic (and, as will emerge, other) events is that such descriptions should, in the place occupied by the atomic event verb, draw only upon the conceptual resources offered by the atomic quality spaces movements in which constitute the events being described. That is, the dynamic properties expressed by the middle terms in canonical descriptions of atomic events should be picked out solely in terms of the concept of a movement from the having of one to the having of another property and in terms of the static properties belonging to the quality space that the event being described is a change in. This idea can be abandoned, for purposes of easy speech, so as to allow one to describe events in an apparently canonical way. However, there is a risk in doing this, for, as will be argued later, the fact that a description looks canonical will tempt one to draw conclusions that would only be proper to draw if the description were actually canonical. And those conclusions have in fact been the source of much controversy.

(A 'very' canonical description of an atomic event is a canonical description of an atomic event in which the event's subject is described in such a way that the description's referring to the entity it refers to does not imply the existence of any other contingent entity. Thus, 'the electron next to this proton' can't be part of a very canonical description of an atomic event whose subject is that electron. An 'extremely' canonical description is a very canonical description of an atomic event in which the description of the event's time of occurrence makes no reference either to any time not included in the event's time of occurrence or to anything that is not a time.)

Non-atomic events come in sorts. Each non-atomic event will have for a canonical description a singular term of the form 'the event composed of $[x_o, \phi_o, t_o]$, $[x_1, \phi_1, t_1]$, . . ., and $[x_n, \phi_n, t_n]$', where the terms following 'of' are canonical descriptions of the atomic events of which the non-atomic event is composed. If $t_o = t_1 = . . . = t_n$, then the non-atomic event in question is a 'synchronic' non-atomic event; if not, it is a 'diachronic' event (and its time of occurence is the shortest interval including t_o, t_1, . . ., and t_n). If in some case, $x_o = x_1 = . . . = x_n$, the event is 'simple'; if not, it is 'complex'. So, for example, a house's becoming engulfed in flames would typically (because generally not every part of the house catches fire at the same time) be a complex diachronic non-atomic event; an atomic object that bounces off a wall and returns by the same path to its place of origin is the subject of a simple diachronic non-atomic event. If an event were composed of an atomic object's simultaneously turning red and getting warm, it would be a simple synchronic non-atomic event.

Canonical descriptions of events describe events by means only of (a) the atomic objects minimally involved in the event or

175

events of which it is composed, (b) the minimal intervals of time at which it or the events of which it is composed occur, and (c) the dynamic properties those atomic objects exemplify, the exemplifyings of which by those objects at the requisite times are or compose the events described. A description of an event will fail to be canonical if it describes the event it does in such a way that the description's referring implies (apart from the way involved objects and times are referred to) either (a) that some event, distinct from the event in question or any of the events of which it is composed, has occurred, is occurring, or will occur, or (b) that some entity, distinct from the ones minimally involved in the event in question or in any of the events of which it is composed (and distinct from any that exist necessarily), existed, exists, or will exist. A description of an event is canonical, if that description would still describe the event it does (apart, again, from the way involved subjects and times are referred to) even if that event, the events of which it is composed, and the objects minimally involved in the event and the events of which it is composed were the only contingently existing things.

4 KINDS OF EVENTS

Events aggregate into kinds. There are properties of events such that if an event has such a property it could not fail to have it (except by not occurring); events have essences. Of course, the property of being an event is one such property; but since that property is had by all events, it does not divide events into kinds.[23] Among the properties I take to divide events into kinds are, in the case of atomic events, properties of the sort 'being an instance of the atomic event type ϕing'.[24] It is of the essence of an atomic event that it be an instance of the atomic event type(s) of which it is in fact an instance; each atomic event must be an atomic object's exemplifying of the dynamic property that is in fact expressed by the atomic event verb in fact true of that object. If, for example, being a movement along some path in space were an atomic event type, then if some atomic event were a moving along that path, then that atomic event could not have failed to have been a moving along that path. And this seems reasonable; for how could an atomic event that was such a movement have failed to have been such a movement? Surely it could not have been, instead, a change in colour! In short, then, my conjecture is that if being an instance of an atomic event type 'φing' is a property of some atomic event, e, then necessarily if e occurs, then e is an exemplifying by some object at some time of φ (where 'φ' is an atomic event verb). So, while events have lots of properties essentially and as essences (e.g., the property of being other than a number), what I shall call a 'property essence' of an atomic event is its property of being an instance of the atomic event type (or types) of which it is in fact an instance. Such properties do divide events into species constituting kinds of atomic event. A property essence of an atomic event can be 'read off' its canonical description; if some atomic event has '[x, φ, t]' as a canonical description, then a property essence of that event is that it be an event of the atomic event type 'φing'.

So, although it is a contingent matter whether or not an atomic event having a certain property essence actually occurs, it is not a contingent matter whether or not an atomic event has a property essence (belongs to the kind) which it in fact has. It is not a contingent matter that an atomic event that actually occurs is an instance of the event type which can be read off a canonical description of that event.[25] But it is a contingent matter whether an atomic event is describable by any of the non-canonical descriptions that in fact describe it, for the correctness of such a description depends, at least in part, on the existence of some contingently existing entity whose existence is implied by the correctness of that description, but is not implied by the fact that that event has a certain property essence.[26] For example, the property of being an event that causes an explosion cannot be a property essence of any event, and 'causes an explosion' cannot occupy the property-place in any event's canonical description, for the fact that an event has such a property clearly implies the occurrence of some *other* event which is an explosion; and the holding of no canonical description of any event can have such an implication. No event that is in fact of that sort (*viz*. events that cause explosions) has to be of that sort; such an event could occur and yet not cause an explosion. Events that are causally related are only contingently so related. However, the atomic event in fact causing the explosion could not have been other than a φing, if being a φing is a property essence of the event which in fact caused an explosion.[27] Properties of atomic events, of the sort 'being a ϕing', which do not correspond to event verbs that can appear in canonical descriptions, are likely to be contingent properties of the events having them, and are not property essences of events. Hence, they do not divide events into kinds. Those properties of atomic events that are property essences, properties that can be read off their canonical descriptions, however, do divide atomic events into kinds.

5   A CRITERION OF IDENTITY FOR EVENTS

We are now in a position to say what the criterion of identity for events should be. To be an event is to be a change, a movement by an object at an interval of time in a quality space. As earlier suggested, it is possible for an object to move in more than one quality space at the same time. But it is not possible for an object to move more than once at the same time in the same quality space; for that would amount to an object's having incompatible properties simultaneously. Indeed, the very idea of such multiple, simultaneous movements by the same object only barely, if at all, makes sense, for the *raison d'être* of dividing qualities into spaces is to be able to say what change by an object at a time a particular, individual event consists in.

A property essence of an atomic event is a property an event has the having of which is its being an instance of an atomic event type associated with an atomic event verb expressing a property the subject of that atomic event exemplifies. And such an atomic event type is just the property of being a movement from having one to having another property in a particular atomic quality space. Such an essence of an event, of course, determines only that an event having it belongs to a certain kind; more than one event can have that property essence. (And, an atomic event may belong to more than one such kind.) What individuates events of that kind, that is, what makes an event of that kind this or that particular event of that kind, is the fact that it is a change of that kind that is a change in some particular object and that occurs at some particular interval of time. If, for example, x were an atomic object, and being a movement from being red to being blue were an atomic event type, then what could possibly show that there could be two movings from being red to being blue that x is the subject of, both of which occur at a certain interval of time? Of course, two atomic events of the same type having the same subject can occur *during* a certain interval of time (x could move twice from being red to being blue during the twentieth century). But, nothing could show that x could move so *at* the same interval. And that suggests that canonical descriptions of atomic events – which describe atomic events solely in terms of their atomic subjects, the dynamic properties expressed by the atomic event verbs which are true of those subjects, and the times at which those subjects have those properties – refer at most to just one atomic event. The occurrence of an atomic event with a certain canonical description guarantees the uniqueness of that description. (Two or more non-atomic events of the same type could occur simultaneously; but for that to be the case, at least some of their atomic constituents would have to be different.) Thus, atomic events are identical if and only if they are atomic events of the same kinds and are simultaneous changes in the same atomic object, if and only if they are simultaneous movements by the same atomic object through the same portion of the same atomic quality space. Since atomic events can have more than one canonical description, atomic events are identical if and only if they have all the same canonical descriptions. Thus, if e_1 and e_2 are atomic events, then e_1 and e_2 are the same atomic event just in case, for every canonical description, '$[x,\phi,t]$', of e_1, there is a canonical description, '$[x', \phi', t']$', of e_2 such that $x=x'$, $\phi=\phi'$, and $t=t'$ (and *vice versa*).[28]

The extension to non-atomic events seems straightforward. Synchronic non-atomic events are identical if and only if they are composed of the same simultaneously occurring atomic events. And diachronic non-atomic events are identical if and only if they are composed of the same atomic and synchronic non-atomic events.[29] All events, according to H, are atomic, or synchronic, or diachronic events; and the canonical descriptions of events describe the events they do in terms of the canonical descriptions of the atomic events they either are or are composed of; and the canonical descriptions of atomic events both specify the kinds to which they belong and individuate them within those kinds. Therefore, the foregoing can be summarized in the following criterion of identity for events:

(E) Necessarily, for any entities, e and e', if e and e' are events, then e = e' if and only if e and e' have all the same canonical descriptions.

Though cast in terms of descriptions, the view (E) expresses does not tie the identity of events to linguistic considerations. (E) merely conveniently summarizes the idea that atomic events are identical if and only if they are atomic events of the same atomic event types whose subjects and times of occurrence are identical, and that non-atomic events are identical if and only if they are composed of all the same atomic events.

I think that (E) meets the conditions laid down in Chapter II which are to be met by any principle qualifying as a criterion of identity for entities comprising a metaphysical category. That (E) is of the right form is obvious. Second, the property expressed by 'is an event' seems to be an essence. No entity having that property could fail to have it; and not everything has it. And a correct existential proof of the existence of events will show that some entities do have it.

(E)'s condition of identity is surely stronger than Leibniz's Law; there are many properties that events have in addition to those the having of which ensure that events have the canonical descriptions they have. Such descriptions, for example, fail to mention anything at all about the causal features of the events they describe. (E) seems also to meet the requirement that a criterion of identity be necessarily true. That requirement is to be met by its being the case that a criterion of identity's identity condition draws on the very concepts to be used in saying what it is to belong to the kind for which the criterion is given. (E)'s identity condition draws on the concept of a thing capable of (non-relationally) exemplifying dynamic properties, the concept of an interval of time, and the idea of a quality space in which things change. The concept of an event I have been pressing is the idea that events are changes; and that idea, I have been urging, is the idea of a movement by an object at an interval of time in a quality space.

(E) does not encompass too much. Its identity condition specifies three kinds of properties the sharing of members of which by events is necessary and sufficient for their identity: properties of having such-and-such an object as subject, pro-

180

perties of occurring at such-and-such times, and properties of being of such-and-such event types. To each event it makes non-vacuous sense to attribute properties falling under these determinables. Moreover, the condition is at least partially exclusive; for nothing but an event can be an exemplifying of a *dynamic* property. And the condition seems minimal, for (i) distinct events can be of the same type and be simultaneous, but only if their subjects are distinct, (ii) distinct atomic events can have the same subject and time of occurrence, but only if they are of different types, and (iii) distinct events can be of the same type and have the same subject, but only if they are not simultaneous. And lastly, though I have no argument establishing the point, (E) seems to meet the requirement of being non-circular.

6 DISPUTES ABOUT EVENT IDENTITIES

A criterion of identity is not an epistemological principle; it does not specify a set of directions or a general technique for discovering when any two singular descriptions of entities belonging to the kind for which the criterion is given refer to the same such entity.[30] That fact notwithstanding, a criterion of identity cannot fail to be relevant to epistemic concerns. A criterion of identity for events embodies and articulates the core of a theory about what it is to be an event; and it does that by specifying conditions under which events are identical. A criterion of identity, in the course of articulating the core of that theory, explains what would in effect have to be discovered when it is discovered that certain events are identical, that certain terms refer to the same event; it does that by saying what crucial properties such events, the events referred to by those terms, must share. So, when a dispute concerning the identity of events arises, a criterion of identity should be of some help in explaining how that dispute arises; and it should be expected to say what in principle it would take to resolve that dispute.

I have been advocating a theory that takes events to be non-repeatable occurrences. Among those who understand events in this way (though, of course, they differ from each other and from me with respect to what it is to be such a thing) are Kim, Goldman and Davidson. And the disagreements between Kim and Goldman, on the one hand, and Davidson, on the other, have been both frustrating and legion. Goldman devotes half a chapter in his *A Theory of Human Action* to counterexamples to Davidsonian claims of action identity.[31] And Davidson, commenting on a paper by R. M. Martin in which Martin advances a view concerning event identity similar to Kim's and Goldman's, writes:

> . . . by Martin's account no meeting is identical with an encounter. . . . No stabbing can be a killing and no killing can be a murder, no arm-raising a signaling, and no birthday party a celebration. I protest.[32]

The view I am advocating provides, I believe, a way to explain why these disputes have arisen.

At first glance, (E), or a version of it that speaks of the content of canonical descriptions of events rather than the descriptions themselves, seems much like the criterion of identity for events proposed by Kim. This is not surprising, since we both more or less accept the idea that events are exemplifyings of properties (though we derive that idea from different underlying considerations). And for a certain class of cases, the atomic events, the proposals look virtually the same and give the same results (except for the fact that my atomic events may have more than one canonical description). Kim and Goldman get their 'standard' descriptions of events (and actions), however, from any sentences of the form 'x ϕs at t', where 'ϕ' is a verb of change, since what such sentences express are targets of explanations.[33] The standard description to be derived from such a sentence is of the form '[x, ϕ, t]' and is to be read as 'x's exemplifying of ϕ at t'. And, on the Kim-Goldman view, if e_1 and e_2 are events, then $e_1=e_2$ if and only if it is the case that if $e_1=[x, \phi, t]$ and $e_2=[x', \phi', t']$, then x=x', t=t', and $\phi=\phi'$. And $\phi=\phi'$ only if every ϕing is a ϕ'ing and *vice versa*. For this reason, no shooting is a killing and no arm-raising a signalling, since not all shootings are killings and not all arm-raisings are signallings. These consequences result from the idea that identical events and actions must be of the same kind, the idea that the kind to which an event or action belongs can be read off a sentence of the form 'x ϕs at t' that reports the occurrence of the event or action making it true, and the idea that an event or action can belong to exactly one kind.

But the latter two of these ideas are false.

My canonical descriptions of events, however, *cannot* be derived from any event-reporting sentence of the form 'x φs at t', even when a sentence of that form is made true by the occurrence of exactly one φing by x at t. In order for a term of the form 'x's φing at t', or 'x's exemplifying of φ at t', to be canonical, and hence for it to be rewritable as '[x, φ, t]', it must be the case that x's φing at t is an atomic event one of whose *property essences* is the property of being a φing. Thus, if for the sake of simplicity we consider atomic events with unique canonical descriptions (that is, that have a unique property essence) it is clear why it is that if an event whose property essence is the property of being a φing is identical with one whose property essence is the property of being a φ'ing, then *every* φing must be a φ'ing, and every φ'ing must be a φing. For identical events must have the same property essence. So, the property essence being a φing just is the property essence being a φ'ing. And the property of being a φing cannot be the property of being a φ'ing unless every φing is a φ'ing and every φ'ing a φing.[34]

An event, e, is a φing if and only if there is an object, x, an interval of time, t, and a dynamic property φ, such that e is x's exemplifying of φ at t. But not every term of the form 'x's exemplifying of φ at t' is a canonical description of e; for that, 'φ' must, in the case of atomic events, be an atomic event verb.[35] Thus, from the fact that e=[x, φ, t] and the fact that e is also a φ'ing, though it does follow that e is an exemplifying of φ' by x at t, it does not follow that e=[x, φ', t]. For it to follow, it would have to be the case of being a φ'ing is a property essence of e. And if that were the case, then (with our simplifying assumption that the events in question have unique canonical descriptions), of course, φ=φ', and any event that is a φing would have to be a φ'ing as well. Therefore, the claim that it is necessary that no event which is a φing can be an event which is a φ'ing unless every φing is a φ'ing and *vice versa* is a claim which, though Kim and Goldman are willing to endorse it quite generally, I endorse only in case being a φing and being a φ'ing are the property essences of the events of which those essences are instances.

But when either the property of being a φing or that of being a φ'ing is not a property essence of the events having those properties, the conclusion Kim and Goldman accept just does not follow. The reason for this is that one of those properties, not being an essence of the event having it, is a property that the event having it has only contingently. An event's having such a property (when it is not a property essence of the event that has it) is contingent upon the contingent existence of entities whose existence is independent of the occurrence of the event having that property, of the occurrence of that event's parts, and of the existence of its minimally involved subject (and its parts). So, any event having such an inessential property can fail to have it, and will fail to have it in any situation in which the independent and contingent entities whose existence is entailed by the event's having that property fail to exist. Hence, this ϕing could be identical with that ϕ'ing, even though not every ϕing is a ϕ'ing (or *vice versa*), if either being a ϕing or being a ϕ'ing (or both) fail to be property essences. And I am inclined to think that many of the cases of disputed event identity are cases in which the events are not described in terms of their property essences.

Some events and actions are describable by the use of causal verbs; 'a's shooting of b at t' and 'c's closing of the door at t' count as such descriptions. In Chapter V, I argued that sentences containing causal verbs, of the form 'x ϕed y at t' (where 'ϕ' is the causal verb), can, in cases where there is no multiple agency, be understood as 'x did something (or was the subject of some event) at t, and what x did (or that event) causes y's being ϕed'. If that is right, it is clear that the property of being a ϕing, where 'ϕ' is a causal verb, cannot be a property essence of any event or action that is in fact a ϕing. For the having of that property by any event or action is contingent upon the occurrence of y's being ϕed, and that is not a part of, but is an effect of, the event or action that is x's ϕing of y. If so, then one cannot argue, for example, that no shooting can be a killing, that no moving of one's arm can be a door-closing, or that no chiming of a bell can be the bell's breaking of a window, on the grounds that there are shootings that aren't killings (or that don't result in deaths), arm-movings that aren't door-closings, or chimings of bells that aren't window-breakings. For such arguments are germane only in connection with events and actions described in terms of their property essences. No action that is in fact a killing is necessarily an action that results in a death; no killing is necessarily a killing, for each killing could have occurred without anyone's dying as a result. Being a killing is not an essence of any action or event. The argument I am offering here does not show that some shootings are in fact killings (I argued for that in Chapter V). What it does show is that the claim that some shootings are identical with some killings is not proved false by the obvious fact that not every shooting results in a death and not every death is brought about by a shooting. What my argument shows, in general, is that events and actions can be causings of their effects, even though they need not have been that.

Can someone's extending his arm out the car window ever be his signalling for a turn? Again, it might be argued that such actions cannot be identical for there are arm-extendings that are not signallings. It is then suggested that such actions are, though distinct, intimately related, and an account may get offered in which it is proposed that a signalling occurs because an arm-extending is performed in circumstances which include a rule such as 'extending one's arm out of the car window while driving counts as signalling for a turn'.[36] But it is countered, the extending of the arm was, on that occasion, performed in such circumstances, and so was, on that occasion, a signalling for a turn. What seems to be going on here is this. Being a signalling is not a property essence of any event or action, for to describe an event or action as a signalling is to describe it in terms of one of its causes, perhaps an intending to follow some rule. Being a signalling, then, is a property an event or action can have, but only if some event distinct from the signalling occurs. Hence, it is not the case that anything that is a signalling must be a signalling; and, therefore, not every extending of an arm out of a car window need be a signalling in order for some such extendings to be signallings.[37]

In a similar way, it cannot be shown that Jones's running of the mile in three and a half minutes and Jones's breaking of the record for the mile cannot be identical, even when he breaks the record by running it (for the only time in his life) in three and a half minutes, by insisting that not every such run is a record-breaking run (the second such run, for example, won't be). For any action that is a breaking of the record for the mile is so only because, in part, there once occurred some other action that was both a running of the world's fastest mile (up to that time) and a running of the mile in more than three and a half minutes. Being

185

a record-breaking run of the mile is a property that an action having it has only contingently; it is not a property that can be a property essence of an action. Thus, it is not necessary that every running of the mile in three and a half minutes be a record-breaking running of the mile in order for one such run to be a record-breaking run.

In each of these three types of case, what seems to stand in the way of saying that the appropriate actions or events are identical and leads to disagreement is the same thing. And that is the tendency to treat each of the event or action 'types' in question (e.g., killing, signalling) as if they were, on my account, property essences of the events or actions that are of that type. But, in each case, it would be wrong to treat them so. And that, in effect, is conceded by those who would insist that such identity claims are false. For what is claimed about such properties, such as that of being a killing, in the defence of the falsity of those identity claims, is that they are properties of the actions and events having them (indeed, the events and actions having them occur) only because other things, quite independent of the events and actions themselves, are in fact the case. But it is for precisely that reason, as I see the matter, that such properties cannot be property essences of the actions and events that have them. Identical events must have the same property essences. They must, of course, share all their other properties as well. But, their sharing of those other properties in common will be, in so far as those other properties are not essential to them, a matter of contingent fact only. If being a ϕing is an essence of an event but being a ϕ'ing is not, then every event identical with an event that is both a ϕing and a ϕ'ing must be a ϕ'ing as well as a ϕing. But not every ϕing need be a ϕ'ing; so not every event identical with a ϕing must be a ϕ'ing as well. None of this, of course, shows for certain that the pairs of events and actions discussed are indeed identical; such certain judgments await resolution of the changes in question to their atomic constituents. But in advance of such resolutions, we can and we do make some good guesses and back them up with good reasons.

VII

EVENTS AND
THEIR ESSENCES

1 INTRODUCTION

A criterion of identity is a principle specifying a necessary and sufficient condition for the identity of entities belonging to the kind for which the criterion is given. In the case of those kinds that are metaphysical categories, such a principle, by satisfying the constraints imposed in Chapter II, can serve as the core of a theory about the entities constituting the category in question, for it leads directly to a principle giving a condition the satisfaction of which is both necessary and sufficient for any entity to belong to that category. A criterion of identity, however, cannot be all there is to a theory about the entities for which it is given, for there are crucial questions about what those entities are like that a criterion of identity does not answer.

A criterion of identity is not, in general, a principle by which one can count the number of entities belonging to the category in question. It is surely the case that a complete theory about, say, physical objects should address the issue of whether spatial connectedness of parts is a necessary condition for those parts to be parts of a single physical object; yet a criterion of identity will not address this issue. Similarly, a criterion of identity for events does not settle the issue of whether there is a single event composed of all the world's avalanches; it will of course say what conditions would have to be met by any event in order for it to be identical with the world's avalanches, *if* the world's avalanches is an event. Whether or not there is such an event, however, will turn on considerations that outrun the resources of a criterion of identity for events. And a criterion of identity is not a principle of 'identity over time' or persistence, though principles bearing such titles do allege to do that work.[1] Indeed, some of the entities for which we provide criteria of identity (e.g., sets and events) do not persist through time at all; so, there is no issue of what the conditions are under which such an entity which (wholly) exists at one time is identical with something which (wholly) exists at another. In the case of events, we can ask when an event which occurs at one time and an event which occurs at another time are temporal parts of the same event. But a criterion of identity will not answer that question, for it is a principle concerning the identity of events and not the notion of being a part of the same event. And, as for entities that do persist, the physical objects for example, the usual criterion of identity does not provide much of a clue as to the conditions under which a given physical object endures.

Given my concerns in this chapter the most important issues with which a criterion of identity is not equipped to deal fully have to do with the counterfactual or modal or essential properties of the entities belonging to the category for which the criterion is given. A criterion of identity for the ϕs has the form:

(1) $\Box(x)(y)(x$ is a ϕ and y is a $\phi \supset (x=y \equiv R(x,y)))$,

where '$R(x,y)$' is the ϕs' condition of identity. That particular ϕs satisfy their condition of identity is fundamentally a non-modal or (to use the possible worlds idiom) intra-world matter. The ϕs' condition of identity specifies types of properties members of which must be shared by identical ϕs. It does not specify all the properties ϕs must have, though it does specify some.

The appearance of '$\Box$' in (1) is justified by its being the case that the types of properties mentioned in the ϕs' identity condition must be importantly and necessarily connected with what it is to be a ϕ. If so, then a criterion of identity for ϕs will imply that if any object is a ϕ, then it must be 'R-ish', where by an object's being R-ish I mean that the ϕ in question non-vacuously has properties belonging to each of the types of property specified in the ϕs' condition of identity.[2] This is so because each ϕ is a ϕ in every possible world in which it exists (since the ϕs form a kind) and because to be a ϕ is at least in part to be a thing having properties from among those specified in the identity condition for the φs. Thus, for example, on the assumption of the usual identity criterion for physical objects, in every possible world in which a given physical object exists, it has some spatio-temporal history, it is spatio-temporal. So, here is one fact about the modal properties of φs that follows from a criterion of identity for the φs: if any entity is a φ, then it is R-ish in every possible world in which it exists.

But two things are clear. First, that determining what the modal or essential features of things belonging to a given category are is an important part of giving a theory about those things, since determining those facts tells us what such things must be like. And second, that not all the essential features of such things can be determined by appeal to those things' criterion of identity. For example, it does not follow, from the fact that a given φ is R-ish in every possible world in which it exists, that it is R-ish in the same way in every possible world in which it exists. Though a physical object must have some spatio-temporal history in every possible world in which it exists, it does not follow that, nor is it true that, there is some spatio-temporal history it has in every possible world in which it exists. And even if it were true that a physical object has the same spatio-temporal history in every possible world in which it exists, that truth would be due to some fact about physical objects not captured in their criterion of identity. Similarly, given the fact that sets are identical just in case they have the same members, and given the fact that each set is membered (including, possibly, null-membered) in every possible world in which it exists, it does not follow that any set has the same members in every possible world in which it exists. That sets do essentially have the members they have is a fact about sets that outruns the facts about sets determined by their criterion of identity.

Principles attributing to φs a property, F, possessed by any φ having it at all in every possible world in which that φ exists are expressed by claims having the following form:

(2) $\Box(x)(x$ is a $\phi \land Fx \supset \Box(y)(y=x \supset Fy))$.

And a claim of that form does not follow from a criterion of identity of the form (1), even when the property F is of the sort specified in the φs' condition of identity.

189

In Chapter VI, section 4, I argued that there is at least one property the having of which by atomic events is essential. I argued that atomic events divided into species whose members shared an essence determined by the portion of the atomic quality space the movement through which was that atomic event. So if some atomic event, e, has as one of its canonical descriptions a term of the form '[x, φ, t]', then the property of being a φing is a property had by e in every possible world in which e occurs. So, the property of being of an atomic event type of which it is in fact an instance is an essence of each atomic event. In this chapter, I want to consider some other candidates for properties that are essences of events. In particular, I will focus on the causal properties of events, on the properties in virtue of which events are changes in the objects they are changes in, and on the properties in virtue of which events occur at the times at which they occur.

2 THE INESSENTIALITY OF CAUSES AND EFFECTS

In 'The individuation of events',[3] Davidson proposed a criterion of identity for events according to which sameness of causes and effects is the condition of identity for events:

(3) $\Box(x)(y)$ (Event x ∧ Event y ⊃ (x=y ≡
  (e)(e')((eCx ≡ eCy) ∧ (xCe' ≡ yCe')))),

where 'Event' means 'is an event' and 'C' means 'is a cause of'. Peter van Inwagen, however, has suggested that, even if true (which he professes to believe), Davidson's criterion is inadequate to certain counterfactual truths about events.[4] It is, he thinks, plainly true both that any event could have had effects different from the effects it in fact had and that Davidson's criterion cannot be used to answer the question that has that plain truth as an answer. However, since van Inwagen does believe that an event could *not* fail to have the causes it in fact has, he proposes what he describes as a 'truncated' version of Davidson's criterion which he thinks is adequate to this counterfactual feature of events; what he proposes is that 'x is the same event as y if and only if x and y have the same causes'.[5] Now, in so far as van Inwagen thinks that his proposal merely truncates Davidson's, it should be represented in the following way:

(4) $\Box(x)(y)(\text{Event } x \wedge \text{Event } y \supset (x{=}y \equiv (e)(eCx \equiv eCy)))$.

But it is clear that something is amiss, for it is claimed that while (3) is inadequate to the alleged fact that events could have effects different from their actual ones, (4) is adequate to the alleged fact that events could not have causes different from their actual ones.

It is obvious that (3) cannot be said to be false on the grounds that events could have had effects other than the ones they in fact had, even if it is true that events could fail to have the effects they actually have. For Davidson's criterion no more implies that events could not have effects different from their actual ones than the usual criterion of identity for sets implies that sets could not have members different from those things that are in fact their members. All that a criterion of identity says is that in each possible world in which any entities, x and y, which belong to a certain kind, exist, x and y are the same entity if and only if they share all the properties of a certain sort (membership-properties in the case of sets, causal-properties in the case of events, as Davidson sees them). But all that is required in order to meet this condition is that in each possible world in which x and y exist, they match with respect to the relevant properties; it is *not* necessary that either x or y have the same properties (from the relevant group) in each possible world in which it exists. So, it does not follow from the claim that necessarily events are identical just in case they have the same causes and effects, that events have the same causes or the same effects in every possible world in which they occur. To settle this latter question about events, we should need to know something about events that is *not* given to us in a criterion of identity for events. So, van Inwagen is correct in thinking that Davidson's criterion of identity is unhelpful with respect to the answering of certain questions concerning the modal properties of events; but this is not true (nor does van Inwagen suggest that it is) because Davidson's criterion falsely implies that events could not fail to have as effects their actual ones, but rather because no criterion of identity for events, having the form (3), could imply that, truly or falsely.

191

But if van Inwagen's proposal is, as he says, a 'truncated' version of Davidson's, then it should be expressed as (4), and is no better off in this respect than Davidson's. First, it appears arguably false; it seems reasonable to believe that distinct events can have all the same causes.[6] But even if (4) were true, it would not imply the claim van Inwagen takes to be true, namely that having the causes it in fact has is an essential property of an event. To obtain results of the sort van Inwagen is interested in defending, principles stronger than those offered by Davidson and van Inwagen are needed, principles that deal with properties events have 'across possible worlds'. What van Inwagen needs is a principle like this:

(5) $\Box(x)(w)(\text{Event } x \land \text{Event } w \land wCx \supset$
$\Box(y)(y=x \supset wCy)).$[7]

Such a claim does say that any event, w, that is a cause of an event, x, in any possible world in which x occurs is a cause of that event in every possible world in which x occurs; and that says that events cannot fail to be caused by whatever actually causes them. And (5) is not entailed by (4).

It should be noted, by the way, that (5) does not imply that such properties as that of being caused by such-and-such events constitute individual essences or haecceities of events; such a stronger metaphysical position would be expressed by something having the following form:

(6) $\Box(x)(z)(\text{Event } x \land z=\{w:wCx\} \supset \Box(y)(y=x \equiv$
$(\exists u)(u=\{w:wCy\} \land u = z))).$

And, of course, if (5) is false, so is (6).

So, it is really a claim like (5) that van Inwagen takes to be true. He finds the idea it expresses attractive, for it matches his and others' intuitions about the 'causal origins' of particulars.[8] And it is the issue of the essentiality of the causes, and of the effects, of events that I now want to explore.

2.1 *The effects of events*

Consider the claim that an event cannot fail to have the effects it in fact has, a claim which, paralleling (5), should be represented in this way:

(7) $\Box(x)(w)(\text{Event } x \wedge \text{Event } w \wedge xCw \supset$
       $\Box(y)(y=x \supset yCw))$.

And consider the following case against (7). Let c be the event that is my driving of my car over a certain stretch of road at a certain velocity at a certain time; and let e be my cat's dying. And suppose that c was a cause of e, for in driving my car on that occasion I ran over my cat who was wandering about on the road. But e surely could have caused *your* cat's dying (e'), since it might have been the case that the veterinarian, at whose establishment our cats were residing at the time, accidentally let out your cat, instead of mine, and your cat wandered on the road in the same way and at the same time that my cat in fact did. Now surely, e≠e', for your cat's dying could not have been my cat's dying.[9] Thus, since c was a cause of e but could have caused e' (and not e), it is not necessary that events have the effects they have in every possible world in which they occur. Therefore, (7) is false.[10]

I regard this case as decisive; but I want to consider a defence of (7) and a revision of the view it expresses. The defence consists in denying that e was an effect of c and in insisting what really had the effect that e occurred was an event, c', composed of my driving my car (c) and my cat's getting out of this cage (f). After all, it might be suggested, if f hadn't occurred, e wouldn't have occurred. But, though c' was a cause of e, it could not have been a cause of e', for *your* cat's dying could not have been an effect of my driving my car and *my* cat's getting out of his cage. However, if this is how (7) is defended, then it is clear that e was no more an effect of c' than it was an effect of c; for my cat, in addition to having to get out of his cage, had to have wandered in a certain direction in order for e to have occurred. Indeed, this pattern of reasoning, designed to rule out certain events as causes of e on the grounds that they are not 'complete' enough to ensure that the cause of e could not have failed to have caused it, will lead inexorably to the view that the only event that caused e was an event composed of every event that was part of any causal chain one of whose effects was in fact e. But then the effects events have essentially, according to this defence, would be just those events whose causes are 'whole causal chains'. However, this sense of 'cause' – where to be a cause of an event is to be the whole causal history of an event – is not the sense of 'cause' employed in any of the claims (3)–(7). Moreover, even if (7) were construed as speaking of whole causal chains, it would then assert that there is no logically possible world in which the causal history of that world is just the same as the causal history of the actual world up to a given time, but diverges thereafter. And surely this is not logically impossible.

Suppose, now, that the following analogy is drawn. Even if it were true (and let us suppose that it is) that children must have the biological parents they in fact have, it would not follow that parents must have the children they in fact have; they could have had other children or none at all. But, if a particular set of parents has some particular individual as a child, then it does seem that in every possible world in which both those parents and that child exist those parents are the parents of that child. The defender of the essentiality of an event's effects might adopt a similar line. The defender might accept the case described above as showing that no event need have had the effects it in fact had; it might have had other effects or none at all. But doesn't it seem plausible that if an event c has e as one of its effects, then in every possible world in which both c and e occur, e is an effect of c? That is, though (7) is being given up, we may be asked to accept this weaker thesis:

(8) $\Box(x)(w)(\text{Event } x \land \text{Event } w \land xCw \supset$
$\Box(y)(z)(y=x \land z=w \supset yCz))$.

It should be noted that (8) not only expresses the weaker thesis about effects – that events have the effects they actually have in every possible world in which they and their actual effects occur – it also expresses a thesis about causes that is weaker than (5); for (8) also says that events have the causes they actually have in every possible world in which they and their actual causes occur. So, if (8) is false, then so are both (5) and (7). And it seems that (8) is indeed false, if the truth of singular causal claims implies the truth of certain counterfactual claims.

I presume that at least some of the events that actually occur are causally related. Now consider a possible world that it like the actual world in that the events occurring in this possible world are the very same events, happening to just the same objects at just the same times, that actually occur. The difference between the two possible worlds is that no events in the imagined world are causally related. But in that case, the assumption that claims of the form 'c caused e' imply claims of the form 'if c hadn't occurred, e wouldn't have occurred' (with suitable allowances for the possibility of causal pre-emption), will allow us to infer that there are counterfactual claims true in the actual world but false in this imagined world. Since a sufficient condition (at least) for the distinctness of possible worlds is difference with respect to the claims true in them, we can conclude that the actual world and the possible world just described are distinct. But if so, then (8) is false, for the imagined world is one in which both events and their actual causes and effects occur but are not causally related.[11] And if (8) is false, then the stronger thesis concerning causes (5) is false as well. For if it is not the case that events have the causes they in fact have in every possible world in which both they and their actual causes occur, then it can hardly be the case that events have the causes they in fact have in every possible world, including those in which they occur but their actual causes do not. (A similar remark applies, of course, to (7).)

2.2 *A counterexample*

Consider the following case against (5), the stronger thesis that events essentially have the causes they in fact have.[12] Imagine a situation in which c, my driving of my car (the c of section 2.1, above), does *not* occur, but in which my cat dies. Now clearly, not every event which is such that had it occurred it would have been a dying of my cat need be the dying my cat actually underwent by dint of the occurrence of c. The dying my cat actually underwent was e; and in some possible worlds, my cat dies; but my cat's dying was not, in that world, e. But in the situation I am now imagining, there was a device which when activated produced in my cat changes indistinguishable from the changes my cat actually underwent in the course of dying by dint of being run over by me. That is, as a result of the action of this device, properties were lost and other properties were acquired by my cat, indeed the very properties the losing and acquiring of which constituted the dying my cat actually underwent as a result of c; and my cat underwent these changes, in this situation, at the same time as it actually underwent them. Only the cause was different; for the actual cause was an event involving my car, while the imagined cause was not. In such a case, I can see neither what the reason would be for saying that the dying my cat underwent in this situation, and my cat's actual dying (e) are not the very same event, nor what the point of saying such a thing would be.

The denial of (5) is the claim that such properties as that of having such-and-such causes are not essential properties of the events which have them. But, in accepting the inessentiality of the causes of events, one is not thereby forced to say that events, in fact caused by certain events, could have been caused by *any* other events whatsoever. One is not, for example, forced to say that Caesar's death (the one he in fact underwent) would still have occurred, even if he had not been stabbed, but had been poisoned instead. Caesar, it seems clear, would *not* have undergone the same death in those circumstances; and this claim seems both true and compatible with the denial of (5). To maintain this position, however, one would have to show that the failure of Caesar's actual death to occur, in the possible situation in which he is poisoned, is due to something other than the failure to occur of the event, the stabbing, that was its actual cause. Now it is true that we have intuitions suggesting that Caesar's actual death could not have been caused by a poisoning, that the eruption of Mt St Helens could have been caused by Nixon's running for Vice President in 1952, and so on. And such intuitions, I think, motivate claims like (5) and (8).

But these intuitions only suggest that there is a relation between events and their causes in so far as their causes belong to certain kinds. Atomic events, I have argued, essentially belong to the atomic event types they in fact belong to. And such types are describable in terms of the properties belonging to the atomic quality spaces those events are movements in. So, an atomic event can, roughly speaking, be described as essentially an atomic object's going from having one to having another, contrary property. What seems clear is that one cannot get an object to go from being red to being blue by whistling (unless whistling is, perhaps, a signal to a painter) and one cannot get Caesar to undergo the very changes he in fact underwent, changes that in fact constituted his dying, by having him ingest poison. But these clarities seem to be founded on what the causal mechanisms are that constitute how our world works. That is, because certain events are essentially changes with respect to certain properties of certain sorts such events can only be brought about, when brought about at all, by events that are essentially changes with respect to properties of certain other sorts. And so it might be plausible to believe that events that in fact have causes must have causes belonging to sorts to which their actual causes in fact belong in every possible world in which those events occur and have causes; for in every such world the event must be constituted by changes with respect to those certain properties with respect to which its subject actually changed. Now such considerations may lie behind one's inclination to accept (8), but they do not imply what (8) asserts. Rather, they suggest, at best, that events that have causes have causes of the sort they in fact have in every possible world in which those events occur and have causes. That is, such considerations suggest a *de re*, transworld version of the thesis 'like events have like causes':

(9) $\Box(x)(y)$(Event x $\wedge$ Event y $\wedge$ yCx $\wedge$ Fy $\supset$
     $\Box(z)(z{=}x \wedge z$ in caused $\supset (\exists w)$(Event w $\wedge$ wCz $\wedge$ Fw))),

where the property expressed by 'F' divides events into causally relevant sorts.[13]

3 THE SUBJECTS OF EVENTS

It is obvious that identical events must be changes in the same subjects; this is a consequence not only of Leibniz's Law, in conjunction with the fact that events have subjects, but also of the criterion of identity for events I proposed in Chapter VI. But again, it does not follow from this that an event is, in every possible world in which it occurs, a change in the same object. Such a claim is expressed by

(10) $\Box(e)(x)$(Event e $\wedge$ x is e's subject $\supset \Box(e')(e'{=}e \supset$
     x is e''s subject)).

And it is this claim that I want to investigate now. Could an event have been a change in an object other than the one it was in fact a change in?

3.1 *A diversion*

I want to begin by asking a different, but related question. Could an event have been a change in an object other than *an* object it was in fact a change in? The answer to this question is *yes*.

Suppose that some event, e, is a change in an object, x, and that it occurs in the actual world, w_0; that is, suppose that for some ϕ (where being a ϕing is not necessarily any event's property essence) e=x's ϕing. And suppose that in w_0, x is a proper part of some object, y. Obviously there is an event, e′, that was a change in y; let e′=y's ψing. Surely my car was the subject of some event just in virtue of the fact that its windshield shattered. But I want here to appeal to a principle adopted in Chapter V, section 3, the Principle of Event Enlargement:

(PEE)　Any event which is a change in any object is a change in any object of which the first is a part.

PEE implies, given the suppositions, that x's ϕing = y's ψing. But now consider a possible world, w_1, distinct from w_0, in which x exists, y does not exist, and x is a proper part of some object z (distinct from y). Now, surely, if events occur in other possible worlds at all, we may suppose that exactly what happened to x in w_0 happened to it in w_1, that x's ϕing, i.e., e, occurs in w_1. But, by PEE, there is an event, z's ψing, which occurs in w_1, and x's ϕing=z's ψing.[14] But, then, since x's ϕing in w_0 just *is* x's ϕing in w_1, and since y's ψing in w_0 just *is* x's ϕing in w_0, and since z's ψing in w_1 just *is* x's ϕing in w_1, it follows that y's ψing in w_0 just *is* z's ψing in w_1. That is, what happened to y could have happened to z instead. Thus, in general, an event could have been a change in some object other than an object it was in fact a change in.

What makes it possible to draw this conclusion is that the changes in y and z occurred in their respective possible worlds only becaue the 'real', that is, the minimal subject of the change, namely x, was part of y in w_0 and part of z in w_1, and because the change in it occurred in both w_0 and w_1. Now surely, y (in w_0) and z (in w_1) were involved in x's ϕing (in their respective worlds). But, the 'real' subject of the event was x. With all this in hand, we can see that the intuitions backing up the argument leading to the conclusion are that, after all, x existed in both

198

situations (w_0 and w_1) and the fact that x was a part of this or that larger object is irrelevant to the occurrence of any event whose minimally involved subject was x. Any inclination to reject this charge of irrelevance would result, I believe, in an inclination to withdraw PEE in favour of the weaker principle: if e is a change in x at t, then there is a change, e′, in any object, y, of which x is a part at t. But I see no clear and independent reason for rejecting PEE. And so we can have cases where an event need not have been a change in *an* object it was in fact a change in. But that still leaves us with the original question: Could an event have been a change in a minimally involved subject other than the minimally involved subject it was in fact a change in?

Suppose I throw a ball (b_1); my throwing of b_1 caused a moving of b_1. Could the moving of b_1, whose minimally involved subject is b_1, have been the moving of some other ball, say b_2? It is true that I could have thrown b_2 instead; and I am prepared to argue that my throwing of b_1 could have been my throwing of b_2. But that is not a matter of allowing events to be capable of having minimally involved subjects other than their actual ones, for the ball I throw (be it b_1 or b_2) is not an object involved (minimally or not) in the throwing.[15] That is, it does not follow from allowing that the throwing of b_1 could have been the throwing of b_2 that one must allow that the moving of b_1 could have been the moving of b_2. Indeed, I do not think there are any persuasive considerations showing that the moving of b_1 could have been the moving of b_2. At this stage, however, this sounds rather like an argument from ignorance; but it may be the case that we can do no better along positive lines, for intuition, it seems to me, comes up short in this matter.

But perhaps what can be done is this. We might try to think of circumstances in which we seem to have the strongest case for saying of some event that it could have had a minimally involved subject different from its actual one and see what it would take to show or deny that the case really is a case of that. What I want to suggest is that we *can* maintain that the actual minimally involved subjects of events are necessarily the minimally involved subjects of them. But, of course, simply finding a way to avoid the alternative may not be especially persuasive; something will have to be said in favour of so avoiding the alternative. Thus, I will construct a case in which it might seem plausible that an event could have a minimally involved subject different from its actual one. But the case will, I believe, fail to be a case of that; and it will be instructive to see why that is so.

3.2 *Some preliminaries and an argument*

I want to allow, without argument, that objects composed of parts (for example, The Ship of Theseus) may undergo over a period of time change with respect to which objects constitute their parts. Indeed, it seems to me clearly possible that, under certain circumstances, an object should undergo a *complete* change of parts, so that *no* object that was a part of it at one time is a part of it at another time. And we can imagine that this happens to The Ship of Theseus, so that while the objects that are parts of The Ship of Theseus at one time are all and only the members of some set s, the objects that are parts of The Ship of Theseus at another, later time are all and only the members of a set s', where s and s' have no members in common. I am supposing that the process of replacement is gradual, that between these two times no ship other than The Ship of Theseus has as parts of any of the members of s, that before the earlier time no ship whatever has as parts any of the members of s', and that between the two times, each member of s' is either a part of The Ship of Theseus or a part of no ship whatsoever. Given all this (and some more, I suppose), we can say that the ship which at the earlier time has the members of s as its parts and the ship which at the later time has the members of s' as its parts are the very same ship, The Ship of Theseus. And if it is supposed that at some still later time, The Ship of Theseus continues to exist but a ship is constructed all of whose parts are members of s (The Ship of Theseus' original parts), then that just constructed ship is *not* The Ship of Theseus, for there is already, at that time, a ship, distinct from the newly constructed ship, that is The Ship of Theseus. We may call the newly constructed ship 'The pseudo-Ship of Theseus'.

Let us now suppose that what actually happens (i.e., happens in the actual world, w_0) is this. The Ship of Theseus has existed from t_1 to t_2 to t_3 with all the same parts, the members of s; it also existed for some time before t_1. At t_3 it sinks for the first and only time. So there was an event, e_0, the sinking of The Ship of Theseus at t_3.[16] But it could have been the case (and was the case in a possible world, w_1) that between t_1 and t_2, The Ship of Theseus underwent a complete replacement of parts, so that from t_2 and thereafter The Ship of Theseus had as parts the members of s'. However, between t_2 and t_3, The pseudo-Ship of Theseus was constructed from the members of s and sailed the very course in fact (in w_0) sailed by The Ship of Theseus. Then, at t_3, The pseudo-Ship of Theseus sinks under precisely the same circumstances, at the very spot, in exactly the same way, and due to the same causes as did The Ship of Theseus in w_0. So, there occurred in w_1 an event, e_1, the sinking of The pseudo-Ship of Theseus at t_3. But, it might be argued, both e_0 (in w_0) and e_1 (in w_1) occurred at the same time, in the same place, as a result of the same causes, and, in addition, involved nothing more than the sinkings of all and only the members of s. So, a strong case can be made for thinking that e_0 and e_1 are the same event. But, since The Ship of Theseus and The pseudo-Ship of Theseus are distinct ships in w_1, The Ship of Theseus in w_0 is distinct from The pseudo-Ship of Theseus in w_1 (despite the sameness of their parts). Thus, since e_0 was a change whose minimal subject was The Ship of Theseus and e_1 was a change whose minimal subject was The pseudo-Ship of Theseus, and since $e_0 = e_1$, we have a case where an event could have been a change in a minimally involved subject other than the one it was in fact a change in. Therefore, it is not an essential property of any event that is a change in a minimally involved subject with exchangeable proper parts that it be a change in the minimally involved subject it is in fact a change in.[17]

This conclusion may seem reasonable in light of hypothesis (H) of Chapter VI, section 2, according to which the only events there are are atomic events and events composed of atomic events. After all, the sinking of The Ship of Theseus in w_0 is composed of the sinkings of the members of s; and so is the sinking of The pseudo-Ship of Theseus in w_1. And nothing else has to happen, other than the sinkings of a ship's parts, in order for a ship composed of those parts to sink. But an additional assumption is required in order to justify the conclusion. And that is, in this particular case, that the sinking of a ship composed of certain parts (a sinking in which all of the ship sinks) just is the sinkings of the ship's parts. The general principle involved is this: if an object is the subject of some event, e, and that object is composed of certain parts, and if e is composed of events which are changes in more than one of e's subject's parts, then e is identical with the changes in its subject's parts.[18] But this principle, in its general form and in its application to the case at hand, is false.

The case just described seems to be the best case for concluding that the minimally involved subjects of events are not essential to the events involving them. I can think of nothing in favour of saying that an atomic event could have had a minimally involved atomic subject other than the one it in fact had; and there seem to be no features of changing things, other than their being partless or not, that seem relevant to the issue. So, if we can avoid, in a well-motivated way, having to accept the case described as one involving an inessential subject, we will have an argument for the essentiality of the subjects of events. And I think my proposal for avoiding that is well-motivated; for in refraining from saying that events can have subjects other than their actual ones, one is forced to give a theory about events composed of other events that will, I presume, parallel what I take to be a theory we must give about physical objects composed of other physical objects. We must give a certain kind of theory about the relation between physical objects and the parts of which they are composed; and that theory must be one according to which physical objects are not identical with their parts.[19] What that composition relation is, that is, what the circumstances are under which some physical objects do compose another, I do not propose to try to specify here; but some such relation there must be and there must be a theory about it.

What makes the case described above seem to work is the assumption that the sinking of The Ship of Theseus (in w_0) is just the sinkings of its parts, the members of s (in w_0). For if so, then since the sinking of another ship could have been those same sinkings, the sinking of the ship could have been the sinking of a different ship. But it seems clear that the sinkings of the members of s could not have been the sinkings of the members of a different set. When we think about the relation between a physical object, x, and its parts, we are not thinking about the relationship between x and another physical object, namely x's parts. There *is* no such object as x's parts; there *are* x's parts. If, however, we insist on thinking of x's parts as being some individual thing, we can, I suppose, think of x's parts as being a 'summational object'. But summational objects are, in an important respect, like sets; the things of which a sum is summed are essential to it, just as the members of a set are essential to the set whose members they are. Similarly, when we think of the relationship between the sinking of a ship and the sinkings of the ship's parts, we are thinking of an event and (at least some of) that event's parts. But in so doing, we are not thinking about the relationship between an event, e, and another event, e's parts. There *is* no such event as e's parts; there *are*, however, events which are e's parts. If we insist, however, on thinking of e's parts as being some individual event, we can, I suppose, think of e's parts as being a 'summational event'. But, summational events, like summational physical objects, are like sets in that the events of which they are sums seem essential to them. But in the case of physical objects, it is just this feature in virtue of which we can say that no physical object is identical with its parts; a physical object can survive a replacement of parts, but its parts (or the sum of its parts) cannot. Similarly, no event is identical with its parts; an event could have had an event as one of its parts that was not in fact one of its parts; but an event's parts (or the sum of its parts) could not have. Thus, a change that comes over a certain object could (sometimes) come over it, even if the subject of that event had had different parts.

Suppose that some object, x, changes, and x is a (partless) part of y. By PEE, that change in x is identical with a change in y. Now, of course, y could have had (partless) z as a part instead of x. Now, if the sort of thing that happened in fact to x had happened to z, then although y would have undergone a change very much like what it underwent when it changed because x changed, the change in y (with z as a part) would have been distinct from the change it actually underwent because the change in z could not have been the change in x. I am taking to be true what I had earlier suggested – that changes in partless subjects could not have been changes in other partless subjects. However, if what happened to y, happened to it (*via* PEE) because of some change in one of its parts distinct from x, then the fact that y could have had z instead of x as a part is irrelevant to whether or not the change in y which actually occurred (when x was one of its parts) was the change in y which could have ccurred (when z replaced x).

In addition, it seems to be plausible to think that if y was the *minimal* subject of some event, then that change in y could still have occurred even if y had had different parts. Consider the actual sinking of The Ship of Theseus. I can think of no reason whatever for insisting, apart, that is, from insisting that the ship is identical with its parts, that that very sinking could not have occurred, if The Ship of Theseus had been different from the way it actually was in so far as it had a certain nail different from one of its actual nails (though as similar to it as one would like). It seems to me unreasonable to think that the sinking of The Ship of Theseus that actually occurred could not have been identical with a sinking of The Ship of Theseus that could have occurred, where the one that could have occurred was a sinking of a ship which (a) was The Ship of Theseus, and (b) was such that when built, one of its builders used a different, though quite similar, nail from the one he in fact used. After all, the sinking of The Ship of Theseus which could have occurred could have occurred at the same time, at the same place, in the same way, and consist in movements in the same portions of the same quality spaces. So, while the sinking of The Ship of Theseus could have had as one of its parts the sinking of a part of the ship other than one of its actual parts, (the sum of) the sinkings of the parts of the ship could not have had as one of its parts the sinking of a part of the ship other than one of its actual parts. The sinking of The Ship of Theseus is not identical with the sinkings of its parts.

If this is right, then one cannot argue that The Ship of Theseus' sinking could have been the sinking of another entity, *viz*. The pseudo-Ship of Theseus, on the grounds that some other entity could have had all and only the parts that The Ship of Theseus in fact had and yet be distinct from The Ship of Theseus. For the grounds, though quite true, are irrelevant. The changes in those parts, the sinkings of the members of s, are not identical with either the sinking of The Ship of Theseus (in w_0) or the sinking of The pseudo-Ship of Theseus (in w_1). Nor can one argue that the sinking of The Ship of Theseus could have been identical with (a sum of) changes in a different collection of parts, on the grounds that The Ship of Theseus could have had different parts at the time of its sinking. For the grounds, though quite true, are irrelevant, because the actual sinking of The Ship of Theseus was not even identical with the sinkings of its actual parts. But the intuitions lying behind our thinking that we had a case of an event whose subject could have been other than it in fact was were that we could have identity of objects through replacement of parts and that we could change an object just by changing its parts. Now, while correct, these intuitions suggested that we should think of changes in objects as just the changes in their parts. But that idea is, I take it, no more or less plausible than the idea that objects are just their parts. Just as we should say that a physical object is composed of, but not identical with, the physical objects that are its parts, we should also say that an event, e, whose subject is an object with parts, is composed of, but not identical with, the events whose subjects are parts of e's subject.

So, while there are good reasons for thinking that the sinkings of the members of s in w_0 are just the sinkings of the members of s in w_1, there is no good reason for thinking that either the sinkings of the members of s or the sinking of The Ship of Theseus in w_0 is identical with the sinking of The pseudo-Ship of Theseus in w_1.[20] And thus, it seems plausible to think of the minimally involved subjects of events as essential to the events whose subjects they are.[21]

An event whose subject is an object with parts and which is composed of changes in that object's parts must be a change in that object. However, since that object can have parts other than the ones it actually has, a change in that object can have parts other than the ones it actually has; a change in that object can be composed of changes other than those it is in fact composed of. Thus, that an event is composed of such-and-such events is an inessential feature of that event.

(Suppose there were physical objects that are 'sums' of other physical objects, their parts. They would, of course, be distinct from those physical objects that are composed of those same parts, since summational objects cannot, while composed objects can, change their parts. Such summational objects would, I suppose, be the subjects of summational events, events that are sums of changes in those objects that are the summational parts of the summational event's subject. A summational event is, of course, essentially a sum of the events of which it is in fact a sum.

205

Would such an event have its subject essentially? If such an event's subject were, say, The Ship of Theseus, then it need not be a change in that thing, for the sinkings of that ship's parts, for example, could have been the sinkings of the parts of another ship. There is no reason, however, to believe that any summational event's subject is The Ship of Theseus, for such events have sums of objects as their subjects, and The Ship of Theseus is not identical with any sum of things. But, if the subject of the summational event is just the sum of the parts, then it does seem that such an event is essentially a change in the sum it is in fact a change in. I regard these parenthetical remarks, however, as merely hypothetical. There are, I suspect, summational events only if there are summational objects to serve as their subjects. And I think that there are no such things. If there were things identical with their parts, they would be distinct from things composed of those same parts, and the things identical with and the things composed of the same parts would occupy the same places at the same times. And I do not see any reason to believe that this is possible or plausible.[22])

4 THE ESSENTIALITY OF TIME

It is, of course, obvious that identical events must occur at the same time; this follows not only from (E) but also from the indiscernibility of identicals in conjunction with the fact that events have temporal features among which are those attributing to events times of occurrence. Thus,

(11) $\Box(e)(e')$(Event e $\land$ Event e' $\supset$ (e=e' $\supset$
(t)(e occurs at t $\equiv$ e' occurs at t))).

But, again, it does not follow from (11) that events occur at the same times in every possible world in which they occur. That the property of occurring at a certain time is an essential feature of any event having it is expressed as follows:

(12) $\Box(e)(t)$(Event x $\land$ t is a time $\land$ e occurs at t $\supset$
$\Box(e')(e'=e \supset e'$ occurs at t)).

And it is this essentialist claim about events that I wish to explore.

First, however, a slightly different issue. Could an event have failed to have occurred *during* a period of time during which it in fact occurred? This question should be answered affirmatively, if it is assumed that time could come to an end. (It would also be answered affirmatively if (12) were false.) Suppose that an event, e, occurs at a time, t. I presume that the following principle, mentioned in Chapter V, section 4.1, is obvious:

(13)   If an event occurs *at* any time, it occurs *during* any
       period of time that includes the time at which it occurs.

Now, let t' be an interval of time that properly includes the interval t; given (13), it follows that e occurs during t'. Imagine, however, a possible world in which e occurs at t, but in which time comes to an end after t but before the end of t'. In such a world, e occurs but does not occur during t', for in that world there is no such period of time.[23] So, an event could have failed to have occurred during a period of time during which it in fact occurred.

The case described is not one in which an event occurs during an interval of time other than one during which it in fact occurred; for in that case, every period of time during which e occurred in the imagined world is an interval during which e actually occurred. But it is easy to construct a case in which this is not so; just reverse the situations. Suppose that e in fact occurs at t in a world in which time comes to an end sometime after t. But now imagine a world in which e occurs at t but in which time either comes to an end at a time later than it in fact does or does not come to an end at all. Then there will be an interval of time, t'', during which e occurs in that imagined situation, but during which e does not in fact occur, for there is in fact no such interval. What these cases show, I suggest, is that such properties as that of occurring *during* such-and-such intervals of time are not, in general, essential properties of the events which have them. (I say 'in general', for if it should turn out that such properties as that of occurring *at* a certain time are essential properties of events, then there will be one period of time during which an event occurs the occurring during which is essential.)

What makes it possible to get this result, apart from the assumption regarding time's coming to an end (about which, mercifully, nothing further will be said here), is that the 'real' time of an event's occurrence is, in general, *not* the time during which it occurs. So long as the history of the universe is longer than that of some particular event, there is no such time as *the* time during which that event occurs. So, it is intuitively clear why, for any non-minimal period of time during which an event occurs, the property of occurring during that period of time is not an essential property of that event. For such non-minimal periods include times during which the event is *not* occurring and are thus, at least to that extent, not relevant to the occurrence of that event; that event could have occurred even if those irrelevant intervals had not existed. But, to return to our original question, could an event have occurred *at* a time other than the time at which it in fact occurred?

4.1 *Two arguments for the inessentiality thesis*

There are many things we commonly say that seem to suggest that an event could have occurred sooner or later than it actually did, and therefore, that what I shall here call the 'inessentiality thesis', the view that the property of occurring at a certain time is *not* in general an essential property of events, is true (that (12) is false). The following are examples of what I have in mind:

(14) (a) I could have been born a few minutes sooner than I was;
      (b) Caesar might have died a bit later in the day;
      (c) The Titanic might have sunk on April 13th, and not on April 14th, 1912, had the infamous iceberg been located a few hundred miles farther east.

The claims in (14), however, do *not* imply the inessentiality thesis. For a claim to do that, it would have to pick out some individual event and say of it that it could (or would, under certain circumstances) have occurred at a time other than the time at which it in fact occurred. But none of the claims in (14) do that, for none say anything at all about any individual event. They say nothing about any individual event in the same way that 'there is a burglar in the house' says nothing about any individual burglar, even when there is in fact just one burglar in the house. In so far as (14a), for example, can be thought to be about events, what it says is that there could have been a birth of me that could have occurred at a time earlier than the time of the event that was my actual birth. But for that to imply the inessentiality thesis, the event that could have occurred at the time earlier than that of my actual birth would have to have been my actual birth. But (14a) makes no such claim. The claim 'there could have been a burglar in your house instead of in mine' does *not* imply that burglars can burgle houses other than the houses they in fact burgle. However, a claim that does imply the inessentiality thesis for burglars is this: the burglar could have burgled your house instead of mine.

Thus, it is now clear which commonly said things are those that may more plausibly be said to imply the inessentiality thesis; they are claims such as these:

(15) (a) My birth could have occurred a few minutes later;
      (b) Caesar's death might have occurred later in the day;
      (c) Had the infamous iceberg been located a few
           hundred miles farther east, the sinking of the Titanic
           would have occurred on the 13th and not on the 14th
           of April, 1912.

These claims do at least appear to pick out an individual event and say of it that it could, or would under certain circumstances, have occurred at a time earlier or later than the time at which it in fact occurred; hence they appear to imply that events do not occur at the same time in every possible world in which they occur.

However, a defender of the view that events can*not* occur sooner or later than they in fact do (the essentiality thesis) will not allow the inessentiality thesis such a facile vindication. The argument from the truth of the claims in (15) to the inessentiality thesis is fallacious.

In order for a term such as 'Caesar's death' to be a proper singular term, in any possible world, it must be the case that the event it, in any such world, designates is the one and only event that is, in that world, a death of Caesar. If we suppose that in some possible but non-actual world Caesar dies exactly once but does so at the age of twelve as a result of a fall from a chariot, then there will be in that world exactly one death of Caesar; and 'Caesar's death' will in that world designate that event. But it would be wrong to think that Caesar's actual death and the event which in this imagined world was Caesar's death are the very same event, even though they are designated in their respective worlds by the same term, *viz.* 'Caesar's death'. 'Caesar's death' and the other event-designating terms in (15) are best thought of as definite descriptions designating the events that, in the possible worlds in which those events occur, uniquely satisfy those descriptions.

The issue, then, of whether or not the sentences in (15) imply the inessentiality thesis turns on the *scope* of the event-designating terms relative to the modal terms in those sentences ('could', 'would'). If 'my birth', 'Caesar's death', and 'the sinking of the Titanic' are construed as having *large* scope relative to the modal words in (15a–c), respectively, then (15c), for example, would be understood as follows:

(15c′)   The event which was in fact the sinking of the Titanic is such that it would have occurred on the 13th and not on the 14th of April, 1912, had the infamous iceberg been located a few hundred miles farther east.

And (15c′) does imply the inessentiality thesis. But if (15c) is read with its event-designating term given *small* scope, it does *not* imply the inessentiality thesis; for so construed there is no implication that the referent of 'the sinking of the Titanic', in a world in which the counterfactual condition in (15c) is met and the referent of that term in the actual world, in which that condition is not met, are the same event. But unless there is such an implication, the issue of the essentiality thesis is not touched at all.

Now it can be granted that claims like those in (15) express obvious truths. But which obvious truths? Those expressed by an interpretation giving the event-designating terms in them small scope or one in which those terms are given large scope? Surely not, I should think, the large scope versions. It is clear, first, that the small scope versions express obvious truths (and are harmless *vis-à-vis* the issue under consideration) and, second, that the inessentiality thesis follows trivially from the large scope versions by a simple application of existential generalisation. Can any claim that implies such a metaphysical principle by existential generalisation alone be said to be an obvious truth? A defender of the essentiality thesis should rightly demand that the inessentiality theorist employing this route to his view present some argument to show that these sentences express truths when their event-designating terms are given large scope. For their truth so interpreted is plainly not obvious, though they are so when those terms are given small scope. But then we are back at the beginning, for it seems evident that no successful argument for the truth of large scope versions of claims like those in (15) could fail to be an independent and direct argument for the inessentiality thesis itself. The short route to the inessentiality thesis, *via* (15), accomplishes nothing. It either begs the question or trades on a scope ambiguity.[24]

4.2 *A valid argument for the inessentiality thesis*

What the inessentiality thesis needs is a direct argument for its truth. Consider this one. Suppose that determinism is false in the sense that there is a substance, X, which when struck with a blunt instrument will explode, though it is undetermined when it will do so. And let us suppose that I strike a hunk of X with a hammer at t and that it explodes seven seconds after t. My wife hears the explosion and becomes concerned. Now, given the hypothesis, that hunk of X might have exploded eight seconds later than it in fact did. Let us then imagine that, in some possible world, it does explode then, that is, fifteen seconds after my striking of X. Now, an inessentiality theorist will say that the explosion that in fact concerned my wife is such that it, that very explosion, would have occurred eight seconds later than it did, had X exploded eight seconds later than it did (though it might have not concerned my wife, for she may by then have moved out of earshot). And the argument for this claim is this. If X had exploded eight seconds later than it did, the explosion that would then have occurred would have had the very causes (my striking of X, etc.) as the explosion that in fact occurred and concerned my wife. And any event which could have occurred and which is such that had it occurred it would have had all the same causes as some event that in fact occurred just *is* the event that in fact occurred. Thus, there is at least one event that could have occurred at a time later than the time at which it in fact did. So, the inessentiality thesis is true.

This argument for the inessentiality thesis is valid. It does, however, have as a crucial premise the claim that each event is such that had there occurred an event having all the same causes as it, it just *is* the event which could have occurred. But this premise expresses what seems to me to be a falsehood. It says that whenever, in any possible situation, the events that actually caused a certain event occur, and they are in that situation the causes of a certain effect then that effect *is* the event they actually caused; that is,

(16) $(x)(s)(x$ is an event $\land s= \{y:yCx\} \supset$
$\Box(s')(z)(s'=\{w:wCz\} \land s=s' \supset x=z)).$[25]

But (16) implies that there is no logically possible world whose causal history (that is, whose events and the causal relations among them) is just the same as the causal history of the actual world up to a given time but which diverges from the causal history of the actual world thereafter, even though the events thereafter have causal antecedents which occurred before the time of the diverging. But what reasons can there be for thinking that there is no such possible world? I can think of three, but none of them seem compelling. One might hold that there is no such possible world because one holds (i) that the causal laws that actually obtain are necessarily true, or (ii) that it is not possible that at some time the causal laws change, or (iii) that it is not possible that the causal laws which obtain are Goodmanesque, gruesome variants of the causal laws that actually obtain. But I do not find any of (i)–(iii) very plausible. And, at any rate, that the causal history of the world could have been different from the way it actually was after a certain time seems plausible on its face. And so, unless there is some further argument forthcoming, it seems eminently reasonable to believe that what (16) implies is false and, hence, that (16) is false. But if so, then the argument under consideration fails to establish the inessentiality thesis.[26]

4.3 *An argument for the essentiality thesis*

I want to present an argument for the essentiality thesis, an argument which, if successful, shows that an event cannot occur at any time other than the time at which it in fact occurs, that each event occurs at the same time in every possible world in which it occurs.[27] I shall defer discussion of the crucial premise of this argument until the next chapter.

Suppose that there is a possible world, w_1, in which a certain object, x, changes *twice* in a certan way at distinct times, t_1 and

212

t_2. That is, there occur in w_1 two distinct events, e_1 and e_2, that are as alike as possible given the fact that e_1 occurs at t_1 and e_2 occurs at t_2. What I mean by 'as alike as possible' is this. An event is a 'movement' by an object, over a stretch of time, from its having one to its having another static property. And e_1 and e_2 are movements by the same object consisting in that object's having and then acquiring the same properties (in the same order); all their qualities are the same. Their times of occurrence are different; but even so, t_1 and t_2 are periods of time having the same length. Now, of course, there will have to be further differences between e_1 and e_2, differences resulting from the fact that they occur at different times. It will, for example, undoubtedly be the case that e_1 and e_2 differ with respect to at least some of their causes and effects (but they are inessential). My hypothesis is that the only respects in which e_1 and e_2 differ, in addition to differing with respect to their times of occurrence, are those respects having to do with their relations to other entities. With respect to their essential properties (apart from the possibility that their times of occurrence are essential) and their non-relational accidental properties, however, e_1 and e_2 are exactly alike; e_1 and e_2 are, as I shall say, 'twins'. Now it seems to me to be clearly possible for there to be two, distinct events that are twins; surely a particular marble could twice roll from one place to another in the same way, at the same velocity, along the same path, etc. So, w_1 seems to me to be a possible world. And both the essentiality theorist and the inessentiality theorist should have no trouble allowing this.[28]

If the inessentiality thesis is correct, however, it need not be the case that e_1 occurs at t_1 and e_2 at t_2 in every possible world in which they both occur. If so, then if the inessentiality thesis is true, then there is a possible world, w_2, distinct from w_1, which is to the extent possible exactly like w_1 except for the fact that in w_2 e_1 occurs at t_2 and e_2 occurs at t_1. Now, an inessentiality theorist might think that even if the time of occurrence of an event is not an essential feature of it there are still limitations on the times at which an event could have occurred, given its actual time of occurrence and some other facts. For example, no event could have occurred at a time at which the object, which was in fact the subject of that event, could not have existed, for if an event could have so occurred, it would have been a change in an object other

213

than the object it was in fact a change in. But in the case at hand, whatever limitations of that sort there may be surely have no application, for the times to which e_1 and e_2 are being shifted, in the shift from w_1 to w_2, are occupied in w_1 by events as like the events shifting into those times as two distinct events can be. If e_1 can occur at t_1 and e_2 at t_2 (as they do in w_1), then, if the inessentiality thesis is true, e_2 can occur at t_1 and e_1 at t_2. Thus, there should be no objection to its being the case that w_2 is a possible world if w_1 is. The fundamental difference between w_1 and w_2 is that e_1 and e_2 switch temporal places. Of course, there will be further differences necessitated by this switch; but these differences will all be a matter of e_1's bearing in w_2 relations to certain entities e_2 bears relations to in w_1 (and *vice versa*).

Now the inessentiality thesis is true only if, on the assumption that w_1 is a possible world, w_2 is a possible world distinct from w_1. That w_1 is possible is clear, since it is clearly possible for an event to have a twin. And that w_2 is distinct from w_1 is also clear, it seems to me. I am assuming that worlds are identical if and only if every proposition true in one is true in the other (and *vice versa*). And, given the way w_1 and w_2 have been described, w_1 and w_2 are distinct, since there are at least two propositions, the proposition that e_1 occurs at t_2 and the proposition that e_2 occurs at t_1, that are true in w_2 but false in w_1. Thus, the inessentiality thesis stands or falls with the possibility or impossibility of w_2. And I shall argue that, appearances to the contrary notwithstanding, the description of w_2 is *not* the description of a possible world. I wish to argue that, from the inessentiality thesis's view about how w_2 is to be described and a principle that seems to me true (about which I shall say something in Chapter VIII), a contradiction in w_2 can be derived. And thus, in so far as the principle I shall propose is true, we must reject the claim that w_2 is a possible world. And it will then follow that it cannot be the case that an event can occur at any time other than the time at which it in fact occurs.

One thing that seems clear about w_1 and w_2 is that they have the same ontologies. Whichever entities exist in w_1, be they physical objects, events, properties, times, sets, etc., exist in w_2 and *vice versa*. This is clear from the way w_2 was constructed. Now let us consider just that subset of all the propositions that are *not* about events. Given the way in which w_1 and w_2 have been described, it is clear that each of the propositions in that subset is true in w_1 if and only if it is true in w_2. This is clear because the fundamental difference between w_1 and w_2 is that e_1 and e_2 switch temporal places. But e_1 in w_1 is just x's having of some dynamic property ϕ at t_1 and e_2, in w_1, is just x's having of ϕ at t_2. In w_2, e_1 is x's having of ϕ at t_2 and e_2 is x's having of ϕ at t_1. In *both* w_1 and 2_2, then, x has ϕ at t_1 and at t_2. So, the propositions which express the facts about the properties objects have at times are the same in w_1 and w_2. The proposition that x has ϕ at t_1 and the proposition that x has ϕ at t_2 are true in both w_1 and w_2. And clearly w_1 and w_2 match with respect to propositions concerning x and its properties at other times and with respect to propositions concerning other objects and the properties they have at times.

Since, by hypothesis, w_1 and w_2 are distinct, there must be propositions whose truth values differ in those two worlds. And the propositions wherein w_1 and w_2 differ must be ones explicitly about events that occur in w_1 and w_2. And the inessentiality theorist will, I believe, agree and insist that such propositions as that e_1 occurs at t_1 and that e_2 occurs at t_2 are propositions explicitly about events that are true in w_1 and false in w_2. But can what the inessentiality theorist insists on at this point really be true? I am inclined to think not. For I think that there is an important sense in which it is true that the facts in any world about events are determined by the facts in that world about objects capable of being the subjects of events, the static properties which they have and then lack (i.e., the dynamic properties they have), and the times at which those objects have and then lack those properties. Once the truth values of propositions concerning the subjects of change, the properties they have, and the times at which they have those properties are settled, the truth values of propositions concerning events are settled. That is, I want to endorse the following principle:

(17)   Possible worlds cannot be alike with respect to the truth and falsity of propositions concerning the existence of objects capable of non-relational change, the possession and non-possession of static properties by such objects, and the times at which such objects possess and fail to possess those properties, and alike with respect to the truth of the proposition that there are events, and yet be

215

unalike with respect to the truth and falsity of propositions concerning which events occur.

Now I have urged that each proposition concerning objects, the properties they have, and the times at which they have those properties is true in w_1 if and only if true in w_2. If so, then by (17), each proposition concerning events is true in w_1 if and only if true in w_2 as well. Thus, since it is true in w_1 that e_1 occurs at t_1 and true in w_1 and e_2 occurs at t_2, it is also true in w_2 that e_1 occurs at t_1 and true in w_2 and e_2 occurs at t_2. But, by hypothesis, in w_2 e_1 does *not* occur at t_1 and e_2 does *not* occur at t_2. Thus, w_2 is a world in which it is true that e_1 does and does not occur at t_1 and true that e_2 does and does not occur at t_2. That is, w_2 is *not* a possible world. But, since it is a necessary condition of the truth of the inessentiality thesis that w_2 is a possible world, it follows that the inessentiality thesis is false. Each event occurs at the same time in every possible world in which it occurs. The essentiality thesis is true.

VIII

THE SUPERVENIENCE
OF EVENTS

1 INDIVIDUAL ESSENCES

My argument at the end of Chapter VII, for the claim that each
event occurs essentially at the time at which it in fact occurs,
depended crucially on the assumption of a principle about the
relation between events and objects capable of non-relational
change, properties such objects have, and times at which such
objects have such properties. More than a few words concerning
that principle are called for. However, I do not have much to say
that would constitute an argument for its truth. The principle
seems to me to be obvious; not, of course, obvious at first glance,
but on reflection. That is, if one has in mind a certain picture of
how events fit into the ontological scheme of things, that
principle will seem a very natural one to espouse. So one of the
things I want to do in this chapter is to provide a sketch of that
picture in the hope that it will inspire one to see things in the way
I do. The picture is to be sketched largely by drawing contrasts
and comparisons; thus I intend in this chapter to be impression-
istic, suggestive, and speculative – the last refuge of a philosopher
who has run out of arguments.

1.1 *Sets and their members*

Consider the following claim about sets and their members:

    (1)   Possible worlds cannot be alike with respect to the truth
            and falsity of propositions concerning the existence of

> particular objects other than sets, and alike with respect
> to the truth or falsity of the proposition that there are
> sets, and yet be unlike with respect to the truth and falsity
> of propositions concerning the existence of particular sets.

That is, possible worlds alike in containing sets at all must be
alike in containing the very same sets, if they are alike in
containing the very same objects other than sets. The reason for
thinking that (1) is true is that the principles determining which
sets there are in any possible world determine which sets there
are in every possible world. After all, possible worlds are not
'worlds'; they are just ways this world might have been. And
since the principles that determine which sets there are determine
that only on the basis of facts concerning which objects there are,
the same sets will be determined by the same objects. And in so
far as that is so, (1) aids in the articulating of the idea that there
is nothing 'hidden' about sets, nothing crucial about sets that isn't
known about a set once it is known what its members are.[1] What
the principle suggests is the idea that sets are determined by their
members in the sense that to be this or that set just is to be a set
with these or those objects as members. For it is hard to see what
could make (1) true that would not also make it true that each set
has the same members in every possible world in which it exists.
And that implies that such properties as that of having such-and-
such objects as members are individual essences of the sets that
have them. That is, if some set, x, has the property of having
such-and-such members, then in every possible world in which x
exists it has that property and in every possible world in which
some set has that property that set is x.[2] However, it does not
follow from this, nor does it seem true, that sets are in some
sense reducible to or are nothing but their members. For the
existence of no set follows logically from the existence of the
things that are, in fact, its members; the axioms of set theory are
not truths of logic. It is just that if there is a set whose members
are certain objects, then all the crucial facts about that set are
settled by the facts about those objects.[3]

1.2 *Physical objects and their qualities*

Consider now the following principle concerning the relation

218

between physical objects and their qualities:

(2) Possible worlds cannot be alike with respect to the truth and falsity of propositions concerning the 'co-exemplifica-tions' of qualities, and alike with respect to the truth or falsity of the proposition that there are physical objects, and yet be unalike with respect to the truth and falsity of propositions concerning which physical objects exist.

The thrust of this principle is that if, in any possible world, there is a physical object, x, that is the unique F, where the property of being F is a property attributing to an object all, or some important subset of all, the purely qualitative features the object in question has, then in every possible world in which there is an object that is in that world the unique F, that object is x. What this principle suggests, however roughly, about physical objects is that there is nothing 'hidden' about them, nothing (crucial) that isn't known about a physical object once its qualities (or its important ones) are known. The principle suggests the idea that physical objects are determined by their qualities (or their important ones) in the sense that to be this or that physical object just is to be something having these or those qualities. And this suggests that there are some qualities, like that of being the unique F, that constitute the individual essences of the physical objects having them; this seems reasonable, since it is hard to see how such a property could individuate 'across possible worlds' without also being essential. However, it would not follow from such a principle that physical objects are in some important sense 'reducible' to their qualities, that physical objects are 'nothing but' their qualities. For the existence of no physical object follows simply from the existence of the properties it in fact has. It is just that if there is a physical object having such-and-such qualities, then the crucial facts about that object are settled by the facts about those qualities it has.

The view expressed by (2) is the so-called Jules Verne-o-scope view of the identification of physical objects across possible worlds, a view according to which picking out some actual individual in some other possible world involves finding an individual in that world that has certain qualities in common with the actual object in question. This view is currently, in some circles, in disrepute.[4] However, I do not wish to get involved in the debate over whether the disrepute (2) finds itself in is well-deserved, though I am inclined to think that it is. What I do wish to point out is that the rejection of (2) does seem to involve the rejection of the idea that physical objects have individual essences that are expressible without recourse to the use of such predicates as 'is identical with Socrates', 'has Socrateity', or 'is the unique Socratizer', and that are given solely in terms of their qualities. And it involves a rejection of the view that there is nothing 'hidden' about physical objects. If (2) and similar principles concerning physical objects are false, then the very idea of what it is to be a given, individual physical object is, in some important sense, inaccessible to us.[5]

1.3 *Events*

Events are non-relational changes in objects; and for an object to change it must, roughly, have a static property at one time and lack it at another. To be an event, then, is just to be a having and then a lacking by an object of a static property at a time (or a having of a dynamic property by an object at a time). To say this is, of course, only to say what it is in general, on the theory I have been advocating, to be an event. It is not, however, to say what it is to be this or that particular event; nor is it to say that events have individual essences (haecceities), that is, properties, F, which satisfy the following schema:

(3) $\square(e)(e$ is an event and $Fe \supset \square(e')(e'=e \equiv Fe'))$.

In Chapter VII, I argued that events are essentially changes in the objects they are in fact changes in. And in Chapter VI, I argued that events are essentially the exemplifyings or havings of certain of the dynamic properties of which they are in fact the havings. However, the individual essences of events, if indeed events have them, cannot be articulated solely in term of the subjects that are essential to them and those dynamic properties of which they are essentially the exemplifyings, becaue if they could be, then either events could not have twins (in the sense of Chapter VII, section 4.3) or events could recur. For, in such a case, if the twin, e', of some event, e, occurred, e' would be e; hence e would, since e and e' occur at different times, have recurred. But if events don't recur, then e could not have had a twin. But, it seems clear that

220

events can have twins and that events do not recur. So, in view of what would have to be the case if the essential subjects and dynamic properties were all that were involved in the individual essences of events, it seems reasonable to think either that events fail to have individual essences or that they do but their times of occurrence figure in. But if the time of occurrence of an event does figure in that event's individual essence, by being essential, it is difficult to see what else (in addition to its essential subject and dynamic properties) could be necessary to the specification of that individual essence. If some event is, in fact, an exemplifying by some object (essential to it) of some (essential) dynamic property at some time, it is, it seems, impossible to conceive of some distinct event's being an exemplifying by that object of that property at that time. And it is difficult to see how an event's time of occurrence could help to individuate that event across possible worlds without also being essential. So I am inclined to see (17) of Chapter VII as true:

(4) Possible worlds cannot be alike with respect to the truth and falsity of propositions concerning the existence of objects capable of non-relational change, the possession and non-possession of static properties by those objects, and the times at which those objects possess and fail to possess those properties, and alike with respect to the truth or falsity of the proposition that there are events, and yet be unalike with respect to the truth and falsity of propositions concerning which events occur.

There does not seem to me to be anything 'hidden' either about what it is, in general, to be an event or about what it is to be this or that particular event. Events are changes, they are the havings of dynamic properties by objects at times; and to be this or that event is just to be a having of this or that (essential) dynamic property by this or that (essentially involved) object at this or that particular minimal interval of time. There just does not seem to be anything more that is needed to pin down the 'individuality' of a particular event. And this suggests that events do have individual essences that are articulated in terms of events' essential subjects, dynamic properties, and times, and that events are completely determined by their minimal subjects, the dynamic properties of which they are essentially the havings, and their minimal times of occurrence. But this, again, does not imply that events are reducible to or are nothing but these other entities; for the occurrence of no event follows from the existence of those other entities. It is just that if there is an event which is an exemplifying of a certain (essential) dynamic property by a certain (essential) object at a certain (essential) time, then all the crucial and important facts about that event are determined by the facts about that object, property, and time.

2 CO-VARIANCE

I would like now to approach the issues just raised in a slightly different, but overlapping way. I hope to generate an idea of how entities belonging to one kind of thing can be so related to entities belonging to other kinds of things that the former can be said to be 'ontologically supervenient' on the latter.

Principles such as (1), (2) and (4) are interesting in that they embody an idea of a correlation of some sort between entities of one kind and entities of another kind (or other kinds): between sets and their (non-set) members, between physical objects and qualities, and between events and objects capable of non-relational change, properties and times.

Let us call a principle a 'co-variance' principle when it is an instance of the following schema:

(5) Possible worlds that are alike with respect to the existence in them of particular entites belonging to kinds K_1, $K_2, \ldots, K_n$ are also alike with respect to the existence in them of particular entities belong to kind K (if they are alike in having Ks in them at all).

Now, when the Ks are taken to be the sets, and $K_1, K_2, \ldots, K_n$ are taken to be comprised of the entities (other than sets) that can be members of sets, what we have as an instance (5) is just (1).

But now, let the Ks be the events, and K_1, K_2, and K_3 be, respectively, the objects capable of non-relational change, the static properties such objects can have and then lack, and times. The result is an instance of (5) that is clearly false. Possible worlds could contain the same changeable things, static properties, and times, and yet not contain the same events, for the same objects need not have and then lack any of the same properties at any of the same times. Indeed, one of those worlds might be such that nothing whatever occurs in it; that is, though that possible world may contain changeable objects, static properties, and times, no object in that world ever has and then lacks any static property.

It should be noted, however, that this false instance of (5) is *not* the same principle as (4), for (4) insists that for possible worlds to match with respect to events, they must not only be alike in containing just the same changeable objects, static properties, and times, they must also be alike in that the objects, properties and times are related to each other in the same way. That is, the same objects must have and then lack the same properties at the same times. So, if one wanted to formulate a schema of a co-variance principle capturing what is embodied in (4), it would not be (5) but (6):

(6) Possible worlds that are alike with respect to the existence in them of particular entities belonging to kinds K_1, K_2, . . ., K_n and with respect to the relations between the entities in them belonging to those kinds are also alike with respect to the existence in them of particular entities belonging to kind K (if they are alike in having Ks in them at all).

Of course, sets and their potential (non-set) members also satisfy this stronger co-variance condition, as well as the weaker (5), since the existence of sets is not tied in any way to their members' being related to each other in any fashion. Thus, while it is true in at least one sense that sets are very much like mere heaps of their members in that no arrangement of 'constituents' is necessary, this is not so of events and objects, properties, and times. Since (5) is false and (6) is true of them, events are not mere 'heaps' of their constituent objects, properties and times; they are 'structured'. The existence of no event follows from the mere existence of an appropriate object, dynamic property, and time, even given that there are, in general, events. Given the general existence of sets, however, the existence of a set is settled once the existence of its would-be members is settled.

That the weaker co-variance principle, (5), fails for physical objects and their qualities should be obvious. So, if any co-variance condition connects physical objects and qualities, it would have to be more like (6); for such a condition would insist that worlds alike not only with respect to containing the same qualities but also with respect to the co-exemplification of them (i.e., the same qualities are co-exemplified), are also alike in containing the same physical objects. But this is just (2) and seems false, since distinct physical objects could have exemplified all the same qualities.

Principles of the form (6), which speak of a relation between entities of one kind and those of other kinds (or another kind), should strike one as similar to more familiar co-variance principles that relate the possession by objects of properties belonging to one sort to their possession of properties of other sorts (or another sort). These more familiar principles seem to be instances of the following schema:

(7)   Objects cannot be alike with respect to the possession of properties belonging to sorts $D_1, D_2, \ldots,$ and D_n, and yet be unalike with respect to the possession of properties belonging to sort S.[6]

Among the true instances of (7) are principles that relate the diameter- to the circumference-properties of Euclidean circles, that relate the properties of being unmarried, of being male, of being of marriageable age, and of having never before been married to the property of being a bachelor, and that relate 'natural' or 'non-evaluative' properties to evaluative properties. Of these three examples, the last is unique in that the other two are 'convertible' while it is not. That is, for example, while it is true that objects alike in being unmarried males of marriageable age who have never been married before are alike in being bachelors, it is also true that objects alike in being bachelors are alike in being unmarried males of marriageable age who have never been married before. On the other hand, while it is true that objects alike with respect to their non-evaluative properties are alike with respect to their evaluative properties, it is not true that objects alike with respect to their evaluative properties are alike with respect to their non-evaluative properties.

3 DEPENDENCE

When it is seen that a relation of co-variance holds, what is seen is something calling for an explanation. Why should it be the case, for example, that objects having the same non-evaluative properties also have the same evaluative properties? Why should it be that possible worlds containing just the same objects that are not sets also contain just the same sets? The explanations offered in different cases may very well be different. In the diameter-circumference case, the explanation has to do with the geometric fact that there is a perfectly general relation holding between the magnitude of the circumference of a Euclidean circle and the magnitude of its diameter: $C=\pi d$. And that formula also explains why the co-variance principle is convertible. In the bachelor case, the explanation is that the property of being a bachelor just is the property of being an unmarried male of marriageable age who has never been married before. Of course, objects exemplifying the former property must be objects exemplifying the latter (and *vice versa*), for the former property is the latter (and this explains the convertibility of this co-variance principle). This is a different explanation from that offered in the previous case in two respects. First, circumference properties are not diameter properties; they just co-vary (in Euclidean circles) in a mathematically necessary way. Second, since the idea of the *dependence* of the possession of one property on that of another is the idea of an asymmetric relation, it cannot be said either that the circumference of a circle depends on its diameter or that a circle's diameter depends on its circumference. But, it does seem true that a person's being a bachelor depends on his having the properties of being unmarried, of being male, of being of marriageable age, and of never having been married before (and not the other way around).[7]

In the evaluative-non-evaluative case, the explanation for the co-variance must be different from those offered in the two previous cases. It is unlike the circle case but like the bachelor case, in that there is a clear sense in which the evaluative is dependent upon the non-evaluative; things have the evaluative features they have because of the non-evaluative features they have (and not *vice versa*). But, it is unlike the bachelor case in a way which is related to the convertibility of the co-variance principle for bachelors and the non-convertibility of the co-variance principle for the evaluative. The non-convertibility of the latter is due to the fact that the dependence of the evaluative on the non-evaluative is a defeasible dependence. That is, though the goodness, for example, of a thing is due to the non-evaluative features it has, its goodness can be spoiled by the addition of another feature. But, the dependence of bacherlorhood on the bachelor-making properties is a non-defeasible dependence; that is, if someone has the properties in virtue of which he is a bachelor, the possession of no other property (in addition to them) is in any way relevant to whether or not he is a bachelor.

What explains the truth of the co-variance principle relating sets and other entities? Here, the explanation begins, I suppose, with a reminder of some of the usual principles of set theory. And what those principles suggest is that there is a relation of dependence (despite the convertibility of the co-variance principle) of some sort or other, holding between the sets and other entities. There is a sense in which the existence of sets, in general, is dependent on the existence of other objects,[8] and in which the existence of some particular set is dependent on the existence of the particular objects that are its would-be members. This dependence ensures that the co-variance principle for sets is satisfied, and it, together with the fact that if there are sets at all they exist in all possible worlds (in which there are entities of any other sort), ensures the convertibility of that co-variance principle.

The explanation of the co-variance of events and objects capable of non-relational change, static properties, and times is different in at least one way from the explanation of the co-variance principle for sets. Given the existence of sets in a given possible world and the usual principles of set theory, the mere existence in that world of objects guarantees the existence in that world of sets of those objects. But given the possibility of the occurrence of events in a possible world, the mere existence in that world of objects capable of non-relational change, static properties and times does not guarantee that in that world any events occur. That events occur in that world is guaranteed only if objects have and then lack static properties at times. The sense in which it is true that the occurrence of events in any possible world depends on there being objects capable of non-relational change, static properties and times is that events occur only because such objects have and then lack static properties at times. And the 'because' is to be understood in terms of the very idea of an event: to be an event is to be a non-relational change in an object. Now, while the co-variance principle for events is convertible, the dependence of events on objects, properties and times is not matched by a dependence of changeable objects, properties and times on the occurrence of events. The non-relationlly changeable things, properties and times are not things dependent for their existence on the occurrence of events; it is surely possible that no changeable thing ever has and then lacks any static property.[9]

4 THE POSSIBILITY OF REDUCTION

Consider the evaluative and the non-evaluative again. A co-variance condition holds: things alike in their non-evaluative features must be alike with respect to their, say, goodness. And a dependence condition holds as well: things that are good are so because of the non-evaluative features, features from among those with which goodness co-varies, they have. One might, in the face of these ideas, be inclined to infer that there must then be some non-evaluative properties the possesson of which by any object ensures that it is good. And having drawn that inference, one would insist that goodness was reducible to, analysable in terms of, or necessarily co-extensive with some (perhaps complex) non-evaluative property. But that inference is fallacious. The fallacious inference is one from the claim that, for each good thing, there are non-evaluative properties that it has the possession of which makes it good, to the claim that there are non-evaluative properties such that any thing's having them makes it good. The fallacy committed is the same one that would allow one to infer from the truth that, for every number, m, there is a number, n, such that $n > m$, the falsehood that there is a number, n, such that for every number, m, $n > m$.

Now despite the fact that such an inference is fallacious, it might be the case that both premise and conclusion are true. This is, I think, how Aristotle saw things when he said that every action aims at some goal and then said that there is a goal at which every action aims (*Nichomachean Ethics*, 1094a). And this is, I take it, how things stand with the property of being a bachelor and the properties of being unmarried, of being male, etc. That is, first, things alike with respect to the possession of those bachelor-making properties are alike with respect to the possession of the property of being a bachelor. Second, for each thing that is a bachelor, there are some bachelor-making properties that it has and the having of which makes it a bachelor; being a bachelor is dependent of the possession of those bachelor-making properties with which the property of being a bachelor co-varies. And third, there are properties, namely those bachelor-making ones, the having of which by any thing guarantees that it is a bachelor. And the reason for that is that the property of being a bachelor just is the complex property of being an unmarried male of marriageable age who has never been married before. It should be noted that if there were, in some sense, no 'complex' properties (but still a property of being a bachelor), then the identification of the property of being a bachelor and the property of being an unmarried male of marriageable age who has never been married before would not be possible. There would be a necessarily true claim saying that anyone having the property of being a bachelor also has the properties of being unmarried, of being male, etc. But there would be no complex property that was the property of being a bachelor; and the property of being a bachelor could not be identical with the properties of being unmarried, of being male, etc., for no thing is identical with things.

Is this how things stand with respect to the evaluative and the non-evaluative? I think not; there seems to be no non-evaluative property, however complex, the possession of which by any object guarantees that it is, say, good. Goodness is only defeasibly determined by the non-evaluative properties with respect to which it co-varies and is dependent; it always seems possible that some otherwise good thing should have its goodness spoiled by the addition of some new non-evaluative property. But if this is so, one might object that this sort of defeasibility is incompatible with the co-variance of goodness and the non-evaluative. For let two good things be alike with respect to the properties with which goodness co-varies; now let one of them, but not the other, possess a further feature that defeats its goodness. Then the co-variance condition will fail, since the two things will be alike with respect to the properties with which goodness co-varies, but will not be alike with respect to being good.

This objection works, however, only on the assumption that the properties with which goodness co-varies and on which goodness depends include *only* the good-making properties, only those properties the possession of which contributes positively towards a thing's being good. And this assumption can and ought to be denied. A thing's goodness should be thought of as determined not only by which good-making features it has, but also by which bad-making features it has. Thus, with that understanding, it seems that while satisfying a co-variance principle and a dependence principle, the evaluative fails to be reducible to or analysable in terms of the non-evaluative. In so far as this is so, we can say that evaluative features are not non-evaluative features, but that they 'emerge' from non-evaluative features. And what emerges is something new and distinct from that from which it emerges. The satisfaction of co-variance and dependence principles by the evaluative and the non-evaluative, but value-relevant, features of things, together with a failure of reduction of the former to the latter, is what I take the 'supervenience' of the evaluative on the non-evaluative to consist in.[10]

Now sets and their members satisfy a co-variance and a dependence principle. What of the possibility of reduction? If there are sets, their existence is established by an existential proof. And the theory of those entities is in part given by the criterion of identity whose identity condition specifies types of properties that both figure importantly in saying what sets are and are connected in important ways with the premises of the existential proof of the existence of sets.[11] In so far as what is established is the existence of entities whose criterion of identity is distinct from the criteria of identity for the entities comprising other kinds, we have a reason to believe that no set is identical with any entity belonging to one of those other kinds. On the usual understanding of sets, sets are not aggregates; they are not pluralities of their members. Thus, while sets co-vary with and are dependent for their existence on the members of other kinds, the sets are not reducible to objects of other kinds. Sets can be said to 'emerge' from their members; and what emerges is something new and distinct from what they emerge from. Sets are, in this sense, 'ontologically supervenient' on their members.

I should think that the situation with respect to events and non-relationally changeable objects, dynamic properties and intervals of time is analogous. Events co-vary with those objects, properties and times (in the sense of (4)), and are dependent on them. But events are not times, dynamic properties or non-relationally changeable things.[12] Nor are event aggregates or sets of such objects, properties and times. The existence of events is established, if at all, by an existential proof whose premises are statements reporting that some object changes non-relationally; events are the changes objects undergo when they change non-relationally. Events are thus the havings of dynamic properties by objects at times. And that part of the theory of events, which is embodied in a criterion of identity for events, shows that events belong to a kind distinct from those to which things other than events belong. And in so far as the events constitute a metaphysical category, there are no entities forming a kind of which the events are a species. So, it seems plausible to think that events emerge from non-relationally changeable things, dynamic properties and times in so far as such objects have such properties at times. And what emerges is new and distinct from what events emerge from. Events are, in this sense, ontologically supervenient on objects capable of non-relational change, the dynamic properties such objects can have, and the intervals of time at which such objects have such properties.

5 CONCLUDING SPECULATIONS

It appears to be the case that sets have individual essences; if a set, s, has such-and-such objects as members, then, in every possible world, a set has those objects as members if and only if that set is s. And events too, it appears, have individual essences: if an event, e, is $[x, \phi, t]$, then, in every possible world, an event is $[x, \phi, t]$ if and only if it is e. But physical objects do not appear

230

to have individual essences. In addition, both events and sets can be said to be ontologically supervenient on other entities. Events and sets emerge from but are distinct from those entities on which they supervene. Physical objects, however, do not seem to be supervenient on any other entities. If these cases are typical, then it would seem that the entities comprising a kind, K, are such that they have individual essences if and only if there are entities, belonging to kinds distinct from K, on which the Ks are supervenient. But if this is so, why is it so?

It should be noticed that the principles specifying individual essences are always ones that specify those individual essences in terms of entities distinct from those for which the principle is given. Indeed, in the cases at hand, those other entities are just those on which the entities that are being provided with individual essences are supervenient. Now, the fact that the Ks are supervenient on other entities is a sign that the Ks are dependent entities, that they emerge from those other entities and are not, in some sense, 'basic' things. In Chapter I, I tried to give a sketch of conditions under which a group of entities form a metaphysical category of things. What the discussion here suggests is that Ks may form a metaphysical category and, hence, be basic in the sense that they belong to no broader kind for which a criterion of identity can be given, without being basic entities in the sense of not being dependent for their existence on the existence of other things. Events and sets may be basic in the former sense and not in the latter. On the other hand, the fact that the Ks have individual essences is, in a way, a sign of manageability. Entities that have individual essences are such that there is nothing hidden, so to speak, about them; what properties they have and could have are facts which are, at least in principle, accessible. (Of course, the individual essences of sets make reference to their members, which may be physical objects, things which fail to have individual essences and about whose individuality there is always something hidden and inaccessible. And, in that sense, there is a limitation on what is not hidden about sets. Similarly for events, whose subjects are physical objects.) How convenient for us! The metaphysically manageable things are the things that emerge. There is a certain air of a set-up here; things look too neatly arranged. It almost appears that doubt should be cast, in the light of this coincidence, on the very

231

idea that these emergent, supervenient things really exist. But, that certain entities are supervenient on others does not show that they are any less real than the entities from which they emerge. It is not as if, being emergent, they could be easily dispensed with, done away with, or done without. Perhaps they can be dispensed with, but it won't be easy. Such entities are said to exist because they figure in the best explanations of how it is possible for what is obvious to us to be true. They can be dispensed with or done without only by finding better explanations. But that, at least according to the friends of such entities, won't be easy.

Another point worthy of note is this. In the case of sets, we know both their criterion of identity and a principle specifying their individual essences. And the concepts drawn on in the articulating of that criterion are the same as those employed in that principle. In a way, this should strike one as quite natural. After all, the criterion of identity provides us with a way of saying what it is to be a set, any set; and the principle tells us what it is to be some particular set. It would be peculiar, I should think, were it to turn out that what it was to be this or that set did not have anything to do with what it was to be any old set. As it turns out, to be a set is to be a thing with members (more or less); and to be this or that set is to be a thing with these or those members. Things are analogous for events. Events are identical (more or less) just in case they are the same change, that is, the exemplifying by the same subject of the same dynamic property at the same time; to be an event is to be a change, an exemplifying by some object of some dynamic property at some time. And a principle giving the individual essences of events draws on these same concepts: to be this or that set just is to be an exemplifying by this or that object of this or that dynamic property at this or that time. So, in the two cases at hand, the principle giving individual essences draws on the same resources as does the criterion of identity, and is to be read off that criterion of identity by 'particularizing' it (in the sense that, e.g., sets are identical when they have the same members, and sets essentially and uniquely have the members they have).

But in the case of physical objects, this parallelism fails to hold. The criterion of identity for physical objects is that physical objects are identical if and only if they have the same spatio-temporal history. If the pattern held, we would expect that each physical object should essentially have the spatio-temporal history it in fact has. But we do not expect this, and it is manifestly not so. Each physical object could have been located at certain times at places other than those at which it was at those times; and a physical object could have had the spatio-temporal history that some other, distinct physical object in fact had. Why does the pattern exhibited by both events and sets not hold in the case of physical objects? Perhaps the reason has something to do with the idea that there are no entities on which physical objects are ontologically supervenient. If there were entities from which the physical objects emerged, then perhaps there would be some hope of pinning down the individuality of physical objects; otherwise, there would seem to be nothing in terms of which to capture that idea.

Perhaps it could be shown that the pattern does hold for physical objects. It would, though, have to be shown that the usual criterion of identity for physical objects is, while perhaps not false, not deep enough. And it would have to be shown that the right criterion will show that physical objects do emerge from entities of other sorts and that physical objects do have individual essences expressible in terms of those entities from which they emerge.

I do not know which entities, in addition to the sets and the events, will turn out to be ontologically supervenient on others. What is clear, however, is that not all entities can be ontologically supervenient on others. There must be some things that are not ontologically supervenient on others; and those things will, I conjecture, fail to have individual essences and will form a kind whose members are things whose individuality is inaccessible to us. But whichever those things are, they are not events.

Appendix

SOME LINGERING ISSUES

I have tried in this book to motivate, explicate, and make plausible a theory about the metaphysics of events. It is not, however, a complete theory. There are difficulties in the theory I have not anticipated or dealt with in a satisfactory way; and there are consequences of my view for other philosophical issues that I have not discussed at all. In addition, there are questions about events, which should be addressed by any theory about events, that I have not addressed at all or at all adequately. In this short appendix, I want to mention a few, but by no means all, of these questions. I should say here that my not dealing at all with certain issues and my dealing only cursorily with others is not an indication that I regard those issues as unimportant or trivial. I fear, in fact, that their depth and difficulty may explain why I have had little or nothing to say about them.

1 THE EXISTENCE OF EVENTS

Perhaps the issue most glaringly left unresolved in this book is the very existence of events. There has been here no serious discussion of an existential proof of their existence, and no serious discussion of the inductive support that should accompany such a proof. My excuse, offered in Chapter I, for this omission is that I have nothing of interest to add to the discussions of this matter already in print; I might also say that I wanted to write a book on the metaphysics of events and not on the semantics of sentences that allegedly entail the existence of events. So, while the very existence of events is left largely untouched in this book, it should be clear how I think that issue comes out in the end. However, if what I have said in Chapters I and II is right, a persuasive case for the existence of events must consist not only of a justification of a claim of validity for an existential proof of the existence of events, but also of a theory of events, turning crucially around a criterion of identity and a related conception of what is to be an event. Perhaps this book should be seen not as one about what events are like but as one about what events would be like if there were any; an exercise in what might be called 'hypothetico-descriptive metaphysics'.

A theory about what events would be like if there were any cannot, however, be seen as independent of the sort of existential proof that could or would be given for the existence of events. Any such theory must somehow be responsive to the considerations in virtue of which it is thought that there are events. I have felt compelled to propose the theory I did in part because an existential proof of the existence of events that I believe will in the end be seen to be valid is one whose premise is some obvious, commonsensical claim reporting that some object *changes*. If such a proof is correct, the existence of events is required in order for it to be possible that certain obvious claims, reporting that some object changes, be true. It would be incredible, I should think, if the events so required were not the changes objects undergo when they change (non-relationally). Thus, it was in part because the events I think there are are among the things that must exist if objects change that I sought a theory of events that would exploit the idea that events are changes.

If one thought that the existence of events figured as part of the best explanation of the truth and meaning of claims of sorts very different from those reporting change in objects, one would expect a rather different theory of events to emerge.[1] There would, of course, have to be important connections and similarities among the theories of events that emerge from the various existential proofs in order that it be the case that those theories are, indeed, theories about the same entities. But how different could such theories be and still be rival theories of events? For there to be a straightforward answer to this question, there must be conditions under which it is clearly true that theories T_1 and T_2 are theories about the same things, but attribute different features to them; and I am not certain that there is a systematic distinction between disagreements over what features to attribute to a given thing and disagreements over which thing is in question. I am confident in varying degrees that the theories discussed in Chapter III are about the same entities my theory is about. But, it is unclear what the full range of competitors really is. My own view is that the range of competitors is limited to those theories that construe the concept of an event to be importantly connected with the concept of change. But, it is not clear how much such a restriction rules out.

2 TOWARDS A THEORY OF EVENT-COMPOSITION

Every event, according to my theory, is either an atomic event or composed of atomic events. (This is short for: every event is either an atomic event or composed of events that are either atomic or composed of. . . .) Indeed, even the atomic events can be construed as composed of other atomic events. Some events are composed of other events occurring in some temporal sequence. For example, an object's moving from a place p_1 to a place p_2 may be composed of that object's moving halfway from p_1 to p_2 and its moving the rest of the way.[2] And some events are composed of events that occur simultaneously. At some times during which a train is moving along the tracks, there occur the engine's moving, the dining car's moving, and so on; and those events occur simultaneously and are the events of which the train's moving at those times is composed. And, of course, there are events composed of others, some of which are simultaneous with others of which are not; the sinking of The Ship of Theseus seems a clear case of this, since some but not all of the ship's parts sink at the same time.

Is it the case that for any events, e_1, e_2, . . ., and e_n, there is an event, e, that is composed of e_1, e_2, . . ., and e_n? It is obvious that this universal generalisation if false.[3] There just is no event composed of the latest eruption of Vesuvius, the flowing of ink from my pen as I write this sentence, and the moving of Jupiter in its orbit in 1944. And there is no event composed of all the world's avalanches.[4] Thus, an important problem is that of stating conditions under which it is the case that when there are events, $e_1, \ldots, e_n$, there is an event, e, that is composed of them. I should like to consider some suggestions as to what those conditions might or might not be.

For an event to be composed of other events, it is not sufficient that those others occur either simultaneously or continuously; there is no event composed of a ball's getting colder and its rotating at the same time, and there is no event composed of that ball's rotating and a match's lighting immediately thereafter. Nor is such a condition necessary. An event composed of other events may be interrupted; my walking from my office to my class may be interrupted by my stopping to talk to a colleague.

Whatever precisely is meant by saying of some events that they are of the same sort, it seems clear that it is neither a necessary nor a sufficient condition of there being an event composed of other events that those others be of the same sort (unless, of course, there are such sorts as 'event of which a certain event is in part composed').[5] Some events of the same sort surely do compose events; my hittings of a tennis ball against a wall one afternoon are the events of which my practising my backhand stroke that afternoon was composed. But, there was no event composed (even in part) of my sneezing on January 22, 1976, and my sneezing on November 24, 1981. That events' being of the same sort is not a necessary condition of their composing some event is shown by the fact that a robot's cleaning of my house is composed of its vacuuming of the carpets, its dusting of the furniture, and its taking out of the rubbish. Of course, the issues of the necessity and/or sufficiency of events' being of the same sort to there being an event composed of them are unclear to the extent that the notion 'some sort', applied to events, is unclear. Brand's analysis of that notion,[6] applied to the present issue, would make the issue of whether there was a certain event composed of others a contextual matter, if being of the same sort were a necessary condition. And this would not be, I should think, a welcome result. A notion of events' being of the same sort may be available in terms of the quality spaces in which things change; but my inclination is to think that the idea that the events of which another is composed must be of the same sort, in that sense, would impose too restrictive a condition on event composition.

It is surely not a sufficient condition for events, $e_1, \ldots, e_n$, to be events of which an event, e, is composed that the e_is have the same subject. There is, it seems obvious, no event composed of a ball's getting colder and its rotating (whether simultaneously or not). Nor is it a necessary condition; the sinking of The Ship of Theseus is composed of the sinkings of its several (distinct) parts.

So far, we have seen only negative results concerning the necessary or sufficient conditions under which events may be those of which another is composed. But a positive result can be obtained that it connected with the subjects of events. According to the theory developed in this book, events are the changes that objects undergo when they change non-relationally. Thus, for each event, there is an object that that event is a change in. So if an event, e, is an event composed of other events, there must be a thing that e is a change in. If $e_1, e_2, \ldots, e_n, \ldots$ are the events of which some event, e, is allegedly composed, and if the subjects of the e_is are not all the same thing, then it is difficult to see how those events could compose an event, e, unless e's subject is a thing composed of the subjects of the events, the e_is, of which e is composed. If the subjects of the e_is are not things of which some other thing is composed, then there is no event composed of the e_is; for in that case, the allegedly composed event would not be a change that any thing undergoes when it changes.

So, there is no event which is Smith's and Jones's greeting each other and which is composed of Smith's saying 'Hello, Jones' and Jones's saying 'Hello, Smith' (on the same occasion). The greeting, if there were such an event, would not be a change in any thing if, that is, there is no thing composed of Smith and Jones. Similarly, consider a double star system, two stars rotating around each other. Since I am not the least inclined to think that there is an object composed of the two stars, I am not inclined to think that there is an event that is composed of the movement of the one star and the movement of the other. Of course, there are the events of Smith's and Jones's greeting of each other, and there are the movements of the two stars around each other; but there is no event which is Smith's and Jones's greeting each other, and no event which is the movement of the two stars around each other.

In dealing with these issues, it is important to keep in mind that the problem is that of finding conditions under which there are events that are *composed* of a plurality of events; the problem is not that of finding conditions under which there are events that *are* pluralities of events; for there are no such events. There is, to be sure, the sinking of The Ship of Theseus, and there are events each of which is a sinking of one of that ship's parts; and the former is composed of the latter. But there is no event that is, i.e., is identical with, the sinkings of the parts.

It is obvious that there are pluralities of events. There is just as much reason to believe that there are the sinkings of the parts of The Ship of Theseus, the world's avalanches, and the fallings of snowflakes in Grosse Pointe on Wednesday as there is to believe that there are the horses in the field, all the world's tigers and the snowflakes that fall. But, while there are the horses in the field, there is no such thing as the horses in the field. And thus, no event can be a change in such a thing, the horses, though there can be events that are changes in them. Similarly, there were the sinkings of the parts of The Ship of Theseus. But if there were an event that was the sinking of those parts, it would surely be an event whose subject was either The Ship of Theseus' parts or The Ship of Theseus. But, it could not be the latter, since identical events must have the same subject and The Ship of Theseus is not identical with its parts. And it cannot be the former, since there is no such thing as the parts of The Ship of Theseus. There are pluralities of events; but no plurality of events is an event.

If there were events which were pluralities of events, it seems clear that their subjects, if they have them, would have to be pluralities or aggregates. But I am inclined to believe that no aggregate of things is a thing. Hence, when an event is allegedly a change in an aggregate, there is no thing for that event to be a change in. Thus, in so far as every event is a change in some thing, there is no event which is a change in an aggregate. Of course one might agree that if every event is a change in some thing and that if no aggregate or plurality is a thing, then there are no events that are pluralities of events. Still, one might then suggest that there are events that are pluralities but that they are subjectless events. And such a suggestion is not the radical one of suggesting that there are events which are in no way connected with changes in things; after all, each of the parts of a 'plural'-event may have a subject. I suppose I see no harm in such a proposal except that it seems entirely gratuitous and ill-motivated.

After all, what reason could there be for thinking that there are events which are pluralities (or aggregates or sums) of other events that would not also be a reason for thinking that there are physical objects which are pluralities (or aggregates or sums) of other physical objects? If there could not be such a reason, then of course either such events do have aggregational or summational objects as subjects or there are no such events. I tend towards the latter alternative.

To the extent that we can sometimes get away with speaking of pluralities as if they were individual things, we can sometimes get away with speaking of pluralities of events as if they were individual events. We do talk of the falling of snow and the boiling of some water; and such talk is facilitated by the ease with which we speak of the snow that fell last night, the water in the kettle and the tea in China as if they were individual things. But talk of matter and quantities thereof is, like talk of the furniture in the room and the horses in the field, really talk of pluralities of things. And in so far as that is so, there can no more be an event which is the tea's brewing than there can be an event that is the grazing of horses. The falling of the snow must be thought of, not as an event composed of the fallings of the snowflakes, since the snow is not a thing composed of the snowflakes, nor as an event which is a plurality of snowflake fallings, but as a plurality of snowflake fallings. Similarly, the gold's melting is not an event but a plurality of events in which each event in that plurality is a change in one of the things the gold is a plurality of.

In this brief discussion of conditions under which events compose other events, the only necessary condition discovered is that the composing events either have the same subject as that of the composed event or have as subjects objects of which the composed event's subject is composed. If there are other necessary conditions or if there are any sufficient conditions, I do not know what they are. We have here an unresolved issue that clearly is of importance and requires more study.

3 SUBJECTLESS EVENTS

By connecting the concept of an event to the idea of an object's changing (non-relationally), I have conceived of events as having subjects, of being changes in things. For each event, there must be a thing it is a change in. And I have been rather strict, as section 2 of this Appendix has demonstrated, about what is to count as a thing and hence as a possible subject of an event. No event is a change in matter, though there are events that are changes in things that are made of matter. No event is a change in things, though an event can be a change in an object composed of those things. In addition, the only things that can be the subjects of events are those which can have and then lack static properties in such a way that in so doing they change non-relationally and survive. Thus, for example, we cannot, I think, take literally talk of a change in 'the situation' or 'the facts'. Such 'things' do not survive change; any change, so to speak, creates a new situation, a new set of facts, a new state of affairs. Speaking of changes in the situation is like speaking of changes in the colour of an object: the colour does not change, redness does not become blueness; rather the object comes to have a different colour. Similarly, the state of the world does not change; things change, thereby creating a new state for the world to be in.

Of course, one cannot always tell what the subject of an event is just by looking at some description of the event. The casting of a shadow is not an event whose subject is a shadow; after all, there are no shadows, there are surfaces on which not much light shines because some object is between it and the light source. A change in 'the weather' surely must give way to changes in air molecules' mean kinetic energy, etc. And an increase in the rate of inflation is surely not an event that is a change in some (impure) number, but is rather to be thought of in terms of events that are changes in consumers and price setters.[7] As for 'changes in the magnetic field' and 'changes in the gravitational structure of spacetime',[8] I am a bit ambivalent. Of course, if there are no such things as magnetic fields or spacetime, then talk of changes in them will have to be parsed out as changes in magnetized objects and things spatio-temporally arranged. Even if there are such things, however, it is unclear whether, for example, spacetime is a thing composed of spacetime points or is just a plurality of such points. If the former, then spacetime could be the subject of an event; if the latter, not.

In any case, notably absent in this book is a direct argument for the claim that all events have subjects, though it is obvious that much that I have had to say about events hangs on the truth of that claim. The concepts deployed in the construction of my theory have made it impossible, I should think, that there be subjectless events, events that are not changes in something. I suppose that I could be said to have argued that there are no subjectless events in so far as I have suggested that events are changes, that changes are exemplifyings, and that there can be no exemplifyings unless there are things that exemplify. If such an argument were accused of being question-begging, I think I would find it hard to see precisely what question was being begged. I do not see how to get a grip on the concept of an event without seeing the concept of an event as bound up with the concept of change; and I do not see how to get a grip on the concept of change without seeing change as what objects undergo. But this is just to insist that the points from which my theory starts (though perhaps not where it ends) are obvious truths. As I see it, to suppose that there are subjectless events is to suppose that there are events that are not changes; and I don't think I understand such a supposition.

Those who think or have thought that events are among the basic entities of the world, in the sense that they are entities the existence of which is not dependent on the existence of entities belonging to other kinds, must, I should think, take the view that there can be subjectless events. What is clear to me is that such entities are not the events for which I have attempted to provide a theory.

NOTES

I EXISTENTIAL PROOFS

1 Of course, if there fails to be a sharp boundary to be drawn between beliefs about what the facts are and beliefs about how to understand the facts, then there will fail to be a sharp boundary between problems identifiable as philosophical and those identifiable as factual or scientific.

2 That there is tension between these ideas is suggested by Robert Nozick, in *Philosophical Explanations* (Cambridge, Mass.: Harvard University Press, 1981), pp. 4–8. But see also Alvin Goldman's review of Nozick's book, in *Philosophical Review*, vol. XCII, no. 1 (January 1983), p. 82.

3 There may be claims, reporting facts of different sorts that may be appealed to. A friend of properties may be impressed not by similarities, but by comparisons, and a friend of events impressed not by change but by causation or recurrence. How different can the facts appealed to by different friends of φs be and it still be the case that it's the same φs they are all friends of? I think there can be no firm answer to questions like this, since, for there to be one, there would have to be a clear distinction between disagreements concerning what φs are like and disagreements concerning the extension of the predicate 'is a φ'. I have a bit more to say on this subject in the Appendix, section 1.

4 In *Acts and Other Events* (Ithaca, New York: Cornell University Press, 1977), pp. 13ff., Judith Jarvis Thomson says that it is obvious that there are actions (which she takes to be a species of event) and that a proof of their existence is unnecessary. However, she does produce (see pp. 13ff.) what amount to two existential proofs. The suspicions she believes likely to be aroused by them – suspicions expressed in the form of questions like 'But what *are* hand-wavings?' – are addressed when the 'significance' argument is under discussion.

243

The fact that a foe of events is likely to be unmoved, when told that there are events because there are fallings and that there are fallings because Jack fell, is beside the point. If the friend of events is right in thinking that his argument is sound and that there really are such things (events) that the foe of events thought there weren't, then an unmoved foe of events is just stubborn.

5 See for example, the 'Comments' on Davidson's 'The logical form of action sentences', by E. J. Lemmon, Hector Castañeda and R. M. Chisholm, in N. Rescher (ed.), *The Logic of Decision and Action* (Pittsburgh: University of Pittsburgh Press, 1967), pp. 96–114; Zeno Vendler, 'Causal relations', *Journal of Philosophy*, vol. LXIV (1967), pp. 704–13; J. Cargile, 'Davidson's notion of logical form', *Inquiry*, vol. 13 (1970), pp. 129–39; R. Clarke, 'Concerning the logic of predicate modifiers', in Davidson and Harman (eds), *Semantics of Natural Language* (Dordrecht: D. Reidel, 1972), pp. 127–41; T. Horgan, 'The case against events', *Philosophical Review*, vol. LXXXVII (1978), pp. 28–47; Altman, Bradie and Miller, 'On doing without events', *Philosophical Studies*, vol. 36 (1979), pp. 301–9; P. M. S. Hacker, 'Events, ontology, and grammar', *Philosophy*, vol. 57 (1982), pp. 477–86; B. D. Katz, 'Perils of an uneventful world', *Philosophia*, vol. 13 (1983), pp. 1–12.

6 First published in *The Logic of Decision and Action, op. cit.*, pp. 81–95; reprinted, with comments, in Davidson's *Essays on Actions and Events* (Oxford: Oxford University Press, 1980), pp. 105–48.

7 First published in *Journal of Philosophy*, vol. LXIV (1967), pp. 691–703; reprinted in *Essays in Actions and Events, op. cit.*, pp. 149–62.

8 'Fairly straightforwardly', for what (5) entails, according to Davidson, is that there is something that was a buttering of the toast by Jones; and that entails that there are actions. Not enough structure is uncovered by Davidson so that (1)'s entailing of 'There are butterings' is explained. That defect is, I believe, easily remediable.

9 Reprinted in David Lewis, *Philosophical Papers*, vol. 1 (New York: Oxford University Press, 1983), pp. 3–9.

10 I do not insist on or require a possible worlds approach to the semantics of modal notions, though *I* shall make free use of the idioms of possible world semantics throughout this book. By my use of modal notions, what I have in mind is a quantified modal logic of the strength of S5, given a Kripke-like semantics in which the Barcan formula – $(x)\square Fx \supset \square(x)Fx$ – fails.

11 See section 1 of the Appendix for what I have in mind by a theory about φs' being responsive to the premises of the existential proof that establishes that there are φs.

II CRITERIA OF IDENTITY AND THE NATURES OF OBJECTS

1 Myles Brand, in his papers, 'Particulars, events, and actions', in

Brand and Walton (eds), *Action Theory* (Dordrecht: D. Reidel, 1976), pp. 133–56, and 'Identity conditions for events', *American Philosophical Quarterly*, vol. 14 (1977), pp. 329–37, was among the first to have interesting things to say about what criteria of identity must be like. Some of my remarks will parallel things Brand has said.

2 See, for example, Eli Hirsch, *The Concept of Identity* (New York: Oxford University Press, 1982), p. 3.

3 That a criterion of identity is such a definition seems to be the view of both Baruch Body, in his *Identity and Essence* (Princeton, New Jersey: Princeton University Press, 1980), p. 64, and J. E. Tiles, in 'Davidson's criterion of event identity', *Analysis* 36 (1976), p. 185.

4 See P. T. Geach's *Reference and Generality* (Ithaca, New York: Cornell University Press, 1962), pp. 39ff. for arguments in favour of the 'relativity' of identity, and David Wiggins's *Sameness and Substance* (Cambridge, Mass.: Harvard University Press, 1980), for replies to those arguments.

5 This isn't quite right, for there is a sense in which the identity condition in Leibniz's Law does specify a proper subset of all the properties existent things can have; it specifies the unit set whose sole member is the relation of having all properties in common. One way around this would be to insist that a criterion of identity's condition of identity be expressed by the use of a quantifier ranging over properties and that in any proper identity criterion, one that is stronger than Leibniz's Law, the quantifier range over only a proper subset of the totality of properties. Thus, in filling out 'R(x,y)', we would get something like this: $(x)(y)(\phi x \wedge \phi y \supset (x=y \equiv (F)(F\varepsilon S \supset (Fx \equiv Fy))))$, where S is a proper subset of all properties. This ploy comes up again in section 1.6 of this chapter.

6 Brody, in *Identity and Essence, op. cit.*, is sceptical, though his scepticism seems ill-founded. In the case of events, it seems inductively based on a survey of a few candidates (Kim's and Davidson's) that he finds defective (pp. 65–70). In the case of physical objects, his rejection of the usual criterion of identity seems based on a confusion of that principle with one concerned with the persistence of physical objects over time (pp. 43ff.).

7 I do wish to point out here that the mere fact that objects that are alike with respect to their spatio-temporal features cannot be unalike with respect to their colour or taste does *not* show that colour- and taste-properties are reducible to, emerge from, or are supervenient on the spatio-temporal properties of objects. I shall have more to say about this matter in Chapter VIII.

8 This is the revision in the form of a criterion of identity alluded to in section 1.1.

9 If the property of being a ϕ and the property of being a ψ are essences, then so is the property of being either a ϕ or a ψ. And, I am assuming that the property of being a physical object and that of being a set are essences.

10 The following will also do: $\square(x)(y)(x$ is a physical object or a set $\wedge$ y

is a physical object or a set $\supset$ (x=y $\equiv$ (if x and y are physical objects, then R(x,y), and if x and y are sets, then R'(x,y)))).

11 Sets have no spatio-temporal history in the sense that they do not have spatial locations at times.

12 My thanks to Peter van Inwagen for pointing out this issue to me.

13 For example, Myles Brand believes that both physical objects and events are importantly spatio-temporal, and, thus, that sameness of spatio-temporal location figures in, for him, the conditions of identity for both the physical objects and the events.

14 Brand makes this point in 'Particulars, events, and actions', *op. cit.*, p. 137.

15 In 'The individuation of events', reprinted in Davidson's *Essays on Actions and Events* (Oxford: Oxford University Press, 1980), p. 179.

16 There is a good discussion of circularity complaints against criteria of identity in D. Katz, 'Is the causal criterion of event identity circular?', *Australasian Journal of Philosophy*, vol. 56 (1978), pp. 255–9.

17 See N. Wilson, 'Facts, events, and their identity conditions', *Philosophical Studies*, vol. 25 (1974), pp. 303–4, and Michael Tye, 'Brand on event identity', *Philosophical Studies*, vol. 35 (1979), p. 82. But see Brand, 'On Tye's "Brand on event identity"', *Philosophical Studies*, vol. 36 (1979), pp. 61–8.

18 See Brand, 'Particulars, events, and actions', *op. cit.*, p. 138.

19 If a criterion of identity for the φs did provide a way of finding out whether any statement of the form 'a=b', when a and b are φs, is true or false, then, since for every φ, a, and any true statement, s, a=(ιx)(x=a ∧ s is true), a criterion of identity would provide a way of finding out whether any statement whatever is true or false. And this is absurd. This argument is Davidson's; see 'The individuation of events', *op. cit.*, p. 172.

20 I hasten to add that it is not a trivial matter to determine whether this constraint is met by a proposed criterion of identity.

21 Tiles, *op. cit.*, p. 185, suspects that something like this is true of events.

22 This sums up how I understand Quine's dictum so that it comes out true. Strawson, however, seems unable to find a metaphysical construal of 'no entity without identity', other than taking it to mean 'every entity is self-identical', under which it is true. See his 'Entity and identity', in H. D. Lewis (ed.), *Contemporary British Philosophy*, Fourth Series (London: Allen & Unwin, 1976), pp. 193–219. Strawson's view, however, seems based on some misunderstandings. He seems to want to take a criterion of identity for the φs as a way of telling when we have one or more than one φ (p. 194); he seems to take every noun phrase (e.g., 'Jones's way of walking') as denoting something, and to think that some of those things (e.g., ways of walking) are such that we do not know or care about their identity conditions (p. 195). A quite different, epistemological construal of Quine's dictum is advanced by Dale Gottlieb, in 'No entity without

identity', Shahan & Swayer (eds), *Essays on the Philosophy of W. V. Quine* (Norman: University of Oklahoma Press, 1979), pp. 79–96.

III SOME THEORIES OF EVENTS

1 One current theory about events that I will not be discussing is Roderick M. Chisholm's (see his 'Events and propositions', *Noûs* 4 (1970), pp. 15–24, and 'States of affairs again', *Noûs* 5 (1971), pp. 179–89). My reason for not doing so has nothing to do with the intrinsic interest that there is in that view; rather it has to do with the fact that I am interested in proposing a view that takes events to be concrete particulars; and I am thus concerned with contrasting my view only with other views that take events similarly. Chisholm's events, however, are abstract entities.

2 See, for example, 'On the psycho-physical identity theory', *American Philosophical Quarterly*, vol. 3 (1966), pp. 227–35; 'Events and their descriptions: some considerations', in N. Rescher *et al.* (eds), *Essays in Honor of Carl G. Hempel* (Dordrecht: D. Reidel, 1969), pp. 198–215; 'Causation, nomic subsumption, and the concept of event', *Journal of Philosophy*, vol. 70 (1973), pp. 217–36; and 'Events as property exemplifications', in Brand and Walton (eds), *Action Theory* (Dordrecht: D. Reidel, 1976), pp. 159–77. A view similar in many respects to Kim's is R. M. Martin's, in 'On events and event-descriptions', in J. Margolis (ed.), *Fact and Existence* (Oxford: Basil Blackwell, 1969), pp. 63–74.

3 See 'Events and their descriptions: some considerations', *op. cit.*, pp. 199ff., and 'Causation, nomic subsumption, and the concept of event', *op. cit.*, p. 223.

4 'Events and their descriptions: some considerations', *op. cit.*, p. 200.

5 *Ibid.* However, we will see some reason to believe that Kim cannot follow through with what he insists on.

6 'Events as property exemplifications', *op. cit.*, p. 160.

7 Jones holds two jobs. Jones *qua* philosopher earns $20,000 per year; Jones *qua* electrician earns $30,000 per year. Therefore, by Leibniz's Law, Jones *qua* philosopher ≠ Jones *qua* electrician. This fallacious argument might be used by someone in the course of explaining a theory according to which there are '*qua* things' which make up the ordinary things with which we are familiar. I imagine that a view of events, markedly similar to this one, could be generated by taking events to be literally the exemplifications, not the exemplifyings, of properties by objects at times. It is a physical object that exemplifies the property of turning red; and so, that object is an exemplification of that property. If one took events to be the exemplifications of the properties that physical objects exemplify at times, one would then take an event to be, not a physical object's exemplifying of a property at a time, but a physical object-in-so-far-as-it-exemplifies-a-property-at-a-time; events would be '*qua* things'. A physical object, on this

view, would be the sequence of the events that happen to it. To the extent that I understand this view, it is clear to me that it is not Kim's; it might be Whitehead's, and it may be related to the Lemmon-Quine view that I discuss in Chapter VI.

8 See, for example, Frege's handling of 'indirect' reference in 'On sense and reference', *Translations from the Philosophical Writings of Gottlob Frege* (Oxford: Basil Blackwell, 1960), P. Geach and M. Black (eds), pp. 56–78; Sheffler's view in *The Anatomy of Inquiry* (New York: Knopf, 1963), pp. 104–5; and Davidson's 'On saying that', *Synthese*, vol. 19 (1968–9), pp. 130–46.

9 'Events and their descriptions: some considerations', *op. cit.*, p. 201, and 'On the psycho-physical identity theory', *op. cit.*, p. 232.

10 See Kim's discussion of Davidson's 'great event' argument, in 'Events and their descriptions: some considerations', *op. cit.*, pp. 206–8.

11 'Events as property exemplifications', *op. cit.*, p. 161.

12 See for example, Davidson's remarks on p. 81 of his 'On events and event-descriptions', in J. Margolis (ed.), *Fact and Experience, op. cit.*

13 See 'Events as property exemplifications', *op. cit.*, p. 157.

14 Davidson makes this point in 'The logical form of action sentences', in N. Rescher (ed.), *The Logic of Decision and Action* (Pittsburgh: University of Pittsburgh Press, 1967), p. 91, and in 'The individuation of events', reprinted in his *Essays on Actions and Events* (Oxford: Oxford University Press, 1980), pp. 167ff.

15 Perhaps that story is that of level generation as expounded by Alvin Goldman, in *A Theory of Human Action* (Englewood Cliffs, New Jersey: Prentice-Hall, 1970).

16 This is not alleged to be a case of causal overdetermination, but of some sort of 'generational' overdetermination.

17 In his 'Events and propositions', *Noûs*, vol. IV (1970), p. 15.

18 See his paper, 'Particulars, events, and actions', in Brand and Walton (eds), *Action Theory, op. cit.*, pp. 133–57, for his theory about how to account for 'the same thing's occurring again' without its literally being the case that any event actually occurs more than once. I find Brand's view on this issue (given on pp. 139–44 of his paper) substantially correct (see Chapter V, section 4, below).

19 In Chapter V, section 4, below, I give an argument for the view that events, in Chisholm's and Brand's sense, do not recur. That they do not recur in the other sense follows from the fact that identical events must have the same subject and the fact that if an event were to occur at different places simultaneously, it would have to have distinct subjects (see Chapter V, note 12).

20 See his papers, 'Particulars, events, and actions', *op. cit.*, 'Identity conditions for events', *American Philosophical Quarterly*, vol. 14 (1977), pp. 329–37, and 'Simultaneous causation', in Peter van Inwagen (ed.), *Time and Cause* (Dordrecht: D. Reidel, 1980), pp. 137–53, esp. pp. 142ff.

21 'Particulars, events, and actions', *op. cit.*, p. 145; 'Identity conditions for events', *op. cit.*, p. 333; 'Simultaneous causation', *op. cit.*, p. 143.

22 'Particulars, events, and actions', *op. cit.*, p. 146; 'Identity conditions for events', *op. cit.*, p. 333; 'Simultaneous causation', *op. cit.*, p. 143.

23 'Particulars, events, and actions', *op. cit.*, p. 147.

24 *Ibid.*, p. 147ff.

25 *Ibid.*, and 'Identity conditions for events', *op. cit.*, pp. 334ff.

26 This point is Ernest Sosa's; he made it in reply to a paper of Brand's, at the Western Division meetings of the American Philosophical Association, in April 1976. The fallacy that drives Brand to the rigidifying tactic is also committed by Marshall Swain, in 'Causation and distinct events', *Time and Cause, op. cit.*, p. 159. For further comments on Brand's criterion, see Michael Tye's 'Brand on event identity', *Philosophical Studies*, vol. 35 (1979), pp. 81–9; and Brand's 'On Tye's "Brand on event identity"', *Philosophical Studies*, vol. 36 (1979), pp. 61–8.

27 See 'Identity conditions for events', *op. cit.*, p. 331, and Chapter II, section 1.8, above.

28 Given the intimate connection between a criterion of identity for the members of a given kind and a principle saying what it is to belong to that kind (see above, Chapter II, section 1.9), to say that physical objects that satisfy the events' condition of identity are identical by dint of such satisfaction is to say that they are events.

29 See P. M. S. Hacker's excellent discussion of these issues in 'Events and objects in space and time', *Mind*, vol. XCI (1982), pp. 1–19. I have learned much from this paper, and that is reflected in the next two paragraphs. Swain, in 'Causation and distinct events', *op. cit.*, p. 161, seems to take the view that Brand does on the analogousness of events and physical objects with respect to spatio-temporality.

30 I will offer a different, though not unrelated reason for this view in Chapter VI, section 1, when I discuss Lemmon's criterion of identity for events.

31 A related point made by Sosa, *op. cit.*, can be expressed in my terms as follows. Where 'R(x,y)' is the condition of identity for φs, things are φs if and only if they are R-ish (See Chapter II, section 1.9, above). What is R-ishness for events, according to Brand? Being spatio-temporal? No, for it does not distinguish between events and physical objects, unless the sense of spatio-temporality as it applies to events is distinguished from the sense in which it applies to physical objects. But, I think that the distinguishing will result in the uncovering of a more basic idea of what it is to be an event, one having to do with the concept of change.

32 Donald Davidson, 'Causal relations', *Journal of Philosophy*, vol. LXIV (1967), pp. 691–703; reprinted in Davidson's *Essays on Actions and Events, op. cit.*, pp. 149–62.

33 *Op. cit.*, pp. 81–5.

34 See Chapter V, section 4.3, below, for my analysis of causal verbs which shows how the idea of causation figures in.

35 See, for example, 'The individuation of events', *op. cit.*, p. 178, and 'Agency', reprinted in *Essays on Actions and Events, op. cit.*, pp.

48ff, 51, 55ff. See also Jennifer Hornsby's *Actions* (London: Routledge & Kegan Paul, 1980), Chapter One.
36 See the Introduction to Davidson's *Essays on Actions and Events*, *op. cit.*, p. 6.
37 *Op. cit.*, p. 179.
38 'Particulars, events, and actions', *op. cit.*, p. 137.
39 *Ibid*.
40 In 'The individuation of events', *op. cit.*, p. 174, Davidson has expressed the idea of the closeness of the concept of an event and that of a change in an object. But it does not serve for him as the idea in terms of which to articulate a theory of events.

IV CHANGE

1 See, for example, Plato, *Parmenides*, 138c, and Aristotle, *Physics*, Book 1, Ch. 5.
2 *God and the Soul* (London: Routledge & Kegan Paul, 1969), p. 71.
3 See McTaggart's *The Nature of Existence*, vol. II (Cambridge: Cambridge University Press, 1927), C. D. Broad (ed.), section 317, and Russell's *The Principles of Mathematics* (Cambridge: Cambridge University Press, 1903), section 442.
4 Again, the existence of times and propositions are issues, not being germane, that will be ignored. I also ignore the following issue: usually, propositions are taken to be such that if true then always true. This cannot be the idea of a proposition operative in the CCC.
5 See the Appendix, section 3, below.
6 I would not offer such an argument, since I accept a principle, the Principle of Event Enlargement, whose rejection this argument requires. See Chapter V, section 3, below.
7 *The Principles of Mathematics*, *op. cit.*, section 442.
8 One must say 'significant', for one can always be faced with vacuous, irrelevant relata, as in the property of being in existence for exactly twenty-five minutes and being either taller than Socrates or not.
9 These changes with respect to the relations the parts bear to each other will not generally be 'relational' changes in the sense of section 7 of this chapter.
10 This view is suggested in Helen Cartwright's papers, 'Heraclitus and the bath water', *Philosophical Review*, vol. LXXIV (1965), pp. 466–85, and 'Quantities', *Philosophical Review*, vol. LXXIX (1970), pp. 25–42.
11 See Richard Sharvy's 'Aristotle on mixtures', *Journal of Philosophy*, vol. LXXX (1983), pp. 439–57, esp. pp. 454ff., for a discussion of the indestructibility of matter.
12 A lot of what I have said in this section, and will say in the next and in section 3 of Chapter VII, rests on the assumption that no thing is identical with its parts or the stuff of which it is made. What follows is a defence of that assumption (though it will not address the concerns of the believers in 'relative identity').

Clearly, if the parts of a thing are not themselves a thing, then no thing is identical with its parts. Nor could a thing be identical with the 'sum' of its parts, for a thing can change its parts (I reject mereological essentialism), while the sum cannot (that's in the nature of mereological sums). The main point is that no objects, x and y, can be identical at any time when it is the case that x exists and y doesn't. But it is surely the case that some things that can survive the loss or gain of a part can exist at times when the things that were once their parts no longer exist; and some things fail to exist at times when their parts do. Similarly, the matter of a thing may outlast the thing made of that matter, and a thing may outlast the matter of which it was once made.

This argument assumes that for any things, x and y, if x and y are not identical at any one time, then they are not identical at any other time either. A defence of this assumption follows.

First, it is clear that just as things have 'ordinary', non-temporal properties at times (my car was blue on Monday), things can also have 'temporal' properties at times (on Tuesday, my car was blue on Monday). And the following principle of temporal shortening (PTS) is obviously true:

(PTS) $(x)(t)(t')((Fx$ at $t)$ at $t' \supset Fx$ at $t)$;

after all, if on Tuesday, it was the case that my car was blue on Monday, then surely my car was blue on Monday; and if on Tuesday my car wasn't blue on Monday, then my car wasn't blue on Monday. With the aid of (PTS), we can prove a principle of temporal expansion (PTE):

(PTE) $(x)(t)(t')(Fx$ at $t \supset (Fx$ at $t)$ at $t')$.

Consider, for *reductio*, the denial of (PTE):

(i) $(\exists x)(\exists t)(\exists t')(Fx$ at $t \wedge \sim (Fx$ at $t)$ at $t')$.

But, then, by EG on (i),

(ii)   Fa at $t_1 \wedge \sim (Fa$ at $t_1)$ at t_2.

But, by (PTS),

(iii)   Fa at $t_1 \wedge \sim Fa$ at t_1.

Since (iii) is a contradiction, (PTE) is established.

Now, assume a 'tensed' version of the Indiscernibility of Identicals (II_t):

(II_t) $(x)(y)(t)(x=y$ at $t \supset (F)(Fx$ at $t \equiv Fy$ at $t))$.
    (1) $a=b$ at $t_1 \supset (F)(Fa$ at $t_1 \equiv F_b$ at $t_1)$ UI,(II_t)
    (2) $a=b$ at t_1 Assume
    (3) $(F)(Fa$ at $t_1 \equiv F_b$ at $t_1)$ (1),(2)
    (4)   let $F_1x=_{df}(t')(x=a$ at $t')$
          (F_1 is the property of being identical with a at all times)

(5)	F_1a at $t_1 \equiv F_1b$ at t_1	UI,(3)
(6)	F_1a	obvious
(7)	F_1a at t_1	PTE,(6)
(8)	F_1b at t_1	(5),(7)
(9)	F_1b	PTS,(8)
(10)	$a=b$ at $t_1 \supset F_1b$	(2),(9)

That is, if a and b are identical at any one time, then they are identical at all times: $(x)(y)((\exists t)(x=y$ at $t) \supset (t')(x=y$ at $t'))$. My thanks to Michael McKinsey for discussing this proof with me and for making helpful suggestions.

13 See Wiggins on phase sortals, in *Sameness and Substance* (Cambridge, Mass.: Harvard University Press, 1980), pp. 24–7.

14 *God and the Soul, op. cit.*, p. 71.

15 See *Theaetetus*, 155b11–14.

16 'On the applicability of a criterion of change', *Ratio*, vol. 15 (1973), pp. 325–33.

17 *The Nature of Existence, op. cit.*, section 309.

18 This derivation was inspired by an example in Kim's 'Noncausal connections', *Noûs*, vol. 8 (1974), p. 48. His example is used below.

19 Geach, *op. cit.*, and Kim, *ibid.*, call what I refer to as relational change 'mere Cambridge change'; Sidney Shoemaker calls it 'McTaggartian change' in 'Time without change', *Journal of Philosophy*, vol. LXXVI (1969), p. 364.

20 Though sets do not change their membership properties (see Sharvy's 'Why a class can't change its members', *Noûs*, vol. 2 (1968), pp. 303–34), it does not follow that they do not change in other, relational respects. It might be argued that some abstract entities do not change at all, by arguing that such entities are 'timeless', in the sense of not having properties *at times*.

21 Michael Slote, in *Metaphysics and Essence* (New York: New York University Press, 1974), p. 16, points out that Moore, Broad and Austin seem to have thought that there is a sense of 'change' in which objects can change without being 'altered'. And one of Slote's definitions of alteration, on pp. 13–14, implies that when an object changes relationally, it alters.

22 'On the applicability of a criterion of change', *op. cit.*, p. 328.

23 *Ibid.*, p. 331.

24 It also rules out arguing that when Jones runs he changes relationally, for he cannot so change unless he lives. Even if living were changing and not just persisting, living is a change in Jones.

25 This latter may not be a change in Socrates, but be changes in Socrates' matter.

26 Does Jones change relationally when he punches Smith? After all, it seems as if Jones could not have so changed unless Smith changed by getting hit. No, he changes non-relationally. It is true that if nothing happens to Smith, then Jones cannot have punched him. That is, in a possible world in which Smith does not change at all, Jones cannot

have changed by punching Smith. But it does not follow from this that the change that actually occurred, Jones's punching of Smith, could not have occurred in that world. It's just that that change in Jones could not, in that world, be described as a punching of Smith. 'Jones's punching of Smith' is a description of a change that correctly describes only if certain other changes occur; the change described could have occurred without those other changes having occurred, but it would not then be so describable. (I have more to say about this in Chapter VI, section 4.) The upshot of this is that one cannot always tell just by looking at a statement reporting that some object has changed whether the object has changed relationally or non-relationally. One settles that issue by discovering whether the change described could have occurred in the absence of other changes to other things, however that change would be described in such circumstances.

27 What can be said about x, that it got to be farther from y, can also be said about y, that it got to be farther from x. But, on my view, in getting to be farther from y, x changed non-relationally, while in getting to be farther from x, y changed relationally. Staring at predicates, again, won't allow us to see which changes are relational and which non-relational.

28 Another interesting issue in connection with motion is this. Of course an object moves when it rotates. Of course, it does not, since it does not change spatial location, only its parts so change. Thus, the separate treatment given to 'place' and 'position' in Aristotle's *Categories*, Ch. 4.

29 The familiar argument is Davidson's in 'The logical form of action sentences', in N. Rescher (ed.), *The Logic of Decision and Action* (Pittsburgh: University of Pittsburgh Press, 1967), pp. 81–95. See my sketch of it in Chapter I, section 2.4.

30 I did so argue, in 'Relational change and relational changes', *Philosophical Studies*, vol. 34 (1978), pp. 63–79, esp. pp. 71–2. I have, as will be seen, changed my mind. The existence of relational changes is, by the way, guaranteed on Kim's view, since, for example, Xantippe exemplified the property of becoming a widow in 399 BC.

31 An arrow in flight has at t_1 the property of being at p_1, but does not have the property of remaining at p_1 at t_1; that is, it is not at rest then. Did Zeno miss this distinction?

32 There is one further point about properties and change that needs making. I will make it in the next chapter.

33 Of course, not the tensed version of that principle used in note 12 of this chapter.

34 Thus the apparent conflict, mentioned in this book's Preface, between the idea of change and the principle of non-contradiction.

35 If change didn't take time, we'd have something that was simultaneously F and not-F; then we'd have a 'Parmenidean' denial of change. But I am interested in a 'Heraclitean' denial of change, based

on the idea that nothing survives the loss of a property.

36 See Quine, *Word and Object* (Cambridge, Mass.: MIT Press, 1960), p. 172; and see Richard Taylor, *Metaphysics* (Englewood Cliffs, New Jersey: Prentice-Hall, 1983), 3rd edn, pp. 63–70, for a defence of the analogousness of the relationship of objects to space and to time.

37 However, for arguments against temporal slice theory, see R. M. Chisholm, *Person and Object* (La Salle, Ill.: Open Court, 1976), Appendix A, and P. T. Geach, 'Some problems about time', reprinted in *Logic Matters* (Berkeley: University of California Press, 1980), pp. 308–11.

38 For an example of this sort of reconstruction, see C. D. Broad, *Scientific Thought* (Paterson, New Jersey: Littlefield, Adams & Co., 1959), p. 63. And for some arguments against it, see J. J. Thomson, 'Parthood and identity across time', *Journal of Philosophy*, vol. LXXX (1983), pp. 210–1, and J. J. C. Smart, 'Time and becoming', in van Inwagen (ed.), *Time and Cause* (Dordrecht: D. Reidel, 1980), pp. 8, 11.

39 Chisholm, *op. cit.*, pp. 142–4.

40 This point is made by Geach, in 'Some problems about time', *op. cit.*, p. 304ff. Geach cites McTaggart, *The Nature of Existence*, vol. II, sections 315–16, on this matter.

41 Quine, I suppose, would number me among the 'unduly nervous'; see 'Things and their place in theories', in his *Theories and Things* (Cambridge, Mass.: Harvard University Press, 1981), p. 10. Quine, however, says nothing that makes me less uneasy about this static conception of change. It is not surprising, by the way, that one who accepts this conception of change would also be attracted to Lemmon's criterion of identity for events (to be discussed in Chapter VI).

V EVENTS AND CHANGES

1 Let 'x is grue*' mean 'x is green before some specified time, t, and blue thereafter'. When t arrives, a grue* thing will both change, by going from being green to being blue, and not change, by remaining grue*. Since every grue* thing is, after t, a blue thing, it cannot be the case that both green (and blue) and grue* are colours, if in saying that, a respect in which things change is specified. Since green and blue are obviously colours, grue* isn't (even if it is a property).

2 My thanks go to David Kaplan, for it was in discussion with him, during a seminar of mine that he visited, that some of the basic ideas leading to the idea of a quality space in which things change arose.

3 The property of being colourless (transparent) must belong to the same space as that to which other colours belong. Similarly for other 'degenerate' properties (e.g., that of being odourless).

4 This proviso comes into play in the discussion, in Chapter VI, section 1.2, of Lemmon's criterion of identity for events.

5 My thanks to Alexander Rosenberg for calling my attention to this point. The importance of the role of scientific theories is felt when I define what it is for an event to be atomic, in Chapter VI.

6 This notion of continuous change should not be conflated with that of a curve's being everywhere differentiable. A particle that moves along a certain straight path and then makes a sharp left turn moves continuously in my sense, so long as it does not linger at any point, for it has a different spatial-location property at each different time. The curve representing the motion, however, is not differentiable at the turning point.

7 I do not know if this is really possible; let us just suppose that it is.

8 The car couldn't have changed in the way it did had the windshield not changed in a certain way; but since the windshield was part of the car, the car's change was not relational.

9 See Davidson's 'The individuation of events', in *Essays in Honor of Carl G. Hempel* (Dordrecht: D. Reidel, 1969), N. Rescher (ed.), p. 228.

10 Consider, by way of contrast, the Principle of Event Contraction (PEC): if an event occurs to any object having parts, then that event is a change in at least some part or parts of that object. Now, when the change in the object occurs just because of a change in a single part, then the change in the whole is the change in the part; this is a consequence of PEE. But when the change in the whole occurs because of distinct changes in distinct parts (e.g., the house is burning because the roof and the basement are on fire), then PEC (but not PEE) requires that the change in the whole be identical with the changes in the parts. And this consequence of PEC is false; I will argue against it in Chapter VII, section 3. PEC was mentioned to me by Robert Grimm.

11 A view essentially the same as this is expressed by Fred Dretske, in 'Can events move?', *Mind*, vol. 76 (1967), p. 488.

12 It is clear, then, that no event recurs in the sense of occurring simultaneously in distinct locations. For an event occurs in a given location only because its subject is located there. Thus, if an event, e, occurs at place p_1 at t and e' occurs at a distinct place p_2 at t, then e and e' must have different minimal subjects. But, since identical events must have the same minimal subject, no event occurs simultaneously in distinct places. This, of course, does not rule out an event's partly occurring in one place while partly occurring in another. That events do not recur, in the sense of occurring again, is argued in section 4 of this chapter.

13 Consider the following argument against the view that mental events are brain events. The minimal subject of a brain event is certainly no larger than the brain; but the minimal subjects of mental events are persons, since no part of a person can be said, for example, to come to believe that grass is green. Therefore, since identical events must have the same minimal subject, and since brains are (usually) only proper parts of persons, brain events can't be mental events.

This argument assumes that, since no proper part of a person can be said to come to believe that grass is green, no proper part of a person can be the minimal subject of a coming to believe that grass is green. But it appears that the only reason for accepting this assumption is something like the following. If an object, x, φs solely because a part of it, y, changes, then y's change must be a φing as well. (Thus, if a change in the brain is to be Jones's coming to believe that grass is green, then that change must be Jones's brain's coming to believe that grass is green; and that is absurd). But this argument is mistaken. It is not generally true that if x changes because a part, y, changes and if x's change is a φing, then y's must be a φing. My blushing surely is my face's turning red; but my face doesn't blush. My car does not shatter when its windshield shatters, though, by PEE, my windshield's shattering is a change in my car. We have here an instance of a 'possession' fallacy, as in 'This cat is a parent and it is mine; therefore, it is my parent': this mental event is a coming to believe and it is a change in a brain; therefore, it is a brain's coming to believe. This fallacious argument cannot be used to show that mental events cannot have minimal subjects that are mere proper parts of persons. Moral: one must be careful when talking about the non-minimal subjects of events. (My thanks to Cynthia Macdonald for bringing this issue to my attention and discussing it with me and to Lawrence Powers for reminding me of other possession fallacies.)

14 *Journal of Philosophy*, vol. LXVIII (1971), pp. 115–32.
15 Whether the location of Jones's shooting must include the location of the pistol raises the same issue as the one now being raised; so we can ignore this complication. Whether the location of a person's action is *smaller* than that of the agent is also an issue that need not detain us.
16 Neil Wilson, in 'Fact, events, and their identity conditions', *Philosophical Studies*, vol. 25 (1974), pp. 303–21, holds that killings are not actions but facts, and hence have no spatial locations. He holds this, I think, because he takes killings to be causings to die, and takes a causing to be a fact that one event causes another rather than as an event that in fact causes another.
17 'Can events move?', *op. cit.*, pp. 479ff.
18 Wiggins makes this same point in *Sameness and Substance* (Cambridge, Mass.: Harvard University Press, 1980), p. 21, n. 12.
19 See R. M. Chisholm's 'Beginnings and endings', in van Inwagen (ed.), *Time and Cause* (Dordrecht: D. Reidel, 1980), pp. 17–25: 'We should not say that there is motion "at an instant" – if that is taken to imply that there can be change of place in an instant' (p. 18). See also W. H. Newton-Smith, *The Structure of Time* (London: Routledge & Kegan Paul, 1980), p. 128. But Michael Slote, in his *Metaphysics and Essence* (New York: New York University Press, 1975), p. 23, says, 'it makes sense to talk of instantaneous events, but not of instantaneous processes'. Events on my theory, however, *are* processes.
20 Similarly, though sets cannot change their members, such things can

change relationally. Myles Brand, in 'Simultaneous causation', in *Time and Cause, op. cit.*, pp. 137–53, believes that events do change non-relationally and can be the subjects of events. But his only reason seems to be that events have and then lack non-relational properties. This, I've argued, is not a good enough reason.

21 Davidson, in 'Events as particulars', *Noûs*, vol. 4 (1970), pp. 25–32, suggests a sense, based on this idea, in which it might be said that an individual event occurred twice. Since events have parts that are events, we might think of all the eruptions of Mt St Helens as a single event of which each such eruption is a part. To say, then, that an eruption of Mt St Helens recurred is to say that two or more parts of that event occurred. I am not much attracted to this solution, largely because I am not inclined to believe that there is any event whose parts are each of the eruptions of Mt St Helens.

22 His account of recurrence is to be found in 'Particulars, events, and actions', in Brand and Walton (eds), *Action Theory* (Dordrecht: D. Reidel, 1976), pp. 139–44. This sort of account is also suggested by some remarks by Davidson in 'Events as particulars', *op. cit.*, p. 28.

23 If an event is uninterrupted, it is occurring at every instant included in the time at which it occurs. But the time at which an event occurs may also be disjointed, and such an event is not occurring at times during the interruption.

24 For a much more careful and thorough discussion of these matters, see Richard Sorabji, 'Aristotle on the instant of change', *Proceedings of the Aristotelian Society*, Supplementary Volume L (1976), pp. 69–89.

25 See Chisholm's 'Beginnings and endings', *op. cit.*, pp. 18ff.

26 I am grateful (sort of) to Patrick Francken for calling my attention to this problem. Moreover, after writing this section, I discovered that the problem has a longer history than I had imagined; Plato and Aristotle seem to have been much troubled by it (see references in Sorabji's paper, *op. cit.*). Apparently, what I have said above, concerning first and last moments, corresponds to Aristotle's views, according to Sorabji's 'second', and preferred interpretation.

27 Eli Hirsch, in *The Concept of Identity* (New York: Oxford University Press, 1982), seems to suggest (pp. 10–15) that if a direct change were composed of dense changes, the latter would have to be changes in the same quality space that the direct change was a change in. I am denying this; indeed this would be impossible if the direct change were a change in a discrete space. Hirsch cites a passage in Kant's *Critique of Pure Reason*, B253–4, that seems to suggest that the view I've adopted is Kant's.

28 See G. E. M. Anscombe, *Intention* (Ithaca, New York: Cornell University Press, 1969), 2nd edn, p. 46, and Davidson's papers, collected in his *Essays on Actions and Events* (Oxford: Oxford University Press, 1980), 'Actions, reasons, and causes', p. 4, 'Agency', pp. 57ff., and 'The individuation of events', pp. 171, 178.

29 See, for example, Alvin Goldman, 'The individuation of action',

Journal of Philosophy, vol. LXVIII (1971), pp. 761–74, and L. H. Davis, 'The individuation of actions', *Journal of Philosophy*, vol. LXVII (1970), pp. 520–30. It should be noted that Goldman cannot make use of Thomson's arguments, since if correct then the shooting and the killing occur at different times, while Goldman's level-generational view (developed in *A Theory of Human Action* (Englewood Cliffs, New Jersey: Prentice-Hall, 1970)) requires that they be simultaneous. See my 'A note on level-generation and the time of a killing', *Philosophical Studies*, vol. 26 (1974), pp. 151–2.

30 'The time of a killing', *op. cit.*, pp. 116–9.

31 *Ibid.*, pp. 119–20. I have replaced names of people with 'a' and 'b'.

32 *Ibid.*, pp. 120ff.

33 Thomson's view is not free of oddity either. Suppose that after a shoots b, a kills himself out of remorse and guilt, and that he dies before b does. Thomson's view will have us say that in such a case part of what a did in killing b he did after he himself has died. Is this not at least as odd as saying that a killed b before b died? I should have thought that dead men neither tell tales nor do anything else. And it will not help to say, as Monroe Beardsley does, in 'Action and events: the problem of individuation', *American Philosophical Quarterly*, vol. 12 (1975), pp. 263–76, that 'activities cease with death, but not necessarily actions' (p. 270). Beardsley apparently believes that actions can go on after the deaths of their agents for he identifies the action of a's killing of b with b's being killed, and he takes the latter to go on until b dies. But, as I will argue, 'b's being killed' is ambiguous, referring in one sense to a state that does not obtain until he dies; but in that sense, it does not refer to a's action.

34 *Op. cit.*, p. 177.

35 *Ibid.*, pp. 177ff.

36 'The time of a killing', *op. cit.*, p. 115.

37 I do not offer this analysis for all cases where a claim of the form 'x φed y' is true. It does not work for 'Smith perceived the tree', since Smith does not generally do anything (intentionally or otherwise) that causes the tree to be perceived. And in a case where Jones digested his lunch, though it may be that Jones's eating of his lunch was something Jones did that caused his lunch's being digested, one does not digest one's lunch by eating it.

38 The failure to make this distinction resulted in Thomson's arguing, in 'Individuating actions', *Journal of Philosophy*, vol. LXVIII (1971), pp. 774–81, esp. p. 777, in the following way. Thomson supposes that Jones gets to work by taking the subway; but she denies that Jones's getting to work is his taking of the subway, on the grounds that his getting to work caused him to become cool (since his office is air-conditioned), while his taking of the subway caused him to become warm (since the subway was crowded and not air-conditioned). But if his getting to work (and not his taking of the subway) caused him to become cool, that must be because his getting to work did not come to pass until he was *at* the office. And that was in part caused by his

taking of the subway. But that getting to work was not his getting to work in the process sense, since that getting to work was an action that terminated in his being at the office. It was his getting to work in the process sense (but not in the state sense) that he accomplished by taking the subway; and in that sense his getting to work caused him to become warm.

39 There may not be such a process. While b is lying in the street, bleeding to death, he is in the process of dying, but he is not then in the process of being killed.

40 'The time of a killing', *op. cit.*, pp. 120, 121.

41 However, though it may be true that I will not eat lunch *unless* you do, it does not follow from this that I will not each lunch *until* you do. Similarly, though it is clear that a does not kill b unless b dies, it does not follow from this that a does not kill b until b dies.

By the way, another possibility concerning the identity of shootings and killings, inspired by talk of relational change, is this. Suppose we accept the fallacious inference from 'unless' to 'until'. It might then be said that a's shooting of b at t_1 was not *at* t_1, a killing of b, but it *became* at t_3, when b died, a killing of b. That is, the shooting changed *relationally* by acquiring at t_3 the property of being a cause of a death, a property, according to this suggestion, no event or action can have *until* its effect occurs. See Jonathan Bennett, 'Shooting, killing and dying', *Canadian Journal of Philosophy*, vol. II (1973), pp. 315–23.

42 The asymmetry and irreflexivity of the by-relation is the asymmetry and irreflexivity of the *causal* relation. In 'a killed by shooting him', 'by' does not relate the shooting and the killing; it causally relates two effects of 'what a did', *viz.*, b's being shot and b's being killed (in the process sense of those terms), the former a less remote effect than the latter. What a did caused b's being shot, which in turn caused his being killed. What a did brought about the more remote effect, because what a did brought about the less remote effect, and that effect caused the more remote effect. This analysis of the by-relation, motivated by my disambiguation of 'b's being φed' and my 'verb-splitting' analysis of causal verbs, is due to Patrick Francken.

43 Since writing this section, I have had more to say about some of the issues discussed therein; see my 'How not to flip the prowler', in LePore and McLaughlin (eds), *The Philosophy of Donald Davidson: Perspectives on Actions and Events* (Oxford: Basil Blackwell, 1985).

VI EVENTS AS CHANGES

1 C. D. Broad, in *Scientific Thought* (Paterson, New Jersey: Littlefield, Adams & Co., 1959), p. 393, expresses this view in these words: 'A thing . . . is simply a long event . . .'. And Nelson Goodman, in *The Structure of Appearance*, 2nd edn (New York: Bobbs-Merrill, 1966), p. 128, puts it this way: 'Our tables, steam yachts, and potatoes are events of comparatively small spatial and large temporal dimensions.

The eye of a potato is an event temporally coextensive with the whole, but spatially smaller. The steam-yacht-during-an-hour is an event spatially as large as the yacht but temporally smaller.' It is not surprising that those who hold a view of this sort are also inclined to believe that physical objects have temporal parts.

2 In N. Rescher (ed.), *The Logic of Decision and Action* (Pittsburgh: University of Pittsburgh Press, 1967), pp. 96–103.

3 (Cambridge, Mass.: MIT Press, 1960), p. 170.

4 In Quine's *Theories and Things* (Cambridge, Mass.: Harvard University Press, 1981), pp. 11–12.

5 *Ibid.*, p. 10.

6 'The logical form of action sentences', reprinted in his *Essays on Actions and Events* (Oxford: Oxford University Press, 1980), p. 125.

7 Reprinted in *Essays on Actions and Events*, *op. cit.*, pp. 163–80.

8 *Ibid.*, p. 178.

9 *Ibid.*, pp. 178–9. A point, irrelevant in this context but which will come up later, to keep in mind is that Davidson says that the warming of the ball is identical with a certain sum of motions.

10 In Brand and Walton (eds), *Action Theory* (Dordrecht: D. Reidel, 1976), pp. 133–57.

11 *Ibid.*, p. 145.

12 The events of which the diagonal movement is composed, on the first suggestion, namely the first and second parts of the trip, do not occur simultaneously.

13 Of course, it would be nice, for the purposes of completing this picture, to have a theory by which to divide the forces that produce motions into sorts, if motions come in sorts (an issue such a theory would settle). But what produces motions are events. And so the issue to be settled here is the same as that of whether horizontal and vertical movements are of the same sort. This situation arises in the next case as well.

14 The discussion of these two cases shows, I believe, what it is that is so plausible about Davidson's causal criterion of identity for events. For if what I have said about the cases is correct, then, though the correctness of judgements about event identity are not determined by truths about causes and effects, decisions about what is to count as an event, as opposed to a vector or aspect of an event, are at least in part determined by considerations concerning the sorts to which the causes of events belong.

15 In light of this, the definitions to follow are relativized to theories. This should not make one think that the account of events based on those definitions makes certain 'facts' about events relative to theory in the sense that what those facts are is determined in part by which theory we happen to accept; they are in part determined, rather, by theories that are *true*.

16 The objects serving as atomic objects persist and have no temporal parts. Thus, when I speak of an object's having or exemplifying a property, P, at an instant or interval of time, t, I do *not* mean that

some object, x-at-t, timelessly has P. Nor do I mean that x has the property of being P-at-t. I take 'x has P at t' to express a two-place relation holding between persisting things and times.

17 The requirement that atomic quality spaces be dense is a consequence of my suggestion (in Chapter V, section 4.2) for dealing with the problem of the time of direct changes.

18 More could have been expected if the atomic events were changes in discrete quality spaces. But then, short of trying to take the idea of an instantaneous event seriously, which I believe cannot be done, the problem of the time at which direct changes occur would have arisen again.

19 Some diachronic events (those satisfying D3*) are atomic. But for simplicity's sake, when I speak of diachronic events, I shall mean non-atomic diachronic events, unless I specify otherwise.

20 'To rot' also picks out an instantaneous dynamic property, for it is true of a log at each moment during which it is rotting; and its being true of it at such moments implies that at surrounding moments it has different rot-related static properties (the log is in different states of rottenness). But that verb also has a dynamic sense in which it expresses a property the log has during the whole interval at which the log is rotting, namely the property of going from being wholly unrotten to being wholly rotten. And it is the dynamic sense with which we are here concerned. Of course, the fact that the log has the dynamic property of rotting is not independent of the fact that it has the instantaneous dynamic property of rotting at moments in the interval of the rotting.

21 Not every exemplifying of a dynamic property expressed by an atomic event verb by an atomic object will be an atomic event; some may involve repetition or lingering, for example. To determine whether a particular exemplifying of such a property by an atomic object is an atomic event, one must determine whether the restrictions in D3* are satisfied.

22 Since an atomic event can be construed as composed of atomic events in some temporal sequence, atomic events not only have canonical descriptions of the form '$[x, \phi, t]$', they also have canonical descriptions of the same form as those of simple diachronic events.

23 For a property to divide events into kinds, it must not only be an essence, it must also be the case that a criterion of identity can be given for the events having that essence. Of course, if there is a criterion of identity for events generally and there are essences had by some events and not others, then there is a (non-minimal) criterion of identity for the events having such an essence. That criterion will look like this: $\square(x)(y)(x$ and y are events $\wedge$ x and y are $\phi \supset (x=y \equiv (R(x,y) \wedge \phi x \wedge \phi y)))$, where '$R(x,y)$' is the condition of identity for events, and ϕ is the essence in question. So, in speaking here about properties that divide events into kinds, I am presuming that there is a criterion of identity for events. I hope to make good that presumption shortly.

24 There are other properties that I take to be essences of the events

that have them; they are the subject of Chapter VII.

25 It is, of course, to be understood here that what is contingent or not must be relativized to the (true) theory, T, against the background of which the atomic quality spaces are determined and events are given their canonical descriptions.

26 I am not interested here in entities whose existence is implied by the ways in which the minimal subjects and times are referred to, though we would be interested in such matters were very or extremely canonical descriptions at stake.

27 Thus, non-canonical event descriptions can lead to the same sorts of scope distinctions and problems that non-rigid designators do. Just as the inventor of bifocals could have failed to have invented bifocals, the event that caused the explosion could have failed to have caused the explosion.

28 On my view, the subjects of events are physical objects; so events have the same subject if and only if those subjects satisfy the condition of identity for physical objects. I have no criterion of identity for intervals of time; 'are included in all the same intervals' sounds like a circular identity condition, and 'are the times at which all the same events occur' is, in the present context, just a bad joke. And, I find myself in no better position than anyone else with respect to a condition of identity for properties. However, it should be said that my goal was to give a theory about events in part by showing how they are related to entities of other kinds; it is not part of that project to give a theory about those other entities. (Criticism of Kim's view on the grounds that he does not give an identity criterion for properties seems to be out of place for the same reason. But see Brand, 'Identity conditions for events', *American Philosophical Quarterly*, vol. 14 (1977), p. 335.) But perhaps the following should be said. Normally, sameness of instances is taken to be an insufficient though necessary condition of the identity of properties. It is not obvious, however, that that condition won't be sufficient in the present context, since it is far from clear that there could be distinct dynamic properties that are definable in terms of the static properties that populate atomic quality spaces and of which all the same atomic events are exemplifyings. This last point was suggested to me by Cynthia Macdonald.

29 Diachronic atomic events are identical if and only if they are composed of the same atomic events.

30 See Davidson's argument concerning this issue, mentioned in note 19 of Chapter II, above.

31 *A Theory of Human Action* (Englewood Cliffs, New Jersey: Prentice-Hall, 1970), Chapter One.

32 Donald Davidson, 'On events and event-descriptions', in J. Margolis (ed.), *Fact and Experience* (Oxford: Basil Blackwell, 1969), p. 81.

33 Actually, as noted in Chapter III, Kim permits virtually any verb expressing a contingent property of things to replace 'ϕ', since both changes and states of affairs are to be explained. But this issue is not

of concern in the present context. Nor am I concerned here with Kim's view that if 'x φs at t' is true, then there is exactly one event, x's φing at t, that makes that sentence true.

34 Without the simplifying assumption, the main point is no different, just more complicated. Without it, if $e_1=e_2$, then for every φ that is a property essence of e_1, there is a φ' that is a property essence of e_2 such that φ=φ' (and *vice versa*).

35 Thus, we can give the following definition: an event, e, is a φing by x at t if and only if there is an object, x, an interval of time, t, and a property, φ, such that either (a) e is x's exemplifying of φ at t, where being a φing is not a property essence of e, or (b) e is x's exemplifying of φ at t, where being a φing is a property essence of e. If e is an atomic event, and condition (b) is met, then e=[x, φ, t], but not otherwise. It seems as if the Kim-Goldman definition of 'e is a φing by x at t' would simply eliminate alternative (a).

36 See Goldman, *A Theory of Human Action, op. cit.*, pp. 25–6.

37 This argument assumes that it is possible for an event or action to have lacked a cause it in fact had. Similarly, the previous argument assumes that an event or action could have failed to have had the effects it in fact had. These assumptions will be defended in the next chapter.

VII EVENTS AND THEIR ESSENCES

1 See, for example, Eli Hirsch, *The Concept of Identity* (New York: Oxford University Press, 1980), p. 3.

2 See Chapter II, section 1.9, above.

3 Reprinted in Davidson's *Essays on Actions and Events* (Oxford: Oxford University Press, 1980), pp. 163–80.

4 Peter van Inwagen, 'Ability and responsibility', *Philosophical Review*, vol. 87 (1978), pp. 201–24, esp. pp. 207–9.

5 *Ibid.*, p. 208.

6 See Myles Brand's case of fission in his 'Particulars, events, and actions', in Brand and Walton (eds), *Action Theory* (Dordrecht: D. Reidel, 1976), p. 137. I used Brand's case in Chapter III, section 4.3.

7 I shall shortly consider a similar, though weaker claim construable as expressing the necessity of an event's having the causes it in fact has. It should be noted that I shall always be taking the causes and effects of events to be events.

8 'Ability and responsibility', *op. cit.*, pp. 208–9.

9 I am assuming here that events essentially have the subjects they in fact have. I will argue for this assumption later in this chapter; and that argument will not depend on the inessentiality of an event's effects.

10 A perhaps more striking case of the inessentiality of an event's (action's) effects was already present in Chapter VI. Jones's killing of Smith is an action one of whose effects is Smith's death. But, Jones's

killing of Smith, i.e., the action Smith performed having the effect that Smith died, could have been performed even if it did not have that effect; though, if it, in certain counterfactual circumstances, did not have that effect, it would not be describable, in those circumstances, as a killing of Smith. Again, the potentiality for scope problems in talk of events is vast; see section 4.1 of the present chapter for a discussion of another such problem.

11 The argument against (8) assumes that the imagined world is, given the possibility of the actual world, possible. Though this assumption strikes me as obvious, it might be accused of being a question-begging one.

12 The case to follow is very much like one employed to the same end as mine by W. R. Carter, in his paper, 'On transworld event identity', *Philosophical Review*, vol. 88 (1979), pp. 443ff. His counterexample, however, assumes that the time of an event's occurrence is not an essential feature of an event. And his argument for that assumption (pp. 445–6) trades, as will be discussed when I take up the essentiality of events' times of occurrence, on a scope ambiguity. So, it would be better if the case for the claim about which Carter and I agree can be made without the assumption I regard as false. The case to follow does do without it, though it does assume the essentiality of the subjects of events.

13 Similar considerations might also motivate an analogous *de re*, transworld version of the thesis 'like events have like effects'.

14 I am assuming that what happens to z in w_1 is of the same sort, a ψing, as what happens to y in w_0. This will be reasonable when z and y are of the same sort. What happens to my car when its windshield shatters should be of the same sort as what would happen to your car if it had my windshield and its shattering occurred.

15 My throwing of b_1 is just whatever I do that results in b_1's being thrown; its minimal subject does not include the ball. See Chapter V, section 4.3.

16 The sinking of The Ship of Theseus I am speaking of is not the event that caused the ship to go down, but the ship's going down.

17 Imagine another situation (in a possible world w_2) in which everything is just as it was in w_1 except that it is The Ship of Theseus (here composed of the members of s') that sails the same course and sinks at t_3 in the same way as it did in w_0. In w_2 there is an event, e_2, The Ship of Theseus' sinking at t_3. But despite the fact that e_0 and e_2 are sinkings of the same ship, under the same circumstances, etc., it might be argued that $e_0 \neq e_2$, on the grounds that, while e_0 involved the sinkings of the members of s, e_2 involved the sinkings of the members of s'.

18 This principle is just PEC, mentioned in note 10 of Chapter V.

19 See note 12 of Chapter IV.

20 And though there is reason to think that the sinking of The Ship of Theseus in w_0 is the sinking of that ship in w_2 (see note 17 above), even though s and s' are disjoint, there is no good reason for thinking

that either the sinking of The Ship of Theseus or the sinkings of its parts in w_0 is identical with the sinkings of the members of s'.

21 This position seems also to be the view of Michael Slote in *Metaphysics and Essence* (New York: New York University Press, 1975), p. 46, fn. 12, and of Kim, in 'Events as property exemplifications', *Action Theory*, *op. cit.*, pp. 172–3. Kim, however, is inclined to deny the essentiality of events' times of occurrence; I take that issue up shortly.

22 Suppose that it were said that summational events are subjectless, and not events with summational subjects, in the harmless sense that while such events have no subjects, all their summational parts have subjects. If there were such events, there would, of course, be no question of whether their subjects are essential them. The condition of identity for such events would be obvious: they are identical just in case they are sums of the same events. And their canonical descriptions are terms of the form 'the event that is a sum of $[x_0, \phi_0, t_0], \ldots, [x_n, \phi_n, t_n]$', where the terms of the form '$[x_i, \phi_i, t_i]$' are canonical descriptions of the atomic events of which the summational event is a sum. But are there summational events? There are, of course, the world's avalanches; but I cannot find any reason for thinking that there is an event that is the sum of those avalanches.

23 If time were to have come to an end at noon last Tuesday, then, though there would have been an interval of time constituting last Tuesday (a shorter than average Tuesday), there would not have been the interval that in fact constituted last Tuesday.

24 In 'On transword event identity', *op. cit.*, Carter employs claims like those in (15) as evidence in favour of the inessentiality thesis. Peter van Inwagen, in 'Ability and responsibility', *op. cit.*, (see esp. fn. 13), also presents an example, like those in (15), clearly intending to have its event-designating term interpreted as having large scope, as an example of an obvious truth that implies the inessentiality thesis. (See also, Slote, *Metaphysics and Essence*, *op. cit.*, p. 106.) But van Inwagen offers no argument for the truth of the claim so interpreted, and so there is no evidence to suggest that a scope fallacy has been committed. Indeed, in correspondence, van Inwagen said to me that he intended to offer no argument, but rather simply to exhibit his belief in the inessentiality thesis. In that same correspondence, he did sketch a direct argument for the inessentiality thesis. And that argument is, with his permission, the subject of the next section.

25 This principle does *not* assert that events essentially have the causes they in fact have, a principle van Inwagen advocated in 'Ability and responsibility', *op. cit.*; (16) is the converse of that principle (see (5), above). The conjunction of (5) and (16) is (6).

26 There are two ways in which such divergence is both possible and compatible with (16): (a) there might be uncaused events occurring in the possible world in question; (b) the temporal distance between events after divergence might be different in different worlds. However, the sort of divergence I am claiming to be both possible

and incompatible with (16) has nothing to do with either (a) or (b).

27 Since the time at which an event occurs is the shortest interval during which it occurs, it would follow from this result that no event could have occurred more quickly or more slowly (as well as sooner or later) than it in fact did. For if an event could have so occurred, it would have occurred *at* a different interval of time from that at which it in fact occurred. I could have written this book more quickly, but the writing of it would have been different; small comfort.

28 No analogous argument can be constructed for the sake of arguing for the essentiality of the minimal *spatial* location of events. For there cannot be events that are twins in the sense that they differ only with respect to their place of occurrence and do not differ with respect to any essential feature except, perhaps, with respect to their place of occurrence, since the subjects of events are physical objects, which can't be in distinct places simultaneously, and since the subjects of events are essential to the events whose subjects they are.

VIII THE SUPERVENIENCE OF EVENTS

1 The word 'crucial' is needed here since which sets are, for example, detested might not be determined by their members but by which person calls attention to them.

2 See Richard Sharvy's 'Why a class can't change its members', *Noûs*, vol. II (1968), pp. 303–14.

3 The conception of sets that is operative here is one that does not take sets to be *sui generis*, that is, that takes the empty set as primitive and then generates other sets. It is rather a conception that takes the 'basic' sets to be ones whose members are not sets, and then generates the rest (even those whose members are just sets or nothing at all).

4 See, for example, Alvin Plantinga's *The Nature of Necessity* (Oxford: Clarendon Press, 1974), ch. VI, and Saul Kripke's papers, 'Identity and necessity', in Munitz (ed.), *Identity and Individuation* (New York: New York University Press, 1971), pp. 147ff., and 'Naming and necessity', in Davidson and Harman (eds), *Semantics of Natural Language* (Dordrecht: D. Reidel, 1972), pp. 266ff. In the latter paper (p. 271), Kripke mentions principles, one concerning the relation between nations and persons, their behaviour, and their histories, and another concerning the relation between material objects and their constituent molecules, which parallel (1) and (2). And he too remarks that such principles do not imply that there can be a reduction of the entities of the former sorts to those of the latter. In *The Nature of Necessity* (pp. 99ff.), Plantinga makes the same points about a principle that amounts to (2).

5 The rejection of (2) constitutes a sceptical answer to Aristotle's question concerning how we can have knowledge of a physical object *qua* individual, given that what is knowable is universal in that the

qualities co-exemplified by a given physical object could have been co-exemplified by some other physical object.

6 (7) is more like (6) than like (5), since it requires that the properties with respect to which the possession of S-properties co-varies must be co-exemplified in the same objects.

7 This is a lesson from Plato's *Euthyphro*: that a property P and a property Q are the same property is not an impediment to its being the case that the possession of P depends on the possession of Q but not *vice versa*. See Sharvy, '*Euthyphro* 9d–11b: analysis and definition in Plato and others', *Noûs*, vol. VI (1972), pp. 119–37.

8 See note 3 above.

9 One might make a case for the dependence of some properties on the occurrence of events by assuming that dynamic properties do not exist unexemplified. If that assumption were true, then if no event, no exemplifying of a dynamic property, occurred, then no object would exemplify a dynamic property; and thus no dynamic properties. The assumption is one I reject. One might defend the dependence of times on events by arguing that there can be no time without change. (But see Shoemaker's 'Time without change', *Journal of Philosophy*, vol. LXVI (1969), pp. 363–81, and H. P. Newton-Smith's *The Structure of Time* (London: Routledge & Kegan Paul, 1980), pp. 19–24, 42–7.) And I think there is no plausible argument for the dependence of objects capable of non-relational change on the occurrence of events, unless one is prepared to argue that all potentialities are eventually realized; but it seems obvious that objects that are capable of non-relational change need never so change.

10 For other conceptions of supervenience, see *Spindel Conference 1983: The Concept of Supervenience in Contemporary Philosophy, The Southern Journal of Philosophy*, vol. XXII, Supplement, Terence Horgan (ed.), and the papers therein referred to.

11 See section 1 of the Appendix.

12 Nor are they temporal parts of such things; I argued for this in arguing, in Chapter VI, against the Lemmon criterion.

APPENDIX

1 Consider Chisholm's events; they constitute a species of the states of affairs, a genus that also includes the propositions. A proof of the existence of such things might be one whose premises were claims attributing 'propositional attitudes' to individuals. And the theory of those entities will reflect the fact that their existence is entailed by such claims; e.g., just as an individual can believe the same thing at different times, events can recur. See Chisholm's *Person and Object* (La Salle, Ill.: Open Court, 1976), p. 117 and elsewhere.

2 Since no event is instantaneous, given any partition of the finite distance between p_1 and p_2 into finitely long segments to be traversed

by an object in getting from p_1 to p_2, there will be at most a denumerably infinite number of events of which a moving from p_1 to p_2 can be construed as being composed; though there is a non-denumerable number of ways of so partitioning that distance.

3 Its falsity is just as obvious as is that of the claim that, for any simultaneously existing physical objects, there is another physical object of which they are the spatial parts.

4 For some more examples and another statement of the general point, see Marshall Swain's 'Causation and distinct events', in van Inwagen (ed.), *Time and Cause* (Dordrecht: D. Reidel, 1980), p. 161. Swain's case (p. 163) of the falling of a row of dominos, construed as composed of the fallings of the dominos in the row, however, is not obvious, since it is not obvious that there is such a thing as the dominos in the row. The importance of this fact is discussed below. Similarly, it is not clear that there is any thing to serve as the subject of a masked ball; this example is Slote's, in *Metaphysics and Essence* (New York: New York University Press, 1975), p. 27; see also p. 28, fn. 21.

5 See Davidson's 'Events as particulars', *Noûs*, vol. IV (1970), p. 28, for a proposal concerning the recurrence of events that requires that there be events composed of events belonging to the same sort.

6 In 'Particulars, events, and actions', *Action Theory* (Dordrecht: D. Reidel, 1976), Brand and Walton (eds), pp. 139-44.

7 See P. M. S. Hacker's 'Events, ontology and grammar', *Philosophy*, vol. 57 (1982), p. 481, for other examples of this sort that I believe can be handled in analogous ways.

8 See Brand's 'Simultaneous causation' in *Time and Cause, op. cit.*, p. 142.

INDEX

Altman, A., 244
Ancient Criterion of Change
  (ACC), 80–1, *see also* change
Anscombe, G. E. M., 257
Aristotle, vii, 109, 113, 228, 250,
  253, 257, 266
aristotelian conception of change,
  see change, dynamic conception
  of
atomic: event (change), 144,
  168–72, 176, 178–9, 236, 261,
  262; event type, 173, 176–8, 190;
  event verb, 172, 173, 174;
  object, 168–71, 175–6, 260–1;
  quality space, 142, 172, 186
  261, 262

Beardsley, M. C., 258
Bennett, J., 259
Black, M., 248
Bradie, M., 244
Brand, Myles, x, 50, 63–72, 76,
  132, 157, 160, 165, 244–5, 246,
  247, 248, 249, 257, 260, 263, 268
Broad, C. D., 250, 254, 259
Brody, B., 245
'by'-relation, 149–50, 259

Cambridge change, *see* change,
  relational
Cambridge Criterion of Changes

(CCC), 81–2, 250
canonical descriptions of events,
  173–6, 177–8, 179–80, 183, 190,
  261, 263, 265; of atomic events,
  173–4; of complex events, 175;
  of non-atomic events, 175; of
  simple events, 175
Cargile, J., 244
Carter, W. R., 264, 265
Cartwright, H., 250
Castañeda, H., 244
causal criterion of event identity,
  28, 72–8, 190–2, 260
causal features of events, 72–6;
  inessentiality of, 190–7, 263, 264
causal verbs, 125, 148–50, 154, 249
change: Ancient Criterion of
  Change, 79–101, 104, 106–10;
  atomic, 144, 168–72, 176, 178–9,
  236, 261, 262; continuous,
  116–17, 120, 169, 255; direct,
  137–44, 257; dynamic
  conception of, 84, 109–10, 138;
  first and last moments of, 133–8;
  general discussion of, 79–110;
  graphs of, 114–18, 162–5;
  instantaneous, 82, 84, 128, 132,
  138–44; interrupted, 84, 117,
  120, 257; non-relational, 95–7,
  102–4, 114, 120, 130–1, 135,
  220, 222, 240–1, 252, 253, 255;

Index

271